Contents

About This Set

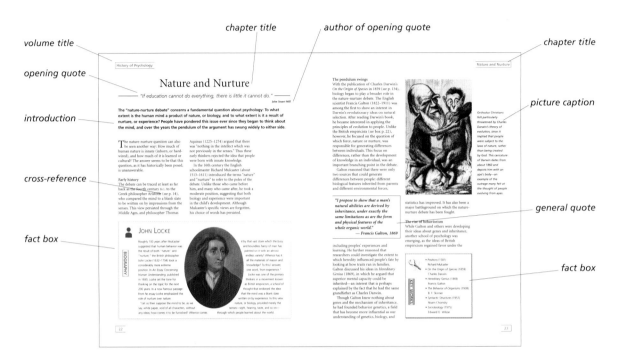

volume title

opening quote

introduction

cross-reference

fact box

chapter title

author of opening quote

chapter title

picture caption

general quote

fact box

These pages explain how to use the *Psychology* encyclopedia. There are six volumes in the set, each one illustrated with color photographs and specially commissioned artworks. Each volume has its own contents list at the beginning and a glossary at the back explaining important terms. More information, such as websites and related reference works, are listed in the Resources section, also found at the back of each volume.

To find articles on a particular subject, look for it in the set index at the back of each volume. Once you have started to read a relevant chapter, cross-references within that chapter and in the connections box at the end of the chapter will guide you to other related pages and chapters elsewhere in the set.

Every chapter has several color-coded fact boxes featuring information related to the subject discussed. They fall into distinct groups, which are described in more detail in the box opposite (p. 5).

The diagram above shows the typical elements found within a chapter in this set. The various types of fact box are explained more fully in the box shown opposite.

THE SIX VOLUMES

History of psychology (Volume One) takes a look at psychology's development throughout history. It starts in ancient Greece when concepts of "mind" existed only as a topic of philosophical debate, looks at the subject's development into a separate field of scientific research, then follows its division into various schools of thought. It also explores the effects of scientific developments, discusses recent approaches, and considers the effects of new research in nonwestern cultures.

The brain and the mind (Volume Two) analyzes the relationship between the mind and the brain and looks at how the brain works in detail. The history of neuroscience is followed by a study of the physiology of the brain and how this relates to functions such as thinking. Chapters tackle the concept of the mind as an intangible and invisible entity, the nature of consciousness, and how our perceptual systems work to interpret the

Developmental Psychology

Grange
BOOKS

This edition published in 2005 by Grange Books
an imprint of Grange Books Plc
The Grange
Kingsnorth Industrial Estate
Hoo, Near Rochester
Kent ME3 9ND
www.Grangebooks.co.uk

ISBN: 1-84013-805-X

Printed in China

Editorial and design:
The Brown Reference Group plc
8 Chapel Place
Rivington Street
London
EC2A 3DQ
UK
www.brownreference.com

For The Brown Reference Group plc
Editors: Windsor Chorlton, Karen Frazer, Leon Gray, Simon Hall, Marcus Hardy, Jim Martin, Shirin Patel, Frank Ritter, Henry Russell, Gillian Sutton, Susan Watt
Indexer: Kay Ollerenshaw
Picture Researcher: Helen Simm
Illustrators: Darren Awuah, Dax Fullbrook, Mark Walker
Designers: Reg Cox, Mike Leaman, Sarah Williams
Design Manager: Lynne Ross
Managing Editor: Bridget Giles
Production Director: Alastair Gourlay
Editorial Director: Lindsey Lowe

Photographic Credits
Front Cover: Photodisc: National Cancer Institute (tr); Photos.com (br); Mark Walker (l).
Ardea London: Frederic Rolland 110; **Corbis:** Lester V. Bergam 8, Bettmann 50, 119, Bohemian Nomad Picturemakers 90, Digital Art 155, Laura Dwight 25, 29, 40, 42, 44t, 61, 64, 66, 67, 71, 77, 81, 94, 98, 111, Ecoscene 21, Owen Franken 27, Tom Gaiilher 23, Shelley Gazin 159, Farrell Grehan 65, Julie Habel 112, Lindsay Hebberd 35, Daniel Laine 116, Robert Llewellyn 60, James Marshall 135, Stephanie Maze 152b, 160, William McCauley 19, Ali Meyer 91, Michael Nicholson 113, Richard T. Nowitz 163, Photex 89, 142, Steve Raymer 162, Albrecht G. Schaefer 36, Leonard de Selva 72, Joseph Sohm/ChromoSohm Inc. 143, James A. Sugar 158, Tim Thompson 44b, David & Peter Turnley 83, David H. Wells 127, 151; **Leslie Garland Picture Library:** Brian Gadbsy 136; **Sylvia Cordaiy Photo Library:** John Howard 124, Humphrey Evans 46; **Hulton Archive:** 150; **Hutchison Picture Library:** Sarah Errington 152t, Michael MacIntyre 31; **Image Bank:** Steve Allen 6, Xavier Bonghi 134, Peter Cade 140, Jan Caudron 156, G. & M. David de Lossy 13, Britt Erlanson 146, G. K. & Vikki Hart 80, Jason Homa 117, Sean Justice 39, 130, Sandy King 106, Romilly Lockyer 20, Marvin E. Newman 104, Real Life 14, Steve Krongard Inc. 157, Ross Whitaker 97, 154, Yellow Dog Productions 34; **Impact Photos:** Chris Moyse 141, Jonathan Pimlott 144, Bruce Stephens 114; **NHPA:** Paal Hermansen 17; **PA Photos:** EPA 102; **Photodisc:** Scott T. Baxter 145, Geostock 56, Jack Hollingsworth 79, Steve Mason 121, Doug Menuez 148, 149, Suza Scalora 133, 161, David Toase 10; **Pictor:** 15, 74, 125, 126, 139; **Rex Features:** Ron Sachs 52; **Science Photo Library:** Alexander Tsiaris 43; **Still Pictures:** David Cavagnaro 48r, Mark Edwards 129, Ron Giling 122, Nicolas Granier 48l; **University of Wisconsin:** Harlow Primate Laboratory 120; **Janine Wiedel Photo Library:** 26, 138; p. 25t courtesy Dr. Philip Zelazo, p. 78 courtesy Dr. Endel Tulving.

CONTRIBUTORS

Consultant:
Sylvain Sirois
Cognitive Neuroscientist,
Center for Brain and Cognitive Development,
School of Psychology, Birkbeck College,
University of London, UK

Authors:
Kirby Deater-Deckard, PhD
Assistant Professor of Psychology,
Department of Psychology,
University of Oregon
Emotional Development, Social Development, & Applications and Future Challenges

Guy R. Lefrançois, PhD
Honorary Professor, Department of Educational Psychology,
University of Alberta, Canada
Memory Development

David Hardman, PhD
Senior Lecturer in Decision Making,
Psychology Department,
London Guildhall University, UK
Development of Problem Solving

Vincent Reid
Developmental Neuroscientist,
Center for Brain and Cognitive Development,
School of Psychology, Birkbeck College,
University of London, UK
Fetal Development

Sylvain Sirois
Cognitive Neuroscientist,
Center for Brain and Cognitive Development,
School of Psychology, Birkbeck College,
University of London, UK
Stages of Development

Janine Spencer
Lecturer, Department of Psychology,
London Guildhall University, UK
Infant Cognition & Perceptual Development

sensations we feel. In a chapter entitled Artificial Minds the volume explores whether or not machines will ever be able to think as humans do.

Thinking and knowing (Volume Three) looks at how the brain processes, stores, and retrieves information. It covers cognitive processes that we share with animals, such as associative learning, and those that are exclusive to people, such as language processing.

Developmental psychology (Volume Four) focuses on changes in psychological development from birth, throughout childhood, and into old age. It covers theories of social and intellectual development, particularly those of Jean Piaget and Lev Vygotsky. It also covers social and emotional development and how they can be improved and nurtured.

Social psychology (Volume Five) studies people as unique individuals and as social animals. It analyzes the notions of personality and intelligence as well as considering how people relate to and communicate with each other and society, and the social groups that they form.

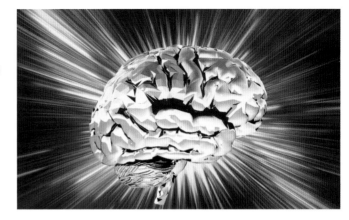

Psychologists using a variety of approaches work in different fields (developmental, social, or abnormal, for example), but all study the brain, trying to figure out how it functions and how it influences people's behavior, thoughts, and emotions.

Abnormal psychology (Volume Six) asks what is abnormality? It shows how the number and types of abnormalities recognized as mental disorders have changed over time and examines specific disorders and their causes. It also looks at diagnosis of disorders and treatments, which can be psychological (talking cures) or physical (drugs and surgery). The social issues associated with abnormality and how society deals with people who have mental disorders are also explored.

 KEY DATES
Lists some of the important events in the history of the topic discussed.

 KEY POINTS
Summarizes some of the key points made in the chapter.

KEY TERMS
Provides concise definitions of terms that appear in the chapter.

KEY WORKS
Lists key books and papers published by researchers in the field.

 FOCUS ON
Takes a closer look at either a related topic or an aspect of the topic discussed.

 EXPERIMENT
Takes a closer look at experimental work carried out by researchers in the field.

 CASE STUDY
Discusses in-depth studies of particular individuals carried out by researchers.

 BIOGRAPHY
Provides historical information about key figures mentioned in the chapter.

PSYCHOLOGY & SOCIETY
Takes a look at the interesting effects within society of the psychological theories discussed.

CONNECTIONS
Lists other chapters in the set containing information related to the topic discussed.

Fetal Development

— *"[Babies] come into the world…uniquely suited to the critical needs of early life"* —

Dr Lise Eliot

When we think of what life must be like for a fetus, we imagine that it must be dark and quiet, with little change in the environment. Recent research has suggested that this is simply not true: The womb has a vast array of stimulating experiences with which to shape the fetal brain. As the fetal brain develops, so too do the fetus's cognitive and perceptual skills.

Human beings are created when a reproductive cell from a man, a sperm, comes together with a reproductive cell from a woman, an egg. This process is known as fertilization. The fertilized egg, or ovum, will go on to develop into a fetus and, at the end of about 38 weeks of a successful pregnancy, a new baby.

CENTRAL NERVOUS SYSTEM

Approximately three weeks after fertilization one-third of the fertilized egg begins developing into what will rapidly become the central nervous system (CNS), consisting of the spinal cord and the brain. That third of the fertilized egg is known as the ectoderm. The ectoderm develops into the epidermis or outer layer of skin and other structures such as hair and nails, as well as the brain and nervous system. A section of the ectoderm begins to fold inward and forms a hollow cylinder called the neural tube.

Along its length the neural tube will develop major specializations within the central nervous system: the spinal cord at

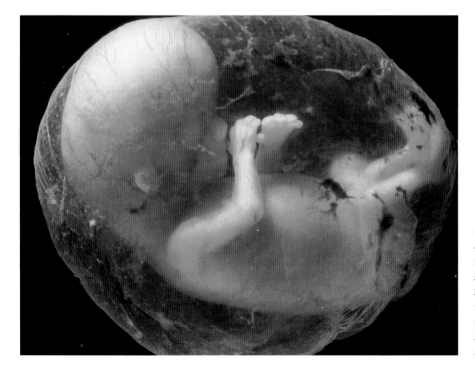

We acquire our cognitive abilities right from our earliest stages of life. Research shows that even as the fetus is growing in the womb, it develops most of the senses that it will use after birth.

The very first stages of our brains appear at about 25 days after conception, with the emergence of the neural tube. At about five weeks the brain stem appears, which will develop into the medulla, pons, and the forebrain. By five to six months the brain stem is developed enough to allow breathing outside the womb. The midbrain is not visible as a separate structure after five months. The major structures of the medulla will form between the seventh and eighth weeks, and the pons appears after the eighth week. The cortex is the last to develop. The first sulci (wrinkles) appear at about 20 weeks.

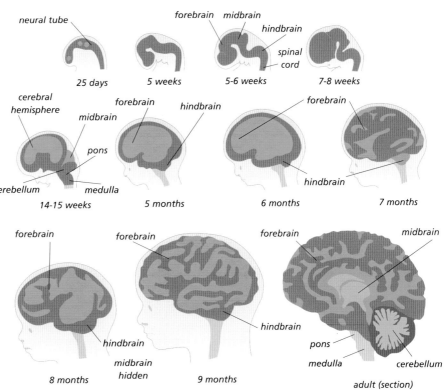

the rear end and the forebrain and midbrain at the front end. The spinal cord end divides into a series of segments, while the front end forms a series of bulges. By five weeks these bulges have formed into the beginnings of the brain. Along its circumference the neural tube develops into the sensory and motor systems. At the front end of the neural tube pathways between different areas of the brain are first detectable at this time. Along its radius, also at the front end, the neural tube develops into the very complex layering of the area of the brain known as the cortex.

Proliferation
Within a matter of days of the formation of the neural tube (25 days after fertilization) the bulges within it, and particularly along the radius, grow larger and begin to form into new cells. After 14 days have passed from the formation of the neural tube, at 5-6 weeks after fertilization, some of these

cells set out on the next stage of brain development. They migrate toward the outer edges of the neural tube (*see* box p. 8) and help thicken its walls, so forming the early stages of what will become the major parts of the central nervous system.

As more cells build up, the journey for newer cells becomes more difficult as they migrate from the inside of the neural tube to its ever-thickening boundaries. To help them reach their destination, some of the new cells develop into a type of cell that moves aside to provide a pathway. These "self-sacrificing" cells are known as radial glial guide cells, and the cells that pass through the "corridor" they have made are known as neuroblasts, primitive cells that will develop later into neurons.

Neurons and glial cells
The developed human nervous system is primarily made up of two types of cells— neurons and glial cells—and each type has its own function. Neurons are nerve cells

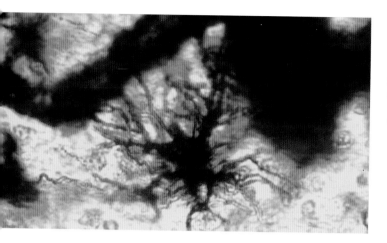

injuries, which leads to neurons in damaged areas of the brain dying due to lack of sustenance.

As well as proliferating and migrating, neurons must also learn how to communicate with each other and must

> "While human brain volume quadruples between birth and adulthood, this is due to increases in fiber bundles, dendrites, and myelinization, and not to additional neurons."
> — Professor Mark Johnson

that communicate with each other on an individual basis or as collections of millions or billions. Glial cells supply energy to neurons. There are over ten times the number of glial cells as there are neurons in the fetal brain.

A scan of an astrocyte, which is a star-shaped glial cell that brings nutrition to neurons and holds them in place. It also "eats up" dead neurons.

In the fetus the majority of neurons have formed by 16 weeks. As they form, they keep migrating to areas of the brain that require more cells, a process that scientists are still trying to understand.

grow communication equipment to do so. Once a neuron has settled into its permanent site, it begins to grow tentaclelike extensions from its main cell body toward other neurons (*see* Vol. 2, pp. 20–39). These extensions are called axons

Neurogenesis

In the developing brain new cells are built in the proliferative zones, which are located in fluid-filled chambers called ventricles. Here the cells that are not specialized—those that are not yet neurons or glial cells—are given their speciality in a process called neurogenesis. By 18 weeks the process of neurogenesis is largely finished, and most cells have migrated to the area of the brain where they will stay for the rest of the person's life. The neurons that have been formed will function until death—in striking contrast to the rest of the body, where cells regenerate to fix damage caused by disease or other harmful environmental effects. Unfortunately, this means that later in life, if the nervous system is damaged, the neurons cannot multiply and regenerate, and so damage cannot be reversed. Furthermore, the energy source of the neurons, the glial cells, can also be damaged by brain

FOCUS ON

CELL MIGRATION

There are two forms of cell migration: cell displacement and cell movement. Cell displacement is a relatively simple process whereby the first cell that is born is pushed outward by cells that are created after the first cell. The oldest cells are pushed to the surface of the developing brain, while newer cells form deep internal structures such as the hypothalamus.

In cell movement, on the other hand, new cells push their way past older cells to form a layer above them. Cell movement is most often seen in the cerebral cortex and in subcortical areas that have a parallel layered structure. They are more complex areas of the brain, where cells are highly specialized. As newer cells arrive on the scene, the previous ones make way for them. In this way the newer cells always end up on top, with the older cells underneath.

The new cells always travel up the same radial glial paths that the previous cells used. To keep this highway free, the previous cells have to move out of the way and allow free passage to the newer cells. If, however, for some reason, they do not do so, the new cells will be obstructed, and the pileup might later result in incorrect connections between nerve cells, which, in turn, might later affect behavior.

and dendrites. Each neuron grows one axon. Axons transmit signals and grow to differing lengths. They stretch out to make connections with neighboring neurons or neurons that are farther removed, such as those at the base of the spinal cord, sometimes a distance of several feet. Dendrites are short and branching; they grow from along the cell body of a neuron and receive signals from other neurons.

Synaptogenesis

The growth of dendrites on neurons is called synaptogenesis. Synapses are the connections that dendrites and axons make with each other so that neurons can communicate with one another. The medium of this communication, or the messenger that carries a message from one neural element to another, is a neuro-transmitter, a small amount of chemical that is released from one neural element to another, across a synapse. One neuron can have as many as tens of thousands of synapses, which would take the possible number of synapses in a human into the trillions. There might also be as many as 100 neurotransmitters darting between the synapses. Synaptogenesis happens at an amazingly fast rate. Lise Eliot suggests in the book *What's Going on in There?* (1999) that between two months after fertilization and two years after birth, 1.8 million new synapses are created every second.

The flip side of this is that the fetal brain makes far more connections than it will eventually need. In later life synapses are pruned. Neuroscientists have found that the critical factor that determines that a synapse should be pruned is whether or not it is used. Synapses are used based on the experiences of the individual, so experience literally shapes the brain. The more electrical activity the synapse is involved in, the higher the chance that it will survive, since electrical activity stabilizes the synapse and fixes it permanently in place.

The creation and pruning of synapses explains two critical factors in human development. First, that the powerful human brain is capable of almost anything. If you speak in many languages to a baby, it will effortlessly learn all the languages that you speak (*see* box p. 11). That is because it still has many synaptic connections related to language. Second, that adults find it harder to learn new cognitive tasks as they get older, since unused synapses that they didn't previously need may have been pruned.

FROM EMBRYO TO FETUS

Eight weeks after fertilization the embryo is referred to as a fetus, a Greek word meaning "little person" or "little man." Limbs are clear, and the face shows the same structures that will be seen at birth. Independent neuromotor activity begins, and the fetus now has control of its movement: The head and abdomen make slight movements. The fetal heart rate increases when the mother is stressed, demonstrating that the fetus is responsive to the environment.

From eight to twelve weeks gestation right up until birth the fetus grows no new body parts; the only development will be in existing parts and their functions.

We are born with all possible neurons at birth and will form no new neurons during our lifetime. However, existing neurons will send out new dendrites to make new synapses. Below left, an artist's representation of dendritic growth in the frontal lobe of a 3-month-old and, right, at 2 years of age.

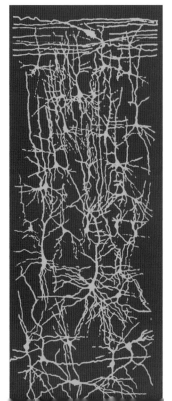
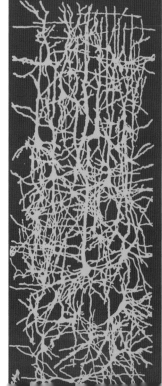

MAKING CONNECTIONS

One question that still puzzles researchers is how does a neuron know to which other neurons it should send its connections? Until recently it was assumed that this question could never be answered. Neuroscientists, however, have discovered that experiences actually shape the way the human brain forms. Each neuron sends out dendrites to neighboring neurons, but only those that are used are kept. When a neuron has migrated to the area of the brain that it has been genetically programmed to migrate to, it sends out a thin offshoot known as a growth cone to "sniff out" the right cells that it should "speak with."

The growth cone sends offshoots in all directions, each trying to detect target neurons. To reach their targets, these offshoots move toward other neurons that emit specific chemical signatures and rely on magnetic fields caused by electrical activity. On contact the dendrite forms a synapse,

Depression might be related to the way that the brain reinforces thoughts. This idea came from researchers studying the fetal brain.

and the cells begin to communicate with each other. With use over time these connections become reinforced. For example, psychologists who have investigated depression in adults have found that people who are a little depressed actually get further depressed because of the way they tend to see even neutral events—such as waiting for a train that arrives a few minutes late—as major disasters. Brain cells registering negative emotions are being reinforced through such active use, pulling the mildly depressed person into clinical depression. Cognitive psychologists David O. Antonuccio, William G. Danton, and Garland Y. DeNelsky recently used this discovery to argue that depression should be treated with psychotherapy rather than with medication. Depressives have to think differently and reinforce brain cells registering positive emotions if they want to recover.

The foundations for the child that will be born have already been laid, from kidneys to brain structures.

The cerebral cortex

The part of our brain that gives us the unique behavior of humans is known as the cerebral cortex. In the adult it appears as the wrinkly surface of the brain. The wrinkles, known as sulci, have been created by folds that give the cortex a vast surface area. Not surprisingly, it is one of the last parts of the fetal brain to develop. That is because it is the most evolutionarily recent addition to the human species (*see* Vol. 2, pp. 6–19).

By five to six months the fetal brain stem has developed to the point where it can support breathing outside the womb. Even at this late stage the cerebral cortex is not fully functional and is still lacking all the wrinkly sulci of the adult brain.

Sulci appear to arrive in three stages. The primary sulci, which all humans have, begin to be defined at approximately 20 weeks. In contrast, the third stage, referred to as tertiary sulci, is specific to the individual person. They do not finish fully developing until a year after birth. Less is known about secondary sulci, although there is increasing research on them. During the first year after birth the infant brain will almost treble in weight.

Myelination

Why is it that adults can think faster than infants? More synapses have been pruned in adults, so their circuits are more streamlined than those of infants; but there is a simpler explanation. You can think of neurons as being rather like wires. The axon is really a wire, and in infants this wire does not conduct electricity very well. That is because in adults axons are covered in a fatty substance, myelin, that insulates the axon in much the same way that a plastic casing insulates an electrical wire.

The process of myelin growth is known as myelination. It is one of the slowest

> *"Myelination begins in the nerve fibers of the spinal cord at just five months of gestation, but not until the ninth prenatal month in the brain."*
> — *Dr. Lise Eliot, 1999*

processes in the brain. It starts in the spinal cord at five months but does not take place in the brain until after the seventh month, continuing up until birth.

Myelination continues through infancy. It is so important that certain cognitive functions will not fully develop until myelination has occurred in parts of the brain related to those cognitive functions. Cognitive functions are any behavior that is driven from the cortex of the brain and is also high-level processing, such as memory recall, language, or reasoning.

ENVIRONMENTAL FACTORS

There are many factors that influence the development of a fetus and baby, including environment and the prebirth behavior of its mother and father, which makes a great difference to their baby's cognitive and emotional capacity.

It is in the first three months that an adverse environment can have the most devastating effects on the developing fetus.

THE FETUS AND LANGUAGE

EXPERIMENT

We need experience to learn a language. But when does this experience begin? A famous study published in 1986 by Anthony DeCasper and Melanie J. Spence of the University of North Carolina shows that the fetus begins to learn about language before birth. In their study some mothers repeatedly read aloud to the fetus the story "The Cat in the Hat" by Dr. Seuss, while some other mothers read the same story but with key nouns changed so that the story became "The Dog in the Fog."

In the first week after birth the newborn babies were given dummies that were connected to a device that recorded their rate of sucking. The babies increased their sucking when they were read the story that they had heard in the womb. They reacted more to the story with the exact words that they had heard in the womb compared to the same story with the nouns changed. Surprisingly, they also reacted more to the exact story read by an unfamiliar voice than to the story with the different nouns read by a parent or familiar voice.

This amazing study shows that the fetus is already listening to language and is learning the characteristics of the sounds that make up speech, but what does it tell us about the fetal brain? Pets hear language all their lives but never learn how to speak or to understand anything but the most simple of words. Human brains are designed to

learn language. During the first sixth months in the womb the planum temporale, the area of the brain related to language production and understanding, begins to grow larger on the left side of the brain compared to the right. (For the majority of people language is located on the left side.) Research with premature babies has shown that by the end of the sixth month, a fetus has a specialized left hemisphere language area: It can hear words better in the right ear, which means that information is traveling to the left hemisphere (the brain swaps information coming from one side of the body to the opposite side of the brain.)

Two further factors indicate that the human brain is wired to learn aspects of language before birth. First, adults can detect phonemes (the smallest boundaries or units of sound in a language) only in languages with which they are familiar. Fetuses and newborn babies, however, can detect these boundaries even in unfamiliar languages, which allows them to concentrate on learning more complex rules of language. Research has shown that newborn babies increase their sucking rate on a dummy when they detect new phonemes, suggesting that they recognize them as new. Second, there is evidence that by the end of the fifth month, a fetus is able to detect the difference between similar-sounding phonemes, indicating that this ability is present in the forming brain.

MULTIPLE SCLEROSIS AND EPILEPSY

The most well-known demyelinating disease is multiple sclerosis (MS). It is a condition in which someone's immune system mistakenly believes that the agent that makes myelin and myelin itself are foreign objects, like a disease. Consequently, the immune system attacks the myelin. Since neurons cannot communicate over long distances without myelin, MS sufferers develop severe motor and sensory problems as they grow up.

Epilepsy is another well-known condition that is often related to myelination. An epileptic is someone who has epileptic fits, or seizures. The seizures can vary depending on the size of the disruption in the way neurons communicate. A small disruption is known as *petit mal*. More serious seizures are caused by large discharges of electrical activity in the brain, resulting in general confusion in the way neurons communicate. This is known as *grand mal*. In the worst instances a *grand mal* can disrupt the parts of the brain responsible for maintaining breathing and can therefore kill a person.

One way to limit the damage of a seizure is to make sure that all the neurons are well insulated. Consequently, pediatricians often suggest that young epileptic sufferers consume a high-fat diet to ensure that myelination of the central nervous system is as complete as possible. Nutritionists suggest that pregnant women consume full-fat milk during pregnancy, because myelin is mostly made up of lipids—a form of fat obtained from milk. In recent years it has been recognized that children up to the age of two should include milk in their diet since myelination is still occurring in many parts of the infant brain.

These factors are called teratogens—environmental factors that can affect the development of the fetus. Teratogens include the age of the mother and the father, the mother's diet, the mother's health, whether or not the mother is stressed physically or psychologically, and chemicals in the mother's bloodstream, such as drugs.

Maternal nutrition

When a woman becomes pregnant, her fetus will depend on her for nutrients from her bloodstream. In order to develop successfully, the fetus must get the right nutrients for specific stages of development. However, since the fetus will take all available nutrients at the expense of the mother, if the mother is low in these nutrients, she is more likely to suffer from a nutritional deficiency than her fetus.

One vital nutrient for brain development is folic acid, a B-complex vitamin. Folic acid is required for the first 12 weeks to help the formation of the fetal central nervous system. If folic acid is not available in the required quantities, then the neural tube might not form correctly, and the resulting baby might have central nervous system problems, such as a damaged spine. Since women often do not know that they are pregnant until four to eight weeks after fertilization, most pediatricians suggest that women of child-bearing age take folic acid tablets or eat cereal each morning that is fortified with folic acid.

Nutritionists also recommend that pregnant women drink milk to increase their levels of calcium, which is vital for the formation of the baby's bones and teeth. The fat from the milk is also important for myelination of the central nervous system, which is crucial for normal development.

Maternal stress

If a pregnant woman is under stress, her emotional state can lead to complications in pregnancy and labor. Some studies have even linked high stress levels to premature babies, low birthweights in newborn babies, and later behavioral difficulties. The reason for this is unclear. However, in 1982 American psychologists Stechler and Halton suggested that stress in the mother might divert blood flow to her major organs rather than sending the blood to the fetus. If this occurs, it is possible that the diversion would cause a temporary oxygen deficiency in the fetus, which might explain these clinical problems. While maternal stress is often suggested as a probable cause for difficulties during birth, we must remember that cause and effect could be reciprocal. It is possible that a difficult pregnancy might cause the mother to be stressed without her even knowing that this is the cause of the stress.

Alcohol

Alcohol is a teratogen. It is highly prevalent in Western culture because of its social acceptance. A small amount of alcohol in a pregnant woman's bloodstream during the first 12 weeks of pregnancy can increase the risk of a miscarriage.

Alcohol in the maternal bloodstream passes to the fetus and anesthetizes the fetus's frontal lobes. As the pregnant mother drinks more alcohol, the proportion of the fetal brain that is anesthetized increases. The anesthetized area progresses from the frontal lobes to the midbrain areas, such as the thalamus, effectively rendering the fetus unconscious.

Calcium and fat are vital to the production of myelin in the fetal brain. Milk provides all the nutrients necessary for myelination.

If the amount of alcohol continues to rise in the fetal bloodstream, then the brain stem will become anesthetized, which will stop the flow of blood to the fetal brain. This will kill the fetus.

Even one evening of excessive alcohol might cause a condition known as Fetal Alcohol Syndrome (FAS). A newborn baby with FAS has a lower birthweight than other newborn babies and later in life might have learning difficulties and other cognitive deficits. People with FAS

> *"[A] Woman's diet and body composition in pregnancy are related to her offspring's risk of raised blood pressure, insulin resistance and coronary heart disease in adult life."*
> — *D. M. Campbell et al.*

characteristically have eyes set farther apart and a slightly larger forehead than is normal, and they often have abnormalities of internal organs, because alcohol interfered with normal cell reproduction before birth. Prenatal alcohol exposure is a leading cause of cognitive deficits in the general population. In the United States during the 1980s two in every thousand babies were severely affected.

Smoking during pregnancy

It was first noted during the 1930s that some babies were born substantially underweight if the mother was a chain smoker. Since then scientists have determined that if a mother smokes while she is pregnant, she dramatically increases the chance of miscarrying her baby or prematurely giving birth. This is significant because premature birth and a low birthweight increase the chance of cognitive deficits and neurological damage for the baby.

A cigarette contains many chemicals, from tar to pesticides. However, scientists who have conducted the most research

Nicotine is a teratogen—something outside the fetus that will affect its development. Even if a pregnant woman does not smoke, if someone smokes near her, the fetus will be "smoking" too.

into the effects of smoking on the fetus have concentrated on the chemical nicotine. Nicotine disrupts the flow of oxygen-filled blood to the fetus by restricting the flow or increasing the flow in bursts. Some scientists suggest that this causes alterations in the fetal "breathing" pattern, which continue after birth and might be related to sudden infant death syndrome (SIDS).

When scientists introduced nicotine into rat fetuses, it seemed to slow down the growth of neurons in areas of the temporal cortex. These areas are related to the use of memory and some spatial skills. The slowing down of fetal brain growth is a matter of great concern, since there are critical periods during which certain areas of the brain must develop—or they will never fully develop.

These areas, such as the prefrontal areas of the brain, are all related to higher cognitive processes that are used during executive functions—cognitive processes that are found only in humans, such as the future planning of actions. The effects of smoking during pregnancy can lead to a lower than average IQ and other cognitive deficits.

FETAL BEHAVIOR AND COGNITION

By the sixth month the fetus already has the ability to live outside the uterus, but cognitive functions are still developing at this time. Knowing when cognitive functions develop is as crucial as knowing what they are.

In the film *Nell* (1994) Jodie Foster plays the role of a woman who has had little contact with other people. As a result her language capability is limited. There are many real-life cases similar to that of Nell, and each one highlights the fact that there are specific times in development before which certain learning must take place. Once that time has passed, some cognitive skills cannot be learned with the same proficiency. These windows in time are called critical periods. These critical periods are related to changes in brain development and synaptic connections. It is during the pruning of synaptic connections, when neural pathways are refined, that the critical period occurs. When pruning ends, the critical period for that area of the brain is over.

There are critical periods for many cognitive skills. For example, complex cognitive skills, such as learning the grammar of language, must be mastered before the age of four. Neurons are pruned even while the fetus learns in the womb. Critical periods for learning how to use some senses, such as taste and smell, occur at this point. Development in the womb is the most important of the critical periods, since it affects the functioning of the brain at an early stage.

Touch

Before babies are born, they are already capable of discriminating between different touch sensations. A fetus thoroughly explores its environment. For example, evidence suggests that a

> *"Along with the other forms of touch, pain is one of the more mature senses the newborn experiences."*
> — *Dr. Lise Eliot, 1999*

A newborn baby likes to be held because the somatosensory system of touch is the most developed fetal sense at birth.

fetus kicks its mother's rib cage because it is a novel sensation. We also know that a fetus sucks its thumb at as early as 12 weeks. The somatosensory system, which is responsible for tactile sensations, or touch, is not fully developed at birth, but is nevertheless in an advanced state. That is why newborn babies are particularly happy when they are held and caressed.

Some researchers have suggested that the somatosensory system is the most developed sense of all the newborn baby's senses. This is surprising in many ways since touch is a complex sense that can take on many forms.

One question that is often asked is whether or not a fetus feels pain. While research is continuing on this topic, we now know that by five weeks an embryo is responsive to other somatosensory influences, such as stimulation near the mouth and nose. The basis for the sensation of pain seems to emerge before the end of the 14th week. We know this because fetuses younger than three months will move away from a surgeon's needle unless they are under anesthesia. Previously, scientists believed that a fetus did not feel pain because its cerebral cortex was not fully developed. This view has changed after research showed clear results to the contrary, and anesthetic is now used during fetal surgery.

Learning in the womb

We now know that a fetus can learn while it is in the womb. One type of learning is habituation. That is when a stimulus is presented repeatedly, during which time it becomes less interesting. Then, when a new stimulus is presented, the interest of the fetus increases. Studies that involve presenting sounds to the fetus have shown that the first time a tone is presented, the fetus will startle, but each subsequent time that the fetus hears the tone, it will startle less and less until it does not respond at all. This has been shown as early as in the fifth month, and all fetuses respond in this way by the sixth month.

Classical conditioning is a more advanced form of learning, and studies show that a fetus also learns this way. It is demonstrated when two stimuli are paired together, and an association is formed between them. For example, if a dog hears a tone just before food is given to it, the dog will learn to salivate when it hears the tone. It seems possible that in mothers who travel to work by train, the sound of the approaching train is learned by the fetus to mean that soon they will be moving to the rocking motion of the train.

CAN A FETUS REMEMBER?

One thing that everyone knows about very early childhood is that it is eventually forgotten: You cannot recall how it felt to have your diaper changed. This phenomenon is known as infantile amnesia. It came as a great surprise to many researchers to discover that the fetus has a fully functioning memory. There are two lines of evidence for this finding: research with fetuses and research with newborn babies.

A simple form of learning is sensory-motor learning. Simple forms of life, such as worms and microscopic organisms, use this form of learning to remember how to act when their environment changes in a specific way. This can also be seen in a fetus: If the mother's abdomen is rubbed on one side, the fetus will move to the other side because it has learned that this is a way of avoiding unwanted stimulation.

Studies with newborn babies clearly show that they remember experiences in the womb. Music that a baby frequently heard before being born will often stop him from crying when it is played. This is not the case with music the baby hears for the first time outside the womb.

Ultrasound studies have shown that mothers who listen to particular music and relax when listening to it condition the fetus to relax to the music as well. Often the fetus will learn to relax to music earlier than the mother if the fetus hears the music repeatedly. This form of learning has been shown in fetuses during the fifth month.

The vestibular system
Between 16 and 20 weeks of their pregnancy most pregnant women can feel their unborn child move. But they only feel this sensation, known as "quickening," when the fetus has grown large enough. The fetus actually moves for the first time many weeks before, and fetal movements are one of the best natural (that is, non-invasive) ways that psychologists have of measuring fetal development.

Motion and balance are some of the most developed senses with which babies are born. That is because they have felt the movements of their mothers and their own movements for many months in the womb. Our sense of movement and balance is perceived by the vestibular system, a series of liquid-filled canals located in the inner ear. At only five months the vestibular system is completely formed and functions in the same way in the womb as it will work for the rest of an individual's life.

As the fetus grows, it slowly runs out of space to move in because the uterus cannot expand beyond a certain point. The maximum amount of room that a fetus has to move in is at the fifth month of pregnancy. Often the fetus will kick or punch to maneuver its body if the mother gets into a position that is uncomfortable for itself, or if it is in distress. From the fifth month of pregnancy the mother cannot sleep on her back because resting on the spinal cord is uncomfortable for the fetus. From the sixth month of pregnancy up until birth, kicking appears to decrease, and full body movements, such as squirming, increase because of the growing lack of space in the uterus. However, head movements increase during this time because the size of the head has grown, and it occupies a substantial amount of room in the womb. Movement of the head and the body are crucial in helping the fetus learn that it is in control of its own body–controlled movement requires substantial learning, since the vestibular system is a complex system. Scientists have found that if a mother is constantly fatigued, the fetus does not move as much as other fetuses at the same stage of development. This can result in lower birthweight, which is linked to lower than average IQ and a higher susceptibility to diseases at birth and even on into later life.

Development of visual abilities
Vision is one of the most complex senses, and that is the reason why it is not fully developed at birth. However, human babies are remarkably well prepared to see the outside world at birth compared to other mammals, such as dogs, cats, or mice. At birth these species still have fused

eyelids, and it can be weeks before their eyes open. By contrast, the eyelids separate in the human fetus during the fourth month of pregnancy.

Studies suggest that vision begins when the eye starts to form in the four-week-old embryo. Visual development starts with the eye and continues to the brain. At eight weeks the optic nerve has formed. It is a pathway in the brain for visual information that will pass to the visual areas located at the back of the brain in an area known as the occipital cortex. It is here that the most complex aspects of visual cognition, such as movement detection, fully develop after birth.

What and where

The visual cortex is not the only part of the brain we require for adult visual cognition. Two independent pathways in the brain, called streams, complement each other in the adult brain. They develop at different times in the fetal brain, but neither of the streams is fully complete at birth. (*see* diagram p. 18)

The "what" stream travels from the occipital cortex to the temporal cortex. It is responsible for our understanding of what an object does and what an object is. Adults with damage to the temporal cortex cannot identify objects despite being able to say what color they are, their size, and other vital aspects of the objects. This stream develops slowly in the fetal brain and is not complete until after birth.

The "where" stream proceeds from the occipital cortex to the parietal cortex. This pathway is vital for an understanding of spatial relations, such as the relationship between where you are sitting and where the door is in the room. People with a damaged parietal cortex have difficulty with spatial relationships and sometimes cannot pick up objects even though they can identify them. This stream is more advanced in the fetal brain and develops from the fourth month.

At birth the "where" stream is more developed than the "what" stream, probably because the fetus has had more

experience with using the "where" parts of the brain than the "what" temporal areas. From the fourth to the sixth month synaptic growth in visual areas in the occipital cortex, and in the "where stream," proceeds at an astonishing rate of ten billion synapses per day. Maximum density of synapses in the "where" stream occurs at four months after birth, while the "what" stream requires another eight months of synaptic growth. This explains why newborn babies are better at some visual tasks, such as tracking an object, than other tasks, such as recognizing the difference between two similar objects.

Taste

Taste is substantially different from other senses, such as vision or touch. Scientifically referred to as gustation, taste is one of the most developed senses at the time of birth. A collection of cells in the fetus's mouth, the taste buds, detect chemicals in the amniotic sac. These cells are tuned to detect specific tastes, either sweet, sour, salty, or bitter.

The first taste buds develop at eight weeks. At around the 14th week nerves from the taste buds are connected to the developing cortex in the brain. From then on the fetus will be able to taste the amniotic fluid surrounding it. In fact, from the sixth month to birth a fetus will

At birth mammals like cats have fused eyelids. By contrast, vision develops early in the human fetus, starting at about four weeks, and the eyelids separate at about four months.

The "what" and "where" pathways in the brain help us understand what we see. The "what" pathway, which travels from the occipital to the temporal cortex, helps us identify what we see. The "where" pathway, which goes from the occipital to the parietal cortex, helps us locate what we see relative to ourselves (see p. 17).

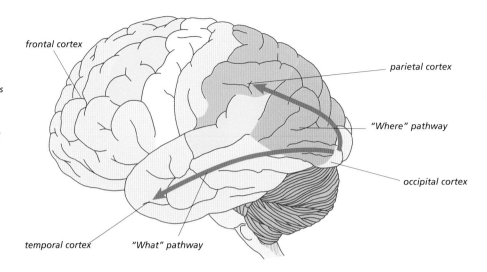

frontal cortex

parietal cortex

"Where" pathway

occipital cortex

temporal cortex

"What" pathway

taste amniotic fluid with its tongue more than once an hour. Amniotic fluid most probably tastes salty, since most of it is actually fetal urine. The salty taste buds send the information to a part of the brain known as the medulla, which is located in the brainstem.

The brainstem is also important for other feeding behaviors, such as swallowing and salivation, and the sensation of taste triggers these behaviors. From the medulla the taste input moves to the cortical areas of the brain. That is where tastes are registered, and the drinking baby is made aware of the sensation of the taste of the amniotic fluid.

Fetal taste is exceptionally important, since some scientists think that the experiences of taste in the womb will influence food preferences later in life. It has not been possible to carry out research into this on people, but it has been performed on animals: Pregnant animals have been fed one specific food, which the baby animal, when weaned, will prefer to other foods regardless of the type of taste, such as sweet, sour, bitter, and salty. This "taste memory" appears to help the newborn feed, since some of the chemicals contained in the amniotic fluid that surrounds the baby before birth are also present in the mother's breast milk.

Smell

A fetus can smell while in the womb. The sensory system that is related to smell is known as the olfactory system. The olfactory system begins to function at between six and seven months, since, up to that time, a plug of tissue inhibits the movement of amniotic fluid into the upper nose. When the tissue disappears, odor molecules bind to the nasal mucus, sending information about the odor to a part of the brain called the olfactory bulb.

The olfactory bulb processes the smell and sends the information to a structure in the brain known as the thalamus. The thalamus, which is important for virtually all senses, functions as a relay station between the detection of the smell and the final goal of the information being recognized by the brain.

From the thalamus the information moves to many different areas, but it must reach the primary olfactory cortex on the surface of the brain before the fetus becomes aware of the smell. Recent research has shown that from the sixth month the fetus smells the food the mother eats, as well as tastes it. There is a period during the development of smell perception when odors are transmitted by fluid in the nasal lining, allowing the fetus to smell in liquid, just as we smell in air.

Hearing

The auditory system, which helps the fetus hear, begins to function well before the end of pregnancy. During the fourth month a fetus will begin to hear sounds from outside the uterus. Even though a familiar voice will have been distorted through the uterus and the amniotic fluid, a newborn will know a familiar voice from a new voice. Stranger still, a fetus of six months and older will blink in reaction to a nearby sudden sound. The first sounds a fetus hears are low-frequency ones, because they most easily penetrate the uterus from the outside.

Sound waves set up vibrations that travel through the amniotic fluid surrounding the fetus. These vibrations are detected by the fetal ear and channeled to the eardrum. In the ear three tiny bones, known as the hammer, anvil, and stirrup, vibrate together. This vibration amplifies the sound and transmits it to the inner ear, which is filled with a gooey fluid.

In the fluid tiny hairs detect the vibration and turn it into electrical impulses. But because the fetus hears sound from the outside world through amniotic liquid, it will hear them rather as we would if we were underwater—muffled compared to hearing them in air.

From the inner ear the electrical impulses are sent through the auditory nerve into the brain. At journey's end the sounds reach the primary auditory cortex on the temporal surface of the brain. It is only when the sound reaches the primary auditory cortex that the fetus is able to perceive it. From four months of age the fetus can hear everything that the mother can hear, although the range is more limited. As the fetus develops, the range of sound that it can hear increases.

At four weeks of pregnancy otocysts, two bumps on either side of the embryonic head, begin to develop into ears. From this point the interior of the ear begins to develop inward. Between 10 and 20 weeks the hairs in the inner ear develop, thereby linking the ear to the brain. Although myelination of the auditory system does not finish until two years after birth, throughout the remainder of the pregnancy (and after birth) the detection of the range of sound (known as frequency) and the volume (known as amplitude) will increase. So at 23 weeks a fetus does not hear as great a range of sounds while hearing music as it will just before birth.

Motor development

Sometimes the fetus kicks or punches at the wall of the uterus. This is known as a gross motor movement, in which a large amount of muscle moves at the same time. Fine motor skills, by contrast, require subtle movements of very few muscles in the hands and arms. Fine motor skills are far less developed in a newborn baby than gross motor skills since fetuses in the womb tend to use gross motor skills far more often than fine motor skills. Motor skills, however, work

For a few months after birth odor is transmitted as a liquid within the nasal lining, allowing babies to smell even though they are in liquid.

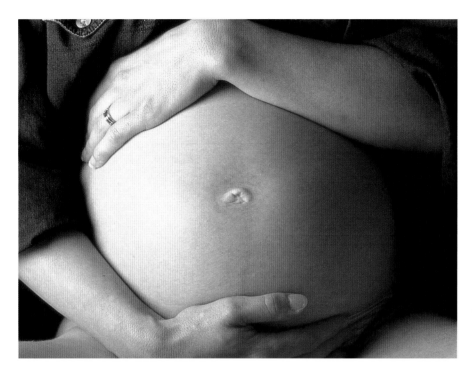

From the seventh month of pregnancy, a pregnant woman should expect to feel at least 10 fetal movements in any 12-hour period.

differently from sensory systems because most motor activity is generated from the brain, whereas the other sensory skills react to stimuli from outside the body.

The motor system matures at a much slower speed than other developmental skills. That is because motor activity is exceptionally complex. Unlike sensory systems, in which information about the world is taken from the world and sent to the brain, the motor system causes changes in that world and also takes in information about the world. This is known as a "feedback" system: Information travels in two directions during the most simple of motions.

Movement and cortical areas

The areas of the cortex that are related to motor activity are divided into three sections: the primary motor cortex (PMC), the premotor cortex, and the supplemental motor area. The PMC is a strip of tissue that contains a map of the human body. The map gives more space to parts of the body with groups of muscles that use specialized movements, such as the face

and lips, compared to muscle groups that perform simple movements, such as the torso. The PMC develops around the eighth week. However, it requires many years of "training" to define the specific areas of the body that are mapped within it.

Voluntary movements are initiated in specific areas of the PMC, each related to different parts of the body. Electrical impulses travel down a special pathway, called the corticospinal tract, to the spinal cord. There motor neurons are activated for the part of the body that the fetus would like to move (*see* Vol. 2, pp. 20–39). Electrical activity is discharged into the muscle of the desired site of action, and the muscle is "excited" into making a movement. This complex system is not fully developed in the fetus and will need many years of development after birth.

The premotor area and the supplemental motor area are related to the planning of movement and other complex movements, and both these areas also require extended periods in which to mature. They are discernible in the embryonic brain by the eighth week following conception.

Gross motor movements

Proprioceptive information tells us where parts of our bodies are in relation to each other. In the fetus proprioceptive information is sent back to the brain from the muscles, giving the fetus almost instantaneous information about where specific body parts are in space.

The fetus does not efficiently process proprioceptive information, which results in a lack of knowledge of where it is in the womb. Consequently, fetuses and newborn babies cannot conduct fine motor tasks such as holding an object. However, they are capable of gross motor movements, such as waving all their arms and legs at the same time.

The other systems of the central nervous system that are related to motor activity, such as the perception of distances, are very well developed, unlike the proprioceptive system.

SCIENCE AND THE FETUS

Since the 1970s medical science has advanced very rapidly, and our understanding of when, how, and why a fetus develops normally has been greatly aided by new technology.

The technology for assessing the hemodynamic (blood volume movement) or electrical activity within the adult human brain is, for ethical and methodological reasons, usually not an option for investigating the fetal brain. For example, in positron emission topography (PET) a radioactive substance is injected into the bloodstream that tracks the use of glucose in areas of the brain. That would not be possible with a fetus because scientists do not yet know the effects of radiation on fetal development, and such a study might be dangerous for the fetus. Instead, scientists use other other imaging techniques that deliver pictures with less information but that are relatively safer.

Ultrasound

The most commonly used form of noninvasive investigation of the fetus is ultrasound. As its name suggests, ultrasound works with sound waves of a very high frequency. When the sounds reach different parts of the womb, depending on the density of those parts, the waves are absorbed in varying degrees and reflected back to the sensor as different levels of frequency. In this way the fetus and its environment are easily reconstructed, allowing for accurate measurement of fetal growth and other important factors, such as the position of the placenta, from which blood flows from the mother to the fetus. Ultrasound is used for a variety of tests during pregnancy to determine if the fetus is

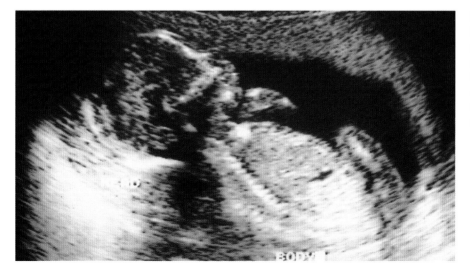

From this ultrasound image radiographers can determine the size and gender of the fetus and identify four chambers of the heart, brain structures, and any visible organs.

EARLY fMRI STUDIES

One pioneer in the area of fMRI is Dr. Penny Gowland from Nottingham University in England. She used fMRI to look at the cognitive processes of the fetus. To overcome ethical dilemmas, she substantially reduced the power of the magnet and decided to look at fetuses at 38 weeks of pregnancy. She decided to look at this stage of fetal development because at this time the fetal head is engaged in the cervix for birth, and that keeps the fetus's head relatively still. She played acoustic guitar music to fetuses and found that temporal lobe areas of the brain reacted to the sound in exactly the same away as they would in an adult. Then she shone a high-intensity light at the mothers' abdomen. She saw no activity in the occipital area of the brain, the region that relates to visual stimulation in adults. However, she did see some activity in the frontal lobe, which can also be seen in newborn babies. This indicated that at 38 weeks the fetus is equipped with many of the cognitive functions needed for life as a newborn.

developing correctly. One of these tests is for the condition known as spina bifida. People with severe cases of spina bifida cannot use their muscles and have little control over their bodies. It is a condition in which the neural tube does not form completely in the first four weeks. The ultrasound test checks whether there is any flow of amniotic fluid into the spinal cord and to the cerebellum. If this is the case, there are gaps in the developing central nervous system that are exposed to amniotic fluid. These areas are slowly eroded, or "washed away," while some of the spinal cord can develop outside the spine and form a cyst or series of cysts. If the ultrasound test shows that the cerebellum appears to be incomplete, then this could indicate spina bifida.

fMRI

Functional Magnetic Resonance Imaging (fMRI) is in many ways at the forefront of adult brain research. Use of fMRI with infants and the unborn child is currently at an early stage (*see* box above). There are two reasons for this: one ethical and the other practical. The fMRI system requires the subject to be examined to be placed in

a magnet with a strong field. Scientists do not yet know what placing an unborn child in a high-intensity magnetic field might do to normal development; and rather than risk harming the child, the utmost caution must be taken before such effects (if any) are known.

The second problem is that fMRI requires the subject to be motionless, otherwise, the image will be blurred. Obviously, it is not possible to ask an infant or an unborn child to stay still.

EFFECTS OF BIRTH

Near the time of birth changes in the hormones in the fetus's brain cause changes in the placenta. It is these changes that trigger birth. Little is known about what happens to a human fetus during birth, but we do know that in sheep the hormone cortisol prepares the fetus's organs for independent life after birth. Cortisol is produced three weeks before birth. The triggering chemical action starts in the brain of the fetal sheep and travels to the placenta. There it mingles with the mother's blood and induces faint contractions of the uterus. Although

> "[We] come into the world with all kinds of mental skills and predispositions, abilities uniquely suited to the critical needs of early life."
> **Dr. Lise Eliot, 1999**

scientists are unsure if the brain of the human fetus triggers birth, this seems more than likely, since the same process appears in other mammals, such as dogs and cats. Cortisol might also be important for preparing the fetus for breathing after birth and might be related to changes in the development of the fetus's lungs.

When we are stressed or frightened, we produce adrenaline and other chemicals. This is known as the "fight or flight" response. During birth a fetus's level of these chemicals increases by 20 times. These

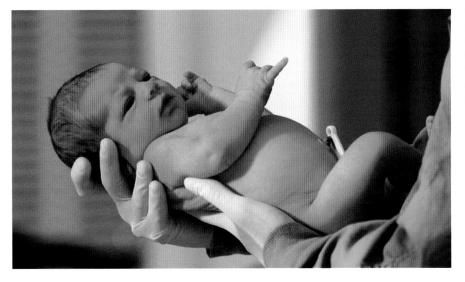

It seems that babies play a part in bringing about a successful birth. Chemicals released during labor help them breathe once they emerge from the womb.

chemicals adjust the fetus's heart rate and uptake of oxygen. Because the flow of oxygen from the placenta is disrupted during contractions, this slowing down protects the brain from damage due to lack of oxygen. These increased levels of chemicals stay in the baby's blood until two hours after birth, during which time they help in many ways.

If newborn babies are delivered vaginally, they are more likely to start breathing immediately after birth than if they were born by cesarean section (the operation that removes the fetus from the womb through the womb wall). Vaginally delivered babies are also more likely to have a higher oxygen level in their blood because the high adrenaline level helps molecules in the lungs absorb air. Vaginal birth also speeds up the metabolic rate, which helps babies maintain their body temperature. Given all these findings, many obstetricians recommend that the mother first go into labor before a cesarean birth is carried out.

KEY POINTS

- 25 days: Neural tube formed. Cognitive abilities begin to develop.
- 5 weeks: Somatosensory system developed.
- 8 to 9 weeks (2 months): Primary motor cortex formed—this means that the fetus can move head and limbs.
- 12 to 13 weeks (3 months): Motor skills developed; fetus can suck its thumb.
- 17 to 18 weeks (4 months): Fetus's movements show vestibular system is functioning. Eyelids separate. Ten million synapses a day added to visual processing streams. Taste buds connect to cortex, activating gustatory system. Auditory system allows fetus to hear.
- 5 months: Vestibular system is complete. Brainstem function could support life outside womb. Fetus capable of habituation, indicating memory abilities.
- 6 months: Fetus tastes amniotic fluid at least once an hour.
- 7 months: Nose fully developed, allowing olfactory system to function. Planum temporale developed, indicating fetus has language discrimination abilities.
- 8 months: Myelination of sensory nerves increases; information processing for all senses increases.
- 9 months: Somatosensory system in advanced state with the exception of proprioceptive abilities. Other senses still developing but ready for life after birth.

CONNECTIONS

- Infant Cognition, pp. 24–39
- Perceptual Development, pp. 40–57

- Stages of Development, pp. 58–77
- Nature and Nurture: Volume 1, pp. 22–29
- Biology of the Brain: Volume 2, pp. 20–39
- Abnormality in Development: Volume 6, pp. 68–91

Infant Cognition

Mental development from birth to literacy.

Adults take many of their thinking processes for granted. Using the telephone or playing a computer game may seem easy, but most of the things that now seem second nature had to be learned. When do we acquire this capacity to stockpile knowledge? How do babies work out effective methods of recognizing external stimuli—the sights, sounds, tastes, feelings, and smells in the world around them? How do they learn to talk and walk?

From the moment of birth human infants seem able to recognize external stimuli and even to discriminate between them. The problem is how to measure these cognitive (mental) abilities in people so young. If adults are asked questions, they can say or write the answers, but babies can do neither. The ingenious methods devised by scientists to overcome this difficulty have produced some enormously revealing results.

It is now generally agreed that infants are born with some innate learning mechanisms. After birth they progress through various stages of development. They start life with reflexive responses to external stimuli; later they learn by imitating others and start to develop concepts. Finally, language emerges.

REFLEXES

It was once thought that neonates, that is, children from birth to about four weeks, were like blank sheets of paper on which nothing had yet been written. Modern research has shown, however, that neonates do have skills from the very beginning of life outside the womb and some cognitive capacity (the ability to learn) even while they are still in the womb. Advances in this area of developmental psychology have also increased knowledge of how people learn things from the earliest days of their lives.

Neonates have very simple interactions with the world around them. Some of the earliest behaviors a newborn baby performs are reflexes. A reflex is an automatic response to an external

KEY POINTS

- The study of infant cognition, or what and how babies learn and know, helps us understand how adults think and interact with other people and objects.
- Developmental psychologists analyze and test babies' behavioral and physiological responses to find out how the infant mind works.
- Concepts are mental representations of ideas and things in the outside world.
- People organize concepts into categories and categories into hierarchies.
- A central argument in the study of infant language development is whether a child acquires language through learning or inborn capabilities. B. F. Skinner said that a child can acquire language only through learning; Noam Chomsky argued that children are born with a Language Acquisition Device (LAD).
- Constructivist psychologists think people are born with few or no innate predispositions and only with general-purpose learning mechanisms.
- Nativist psychologists think we are born with various innate predispositions and strongly biased or constrained learning mechanisms.

stimulus. Reflexes help both physical development and cognitive processing (the acquisition of knowledge).

Babies are born with many reflexes. Some, such as the breathing reflex, remain with them for life, while others disappear within the first few months as the cerebral cortex (the outer structure of the brain responsible for intelligence) develops. One example of the latter type is the Moro reflex, also known as the embrace or startle reflex. If children hear a sudden

> "Every generation rediscovers and reevaluates the meaning of infancy and childhood."
> — A. Gesell and F.L. Ilg, 1943

loud noise or unexpectedly lose support, they will react with an embracing motion that allows them to grab and hang onto the parent. This is crucial to their survival when they are newborn, but becomes redundant later and is hence discarded.

Several reflexes foreshadow and lay the foundations for motor development (the ability to use the limbs purposefully). If infants are held in an upright position with their bare feet free to touch a surface, they will make stepping movements as if trying to walk. This reflex also disappears by the time they are about two months old, but the neurological mechanism responsible for it is the same as that used later when children do begin to walk.

IMITATION

People are equipped from birth with a general mechanism that helps them pick up and retain information. One of the most important parts of this learning mechanism is the ability to imitate. In *Play, Dreams, and Imitation in Childhood* Jean Piaget (*see* pp. 58–77) claimed that this skill emerges slowly during the first two years of life. But in the 1970s Andrew Meltzoff showed that even very young babies can imitate some facial expressions and may be able to reproduce

CASE STUDY

STEPPING EXERCISES

Research has suggested that a primitive reflex, the stepping reflex, is related to motor development. In 1993 Philip Zelazo of Harvard University, and colleagues at Boston University reported that babies made to do stepping exercises in the first few months of life walked earlier than babies who were not given these exercises. The role of reflexes in learning is debatable, but it is clear that they are usually reliable indicators of normal brain development.

Philip Zelazo believes that the stepping reflex helps infants sit and walk.

fairly complex emotional expressions such as happiness and sadness. In further research published in 1990 Meltzoff noted that two-day-old infants will copy the head movements of adults. By the time babies are two weeks old, if an adult sticks out a tongue, they will stick out theirs. Babies learn new behaviors and actions by mimicking others.

The fact that two-week-old babies can imitate is interesting enough; what is even more significant is that only about a month later in their lives, they can do it

This baby is three months old; he smiles as his mother leans over to play with him. Infants learn facial expressions such as smiling by copying the adults around them, and there is some evidence that they can remember and repeat these expressions spontaneously from about six weeks of age.

some time after they saw the original action on which their response is based. This is known as deferred imitation. Piaget believed that babies could not perform deferred imitation until they were about 18 months old, and that they did not develop mental representations until later in childhood. This theory too was discredited in 1994 by Meltzoff and M. Keith Moore, who conducted an experiment in which six-week-old babies were shown adults sticking out their tongues or opening and closing their mouths. All babies may stick their tongues out or open and shut their mouths from time to time. However, the infants who had observed adults performing these actions performed them spontaneously up

> "For a small child there is no division between playing and learning....The child learns while living and any part of living that is enjoyable is also play."
> —Penelope Leach, 1977

to 24 hours later, and they did so much more frequently than infants who had not seen adults behaving in this way. In related tests babies who had seen adults sticking out their tongues only, without opening their mouths, performed this action more than other infants. Those who had seen adults only opening and closing their mouths imitated this action but did not stick out their tongues.

In order to demonstrate deferred imitation, a baby must have some kind of mental representation—that is, an image or idea that is stored in the memory and can be accessed at will. The development of mental representations means that babies must be able to remember actions or objects simply by thinking about them and be able to act on that knowledge.

By the time babies are about nine months old, they can imitate many more complex actions, such as pressing a button on a toy so that it makes a sound. By the age of 14 months the length of time that children are able to remember an action they have observed and then imitate it has increased to four weeks or longer.

Responding to stimuli

Neonates cannot talk or write, but they can control their eye movements from birth, and researchers use this behavior to test what babies know. Babies also have physiological responses that can be measured, such as the amount of activity that takes place in their brains when they are shown a moving object. Newborn babies will follow with their eyes a simplified pattern, such as a face, if it is moved slowly sideways out from the midline of their vision. This response is known as tracking. Researchers can record changes in the baby's visual sensitivity by examining differences in his tracking responses—that is, the way the eyes move—to different stimuli.

By the age of nine months old babies are capable of imitating complex manual actions such as pressing a button on a toy. This child has learned, by imitating adults, to choose the button that makes an appealing noise.

Although this technique has proved that even the youngest babies can see, it cannot be used to establish whether they actually understand what they are looking at. That is determined through habituation studies in which babies are repeatedly shown the same stimulus (*see* pp. 42–43). At first they show interest and fixate on the object; but as they become familiar with the stimulus, they are less and less responsive to it. When the babies eventually spend less than a certain amount of time looking at the stimulus, they are said to be "habituated."

Once babies have become habituated to the stimulus, they are given a new one, and their responses to both the old and the new stimuli are measured. For example, young babies will show the Moro reflex in response to a loud sound. After they have been exposed to the same sound several times, they will stop reacting in this way. When exposed to a new sound, they show the Moro reflex again. This proves they know how to differentiate between familiar and unfamiliar things.

However, the habituation technique has various limitations. Babies are slow to respond and tire easily, and each experiment can take up to an hour. The technique most often used to test what babies know is the forced-choice preferential looking procedure, which capitalizes on the tendency of infants have of looking more often at displays they find "interesting" than at ones that do not grab their attention.

A forced-choice preferential looking procedure has two parts. During the first part (known as the trial phase) the experimenter will show the baby several stimuli for a fixed period of, say, 20 seconds until the baby becomes familiar with them. These stimuli could be different female faces. In the second part of the experiment (the test phase) the experimenter will show the baby two fresh stimuli: one a new stimulus from the familiarized category (for example, a different female face) and another from a new category (for example, a male face). The researcher then records whether the baby looks at the new category stimulus for longer than the familiar category stimulus. If the baby shows a preference for the new-category male image, this implies that the baby has already formed some kind of representation of the familiar stimulus of the female face and no longer needs to keep looking at it.

Another widely used method of infant cognition research is the event-related potential technique, which involves placing electrodes over various parts of the scalp to measure the baby's brain responses to various stimuli (*see* box overleaf).

A young baby looking at his mother's face. Babies can control their eye movements from the moment they are born. Psychologists can test how much children recognize by testing their tracking abilities, that is, their capacity to follow a moving object such as a face with their eyes.

RECOGNIZING CATS AND DOGS

How do infants form concepts, and can this be measured? In 1997 Janine Spencer and her colleagues at University College, London, England, studied the abilities of four-month-old infants. The stimuli were 36 color pictures of cats and dogs. These pictures were placed to the far left and right of the children's field of vision, and their responses were measured by noting whether their eyes moved from one stimulus to the other. A previous study had shown that the infants could differentiate cats from dogs, but in these experiments the researchers wanted to find out what visual information infants use when they do this.

First, the babies were shown six pairs of either cats or dogs to familiarize them with one type of animal. They were then shown a pair of hybrid animals in the preference test trials. The stimuli for the preference test included six sets of hybrid cat-and-dog pictures made up of various cats and dogs that were different from those the babies had seen in the familiarization part of the test—some had the head of a cat on the body of a dog, others the head of a dog on the body of a cat. The logic behind this is that during the familiarization part of the experiment babies are thought to form an idea of a typical dog or cat, so when they see one they have not seen before, they will recognize it as another cat or dog rather than as a completely new object.

When researchers compared the lengths of time the infants looked at the different hybrid (those with mismatching heads and bodies) stimuli, they found that the infants spent longer on those with a new head than on those with a familiar head and a new body. These preference results suggest that information from the head and face region rather than the rest of the body is essential for infants to distinguish between animal species such as these.

A concept may be defined as a way we group different objects into categories in order to think about them and to recognize them when we see them again. It is a mental image of something and may be a concrete image (such as of an animal) or an abstract one (as of happiness). We can form concepts of groups of events, objects, and situations that we regard as different but somehow related. For example, if we have concepts of three people, Daniel, Carly, and Susan, together with a concept of Daniel being Carly's father, and a concept of Susan being Carly's sister, it is possible for us to think about the concept of Daniel being Susan's father.

Our knowledge of the world is divided into concepts that represent various categories of objects or thoughts. In other words, our concepts divide the world into classes, such as "friends" or "family," "animals" or "fish." In order to have the concept "ovens can burn," we must have two mental pictures: one of ovens, the other of what a burn is like. This is regardless of whether we have ever seen an oven or been burned ourselves.

A concept, then, is the mental image of a category. People can and must divide their knowledge of the large number of objects and information in the world into a manageable number of categories. This has the advantage of reducing the amount of information that people must remember. It also enables them to recognize new stimuli as members of an already familiar category. Thus, for example, if we have a concept of a "flower," we can recognize a new type of rose as a flower even if we have not seen it before. Without concepts, every time we came across something new, we would have to form a new mental representation of it along with a new word to describe it.

A further function of concepts is that they allow us to go beyond just knowing what something looks like. When we see a particular dog for the first time, the only knowledge we have about it is what it looks like. However, we draw on our preexisting concept of "dog" to go beyond its basic appearance. For example, even if the dog has a wagging tail, which is generally accepted as a sign of friendliness, if our concept of "dog" tells us that dogs who wag their tails are sometimes ferocious, and that some may even be dangerous, we will link our knowledge of what dogs look like with our previously acquired knowledge of what dogs can be like.

Development of concepts

Since the late 1980s psychologists have been particularly interested in the origins and development of these concepts. Some have suggested that thinking depends on a thought system that can categorize things in the world. For example, when children start learning to read and write, they must already have a concept of what

> *"...some 'information' or 'programs' are built-in at birth (for example, the child does not have to learn how to suck...)"*
> — *Cleverley and Phillips, 1986*

the words they are reading mean. The main area of research is focused on what categories infants learn, and how they come to learn them.

People seem to put many categories of objects into hierarchies. In 1975 Eleanor Rosch of the University of California, Berkeley, conducted studies of how these hierarchies are structured. She found that they tend to build up from a single instance, such as "my dog," to increasingly abstract concepts, such as "dogs." We can retain a mental image of how dogs look even though it is highly generalized and glosses over the vast physical differences between, for example, chihuahuas and St.

A child points out a flower to his mother. Infants develop concepts and can categorize objects at about 3 or 4 months. At 12 months this child will only be able to say a few words, but over the next few years he will develop an extensive repertoire of words.

Bernards. But we cannot form images of very large classes. We may know that all dogs are mammals, but we can have no generic image that covers every mammal species from bats to dolphins because the category is too large and diverse to be retained in the mind as a single entity. Thus the basic level of recognition is based on how alike members of a category look. This is known as perceptual similarity. Rosch and her colleagues said the basic level has the greatest psychological significance.

Children use basic-level terms when they first learn to refer to objects. In fact, it has been shown that by the time babies are three to four months old, and possibly even earlier, they are able to categorize objects at the basic level. They do so by observing what the objects look like.

How do babies learn to categorize objects they have never seen before and about which they have no sensory information? This question has long been a subject of debate among psychologists. Many claimed that all conceptual categorization is based on visual perception. But in the early 1990s Jean Mandler of the University of California, San Diego, argued that perceptual and conceptual categorization are basically independent. She began by suggesting that if the way things look is the basis for developing conceptual categories, then infants should be able to distinguish between objects that are visually different. Yet her experiments showed that although nine-month-olds could make categorical distinctions between some broad categories (for example, they could reliably tell the difference between birds and airplanes), they could not necessarily distinguish between some basic-level categories, such as the difference between dogs and rabbits. Mandler concluded that the fact that infants could not be relied on to take account of visual similarity in making categorical distinctions shows that conceptual knowledge is different in kind from perceptual knowledge.

In 1996 Paul Quinn and Peter Eimas at Brown University drew these opposed views together by suggesting that babies form categories through the use of both visual and conceptual information. Early in life babies receive most of their information about the world through what they see and thus form most of their categorical groupings on the basis of visual similarity. As children develop, they learn more about objects in the world, and their ability to make categories becomes increasingly conceptual in nature.

LANGUAGE

Learning to speak plays an important part in the development of children's abilities to form concepts and identify categories of objects. As soon as children develop verbal skills, they are able to use language to define and categorize what they see. There is a complex relationship between the development of thought and language (*see* pp. 58-77).

When we use language, it all seems very simple. Say the word "handbag" quickly. The sound that is often produced is "ham bag." According to cognitive psychologists such as Steven Pinker (*see* Vol. 1, pp. 134–143), our ability to use language has evolved with the main purpose being to communicate meaning: it does not matter whether we say "hambag" or "handbag" as long as the person we are talking to understands what we mean.

Many scientists believe that the ability to use language played an important role in our evolutionary success over other species. We acquire language at birth if not before. Within a few days of birth babies can distinguish between the languages they heard while they were in the womb and other languages. For example, if the mother always spoke Japanese while she was pregnant, then the newborn infant shows a preference for Japanese over any other language. If the baby also heard another language, say Italian, before being born, that baby would show a preference for both languages.

> *"Evolution, having made the basic computational units of language innate, may have seen no need to replace every bit of learned information with innate wiring."*
> —Steven Pinker, 1994

Between the ages of seven and ten months babies begin to babble, making noises such as "ba ba ba" or "da da da." These are not random noises: They are phonemes. Phonemes are the smallest units of speech, and all words are made up of them. Changing a phoneme changes the meaning of the word; for example, the phonemes "s" and "k" have no meaning as such, but change the word "sit" to "kit."

Up to the age of about 12 months infants babble using all possible phoneme sounds. This is significant because it means that mentally normal infants can learn any language to which they are exposed. So if infants from England are taken to India and there hear mainly Hindi, they will end up speaking Hindi as fluently as they would have learned English if they had lived in England. By the time children near their first birthdays, they will normally have learned to say a

few words, such as "mamma," "dada," and so on. The number of words they will learn grows rapidly in the first few years of life. When they are six years old, they have learned between 6,000 and 9,000 words. In fact, children learn more in their first few years of life than they will ever learn in such a short time again. Learning can be severely delayed in children who have been deprived of human contact during their first year: They acquire some words but have difficulty with language structure.

Words and meaning

Knowing how to say a few words is not the same as being able to communicate using language. Language involves understanding what the words mean individually and in relation to other words. How do children come to speak and understand the language to which they are exposed? When infants point to an object and say "nana," meaning "banana," how do they know that the word used to refer to that object is the correct word? How do they know that the word "banana" refers to the actual fruit? Researchers have come up with many different theories to explain how children learn the meaning of words.

In the early 1980s Jerome S. Bruner (born 1915) suggested that when parents talk to their young child, they get the child to look at any object they are referring to. But this is not always possible. The child may be looking at a different object at the time of labeling. For example, if the mother points to a bowl of mixed fruit and says "banana," how can the child tell which fruit she is talking about? Researchers have found that if there is a small time lapse between presentation of the word and presentation of the object with which it is associated, the child is more likely to learn the word. But even if infants can associate words with objects, the question remains: How do they then go on to understand what a word means?

If an American child were to be taken at birth to live in India, he or she would naturally grow up speaking Hindi, and it would thus be the child's native language. Yet his or her mother tongue would still be English, and some research suggests that children who have been relocated, even at such an early age, already have a predisposition toward the parents' language.

Constraints

In 1988 Ellen Markman and Gwyn Wachtel proposed that there are innate or inborn constraints on learning word meanings, and that babies are born with an instinct to make certain assumptions when they hear new words.

The first such assumption is termed the whole object assumption constraint. When infants hear a new word to refer to an object, they assume it refers to the whole object. They do not consider the possibility that it may refer to a part or parts of the object or to what it is made of. For instance, if someone says "tail" and points to a dog, the infant assumes that the person is referring to the whole dog, not just to its wagging appendage.

Another constraint is taxonomic, that is, concerned with classification. For example, children may assume that "cat" and "dog" are from the same category because they are both animals, but have greater difficulty in making the link

> *"As each successive word is learned it further constrains the meanings of the yet-to-be-learned words, thereby helping children figure out their meaning."*
> — *Ellen Markman, 1993*

between "door and "key," which, though often related, have no obvious visual similarity to link them. Infants assume that labels refer to objects within the same category and not to objects that often go together but are from different categories.

One of the most important constraints is that of mutual exclusivity, which prevents infants from giving more than one label to any object. Pairs of words such as "dog" and "pet" cannot coexist in their minds. The mutual exclusivity constraint is easy to demonstrate in children from the age of about 18 months, but it gives no clue as to how, by the age of about four, children have learned to make distinctions between words that refer to parts of objects, such as "tail," and those

that refer to the objects themselves, such as "dog." Research by Markman and Wachtel into how children learn new words suggests that they assume that any new word describing an object refers to the whole object. They do not recognize two words used to describe the same object; for example, they may know the word "bus," but be unable to comprehend that it may also be described as a "vehicle." When they hear a new word to describe an object with which they are already familiar, they think the new word refers to a part of the object.

Some psychologists think it is possible that children do not have innate constraints at all. Rather, they have only biases to favor some assumptions over others. A bias is not as strong as a constraint. According to this argument, if circumstances alter, children will adapt and learn new words in a different way. The inference is that, if we can learn in different ways, we cannot be programmed to behave in any particular way. But that is questionable. Infants show a bias to track faces from as early as a few hours after birth, before they have had a chance to learn anything about human physiognomy—there evidently is an innate program, but it is probably less limiting than some psychologists originally thought it was.

Innate or learned?

So far we have looked at some of the developmental milestones that infants pass during their first year of life, including how they begin to develop cognitive knowledge. One of the main questions that remains concerns the extent to which cognitive development is controlled by innate and environmental factors. Are babies born with some predispositions to behave as they do?

Early researchers on language development were divided on this question: Some believed that language was acquired incidentally through general learning processes; others maintained that it came about as a result of innate predispositions. There is no doubt, however, that fully functioning adult language is extremely complex. The child's

> *"Education is what survives when what has been learned has been forgotten."*
> —B. F. Skinner, 1984

mind must be able to grasp an adult level of complexity. Learning a language involves making new connections between nerve cells. If we were born with all the

connections between neurons fully formed, we might not be able to learn anything new. It is generally agreed that the structure of the brain in the areas responsible for language is important. If there is too little structure, language development will be inhibited; and if there is too much structure, language-learning abilities will be rigid, and the child may be unable to adapt to a particular language.

Learned argument

In the 1950s a debate raged between two schools of thought about language development. One group of theories was

LANGUAGE GROWTH

EXPERIMENT

In recent years experiments have provided strong evidence that exposing children to complex language early on helps their development of language skills. In 1987 Ric Cromer of the Cognitive Development Unit at University College, London, England, wanted to find out if experiencing different ways of using language stimulates the way we organize our language processing. To this end 60 mentally normal English-speaking children took part in an experiment. Seventeen of the children were aged seven years, thirty-three were aged eight years, and ten were aged nine years. Each child was shown how to operate a wolf and a duck puppet, one in each hand.

The children were asked to make the wolf bite the duck and to make the duck bite the wolf. There were 10 different sentences used in the study to tell the children what to do. Five of the sentences instructed the named animal to do the biting, and five required the nonnamed animal to do the biting. These are the sentences that were used:

1. The wolf is happy to bite.
2. The duck is keen to bite.
3. The wolf is easy to bite.
4. The duck is exciting to bite.
5. The wolf is delightful to bite.
6. The duck is anxious to bite.
7. The wolf is willing to bite.
8. The duck is hard to bite.
9. The wolf is glad to bite.
10. The duck is fun to bite.

The experiment required the children to listen to the sentences and act them out using the puppets. They were always told that they had completed the correct action, even if they had not.

The same test was repeated the following day, and all the children were tested every three months for a year. Ric Cromer's hypothesis was that children who experienced the structure of these sentences for a year would show the same language comprehension as adults. He also believed that the children he tested would show much better language comprehension than other children of the same age.

When the children were exposed to this linguistic structure every three months for one year, their linguistic knowledge was reorganized. After a year the children in the study aged eight years performed like eleven-year-olds. Furthermore, more than half of the nine-year-old children performed like adults—who were defined in this context as people with a reading age higher than that of the average fourteen-year-old. This supported Cromer's hypothesis that exposure to the structure of these sentences enhanced the language comprehension of the children in the experiment.

The findings also suggest that children develop some parts of their linguistic systems without any feedback from adults. In other words, exposing children to complex sentences encourages them to concentrate on a particular aspect of grammar that is important for the development of their own language skills, and that occurs without any adult supervision or intervention.

headed by B. F. Skinner (*see* Vol. 1, pp. 74–89) and the other by Noam Chomsky (*see* Vol. 1, pp. 118–125). For Skinner every focus of psychology, whether it be personality, language, or any other topic, can be explained by observable behavior alone. Making assumptions about brain processes or about people's inner thoughts and feelings was no way to study psychology, according to Skinner. In his view people behave in response to prompts from their external environment. This exposure to the environment provides the conditions for learning. In other words, we are born into the world with an innate ability to learn, but everything we learn depends on the environment in which we live.

Skinner is noted mainly for his contributions to the study of animal behavior. In 1957, however, in his book *Verbal Behavior* he attempted to give a working explanation of how children learn language. Specifically, he was interested in the variables that control what he termed language behavior and in specifying how they interact with each other to determine a particular verbal response. He argued that the determining variables could be described entirely in terms of "stimulus, reinforcement, and deprivation." For Skinner the acquisition of language, like any other form of learning, was based on experience. According to behaviorist theory, we learn language in the same way as we learn other kinds of behavior, through what Skinner called "operant conditioning."

At first, babies utter sounds at random. People around them reinforce the sounds that resemble adult speech by displaying approval—smiling, paying attention—and by talking to them. Thus encouraged, the babies repeat these reinforced sounds. Infants also imitate the sounds they hear adults making, and the adults encourage them to make them again. As this process of reinforcement continues, infants learn to produce meaningful speech by generalizing from their experience. For

AGE AND LANGUAGE LEARNING

CASE STUDY

Children around the world learn language at approximately the same age. In 1967 Erik Lenneberg proposed that there is a critical timespan during which children can learn language. By the time a child reaches puberty, the different areas of the brain have become specialized for different functions. This means that if children do not acquire a language by puberty, Lenneberg believed they never would.

In order to test whether or not there is a sensitive period for learning language, researchers began to study the language skills of children who had been abused and had experienced little human contact. Take the case of Genie, a little girl from Los Angeles, California. At the age of 20 months Genie was locked in a room in her parents' house until she was nearly 14 years old. No one was allowed to talk to her. If she made any noise at all, her parents would beat her. Genie's environment was emotionally as well as linguistically deprived.

Once Genie was found, over a period of years she was taught to speak. Her comprehension and vocabulary

Research suggests there is a critical time for language learning: if children have not learned to speak and read by the age of puberty, it is unlikely they ever will.

developed well, but her grasp of grammar never developed to the same extent as that of normal children. Findings from other similar cases seem to support the idea that there is a critical period for learning the structure of language.

instance, infants can often be heard babbling noises that sound very much like words, such as "dada-dada-dada." When parents hear their children doing this, they praise them, saying, "Yes, daddy!" and pointing to the father.

In contrast to Skinner, Noam Chomsky in his 1957 book *Syntactic Structures* argued that although reinforcement and imitation do to some extent contribute to language development, they do not fully explain it. First, the rules of language and the fine distinctions in the meaning of words are so numerous and complex that they could not all be acquired simply by reinforcement and imitation. Second, behaviorism cannot explain how children can make up new words, such as calling a sprained ankle a "sprankle."

Language acquisition device

Young children around the world seem to learn language at about the same age. They also do so without receiving enough feedback to teach them the rules of language. Chomsky suggested that children must be born with an innate mechanism in the brain, which he termed the language acquisition device (LAD). The LAD is triggered when children have learned enough words to form sentences and understand what they mean. That helps them acquire a fully functioning language. It does not matter which language children hear, the LAD has what Chomsky called a universal grammar. So children of the Shimong tribe have no more trouble learning their native language than children born in the United States do learning English.

Pidgin and Creole

In *Language and Species* and *Language and Human Behavior* Derek Bickerton, a linguist at the University of Hawaii in Honolulu, showed that part of the evidence for an innate predisposition to particular grammars is the way children convert pidgins into creoles. By definition a pidgin is a simplified language, and creole is any language made up of

elements of two or more other languages and used for contacts, especially trading contacts, between speakers of the other languages. It does not constitute the mother tongue of any speech community. Pidgin languages have very little grammatical structure, and their word order is changeable and haphazard. There are none of the compensating inflections found in many languages. Inflections are alterations to words to indicate tense, number, gender, or other grammatical differences—in English, for example, one man (singular) becomes two men (plural);

This Shimong girl will have no more difficulty learning her native language than children born in any other parts of the world will have learning their native languages. Young children also seem to learn language at about the same age.

PIDGINS AND CREOLES FOR THE DEAF

Further evidence for an innate predisposition to learn language comes from work with deaf children. Before 1979 deaf children in Nicaragua were not taught sign language; instead, they were forced to lip read. In the playground these children came up with a makeshift sign system they used at home. It is now known as LSN (*Lenguaje de Señas Nicaragüense*, Spanish for Nicaraguan Sign Language). LSN does not have a consistent grammar—it is a pidgin sign language. Children who were four years or younger when they joined the school were exposed to the already existing LSN. As they grew up, their mature sign system turned out to be quite different from LSN. It had a consistent grammar. Like a real language, this new creole sign language allowed children to be far more expressive in their conversations. Due to these significant developments this language is now recognized as distinct from LSN and is referred to as ISN (*Idioma de Señas Nicaragüense*). Basically, ISN is a creole that the deaf Nicaraguan children spontaneously created from their knowledge of pidgin LSN.

I swim today (present tense), but I swam last week (past tense). Pidgin utterances, on the other hand, are restricted to short and simple word-strings.

Pidgin languages provide such an impoverished environment in which to learn grammar that it is all the more amazing that children should grow up to convert them into sophisticated and versatile linguistic tools, known as creoles. Creole languages often have their origin in extended contact between two language communities; they incorporate features from each and constitute the mother tongue of a community. In a single generation, though not necessarily the first, children brought up hearing only a pidgin language develop a complete new language with its own rules of grammar and none of the limitations of pidgin. Creole vocabulary is drawn from a pidgin, but the rules of its grammar are new because pidgin languages do not have these principles in the first place. Derek Bickerton found that the grammars of creoles all around the world are remarkably similar even though they arise independently. Such rapid universal processes strongly suggest that children do not learn language only as a result of imitation and reinforcement.

THE MODULAR MIND

For many years developmental psychologists were divided into two opposing schools of thought on how a child's thinking develops. On the one hand, constructivists, such as Jean Piaget, believed that infants were born with almost no innate predispositions, and that

Pidgin and creole languages are common in places such as the island of Malaita, Solomon Islands, where more than one language is spoken. The blond and red hair of these children is also the result of the mixture of ethnic groups over the generations.

their cognitive processes were "constructed" after birth. On the other hand, nativists, such as Noam Chomsky, believed that infants were born with a lot of innate knowledge or genetic predispositions toward learning.

Yet some people think that it is possible to have a theory of development that respects both these views. In fact, combining these two conflicting ideas may be essential for a coherent theory of human cognition. In 1985 the American philosopher Jerry Fodor claimed that it is possible to think of the mind as being made up of two different types of system for thinking: input systems and central systems. The job of an input system is to understand sensory input, such as the information that reaches our brains through our eyes or ears. Once the input system has made sense of the incoming information, it can be passed on to the central thinking systems.

Fodor suggested that all these input systems are modular, that is, self-contained and separate from each other. If one is damaged, it does not have any effect on the others. And what goes on inside a module, such as the seeing module, is not available to other parts of the brain until the module has finished processing it. He argued that we are born with the structure already in place for the development of these mechanisms. He also said that these mechanisms must work very rapidly and automatically. For example, when someone speaks to us in a language we know, we cannot help but hear it as a sentence in that language. According to Fodor, these input systems have evolved to process relevant information from the environment.

Innate modules
In contrast to input systems, central systems are slow, higher-level processes that have access to information from anywhere within the cognitive system. The main idea of Fodor's theory is that babies are born with these innate modules in place. Professor Annette Karmiloff-Smith

of the University of London, England (who was a student working with Jean Piaget), came up with a modified version of Fodor's theory to explain children's cognitive development. She made a distinction between innate modules, which have specific functions, and

> "We thus make a fundamental distinction between competence (the speaker-hearer's knowledge of his language) and performance (the actual use of language in concrete situations)."
> —Noam Chomsky, 1965

modularization, that is, the process by which the brain becomes specialized only as a result of developmental changes. So babies are born with some innate predispositions. However, without specific environmental input these predispositions will never be realized. The environment does not simply trigger the development of these innate predispositions, it actually affects the resulting structure of the brain. According to Karmiloff-Smith, a modular mind is the result of, and shaped by, cognitive development.

Redescribing knowledge
The second part of Karmiloff-Smith's theory is known as representational redescription. She argued that in order to increase our knowledge, our minds can use any information we have already stored in our memory (innate or not) to modify our mental representations. This re-formed knowledge, in turn, results in the development of new modules that are specialized for receiving different kinds of sensory information.

The development of different types of knowledge, however, does not progress equally, according to Karmiloff-Smith. It depends on the individual; for example, for some children knowledge of math develops more slowly than their understanding of grammatical rules.

Psychologists and others have often observed that when children are learning a new type of knowledge, they first succeed in a task, even though they are not aware that they have the relevant knowledge to do it. For example, four- to five-year-olds can successfully balance both evenly and unevenly weighted blocks on a narrow bar. Later, they form a mental representation of how they believe the task can be performed. At this stage they are not paying attention to any external stimuli, but developing their own theory of how to achieve their objective. The classic result of this deeper thought process is that by the time they are six to seven years old, they can balance only the evenly weighted blocks—they have apparently gone backward, losing a skill they previously seemed to have mastered. Toward the final stage, as they approach maturity, the children once again take

> "At different moments in development, then, children alternate between focusing on data and on theory."
> — Annette Karmiloff-Smith, 1992

notice of external information, only this time they try to reconcile it with their previous theory. Consequently, by the age of eight or nine they can again balance both the evenly and the unevenly weighted blocks. In this way they develop a new and more complete representation about particular domains of knowledge.

The children's behavior on the block task follows a U-curve. Although they are able to solve what seems a complex problem when they are young, a year or so later they are no longer able to solve the same problem. Yet by the time another year or two has gone by, they can solve the problem again. This looks like a U-curve because the behavior looks good to start with, gets worse, and then gradually gets back to how it looked at the outset. However, it is the underlying change in internal thinking that is crucial to understanding how the children's knowledge is developing. This modification of internal thinking is called representational change—in the block test the crucial change is that the child has developed an understanding of balance.

A dynamic process

Unlike Fodor, Karmiloff-Smith believes that the development of infant cognition is a dynamic process. Children may be born with an innate predisposition to learn, but according to Karmiloff-Smith, it is only a very small part of the larger process of developing different domains of knowledge—recognizing objects, categorizing sets of objects as being of the same kind, and communicating through the use of language. From birth children display a whole array of cognitive abilities such as imitating movement, recognizing face shapes, and identifying sounds. Initially these skills are unrelated, but gradually the different domains of knowledge start working together. Education and play, influenced by the culture in which the child lives, shape how the different domains interact.

FUTURE RESEARCH

Determining what infants can perceive and how their cognition develops is the fundamental task facing cognitive psychologists. A major current debate is between psychologists such as Renée Baillargeon and Elizabeth Spelke who believe that infants develop cognitive abilities such as concepts and reasoning at an early age, and those such as Richard Bogartz who believe that children do not develop these abilities until they are older. Cognitive psychologists dispute the view that babies under about 12 months of age have a definite notion of concept, for example. Their claims that younger children lack certain cognitive abilities are countered by critics who believe that the research methods used are not sensitive enough to measure the cognitive systems of children at a younger age.

A young girl and her father playing with building blocks. At the age of about four children can balance blocks of both even and uneven weight. A few years later they appear to have taken a reverse step and are able to balance only even-weight blocks. In the final stage they can balance blocks of even and uneven weight again, as their thought processes have developed to a level where they can solve the problem.

Infants learn more in their first few years of life than they will ever learn in such a short time again. Although the course of the development of cognition is not yet fully charted, it is clear that, by continually studying the way infants behave, and improving research methods, cognitive psychologists will be able to understand more and more about the extraordinary nature of the human mind.

CONNECTIONS

• Perceptual Development: pp. 40–57
• Stages of Development: pp. 58–77

• Nature and Nurture: Volume 1, pp. 22–29
• Cognitive Psychology: Volume 1, pp. 104–117
• Perception: Volume 2, pp. 62–85
• Nature or Nurture: Volume 5, pp. 142–163

Perceptual Development

——— *"Perceptual abilities…change with development and experience."* ———

D. J. Kellman & M. E. Arterberry

Perception is the bridge between the mind and the external world. By perceiving sensory information, we form beliefs and ideas about how the world works. Perceiving the world may seem easy, but it is possible only through a large number of complex biological processes, many of which are still only partially understood and are the subject of ongoing research.

Psychologists distinguish between sensation and perception. Sensation is the measuring ability of our five main senses (hearing, sight, smell, taste, and touch) and other senses to pick up information about the body. The data thus gathered are sent to the brain, where they are interpreted—that is perception. Sensation is inborn: We know that newborns' sensory organs (ears, eyes, nose, skin, and tongue) function effectively from birth. However, less is known about the extent to which infants can perceive objects and events. In 1890 William James (1842–1910) suggested that the newborn's sensory world is a "booming, buzzing confusion." It is only through experience that the developing child can learn to distinguish between the information from its different senses. Perception is a learned process, at least to some substantial extent.

VISUAL PERCEPTION

How and when do infants learn to perceive? Psychologists are eager to measure the growth of perception in infants, but infants are not easy to test. In the first few months of life they spend a lot of time

Newborn babies spend a lot of time eating and sleeping. They are alert only for short periods and have little perceptual ability. What ability they do have is difficult to establish, since they have no means of telling us.

eating and sleeping. They cannot talk, they are unable to follow verbal instructions, and they cannot point out objects. We cannot tell what they are thinking and can only guess their moods, what they are feeling, and infer their perceptions from observing how they behave.

As children grow up, it is easy to assume that just because they can talk, they can understand verbal instructions in the same way that adults do. But that is not always the case. Children's language production often develops before their comprehension: They mimic the noises of

> *"It remains to be seen exactly how attention can distinguish between objects represented by populations of neurons that are so intimately entwined."*
> — *Jochen Braun, 2000*

adult speech before they fully understand it. Consequently, researchers have had to devise a range of novel and ingenious measures to study how children's perceptual abilities develop.

Many of the techniques used to test the development of infants' visual perception rely on watching their eye movements. When adults read or look at something, their eyes flick rapidly from one place to another. For example, in reading this sentence, you will make many rapid, jerky movements with your eyes. However, it will feel as if your eyes are moving smoothly from one word to the next. These rapid eye movements are known as saccades (the word comes from the French for "a jerk on the reins of a horse"). From the age of about one month infants can make saccadic eye movements almost as well as adults. Before this age most evidence suggests that infants often fail to move their eyes toward the correct target, although some researchers have recently suggested that even newborns can make saccadic eye movements for short periods. The most common methods of studying

infant vision rely on the behavioral techniques of preferential looking and habituation that measure overt behavior.

Preferential looking

In the classic preferential looking test two stimuli are presented to a child at the same time. The objects are placed in front of the infant at eye level on either side of the midline (one to the left of the nose, the other to the right). Researchers then measure how long the child looks at each stimulus, either by videotaping the experiment or by watching through a peephole. If the child looks at both stimuli for the same length of time, that is probably because the infant cannot tell them apart. However, if the child looks at one stimulus for longer than the other, then he or she is probably differentiating between the two stimuli.

Another preferential looking test is used to ascertain whether infants can perceive illusory contours (imaginary shapes). In the diagram in the box on p. 42 the shaded circle forms an illusory sphere, but it is difficult to find out whether infants can see it. However, researchers have developed a test in which infants are placed in front of a screen onto which two lines are projected. If the lines move at different speeds, one gives the illusion of an edge, and the other does not. Two-month-old infants showed a preference for the illusory contour.

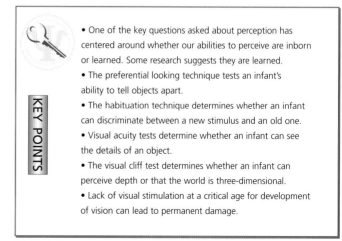

KEY POINTS

- One of the key questions asked about perception has centered around whether our abilities to perceive are inborn or learned. Some research suggests they are learned.
- The preferential looking technique tests an infant's ability to tell objects apart.
- The habituation technique determines whether an infant can discriminate between a new stimulus and an old one.
- Visual acuity tests determine whether an infant can see the details of an object.
- The visual cliff test determines whether an infant can perceive depth or that the world is three-dimensional.
- Lack of visual stimulation at a critical age for development of vision can lead to permanent damage.

Habituation

Infants will fixate on objects and people until they become familiar with them. They then lose interest and look away. Try holding a brightly colored toy in front of a crying baby. Often, the introduction of this new object will stop the baby crying. It will stare at the object, forgetting the reason for crying. After a while, however, the baby may become used to seeing the object, remember being upset, and start crying again. This process of fixating on an object or person for a while followed by a lack of interest in the object or person is termed habituation.

Studies of habituation have provided a wealth of information about the development of perceptual processes. For example, infants will be shown stimulus A for a set period over and over again. Once they have become "habituated" and show

Holding a brightly colored toy, such as this yellow duck, in front of a crying baby is often a successful way of stopping her from crying, but then she will lose interest in the toy and start crying again. This process, called habituation, has been studied to reveal how perceptual processes develop in young children.

VISUAL ILLUSIONS

FOCUS ON

Visual illusions are one of the most exciting ways to gain insights into how our brains make sense of the world. Most of the time we have no difficulty recognizing objects for what they are, but sometimes we can be fooled. A stick, for example, will appear bent when it is placed in water. This illusion is caused by the process of refraction (bending) of light as it passes from air to water. Similarly, a mirage is caused by light passing through layers of hot air above a heated surface, creating the illusion of a pool of water on desert sands or a highway.

Other illusions occur because of the way our brains process the visual information hitting our eyes. For example, if you stare at a rotating wheel for a minute, then look at a static object, the static object will appear to be spinning, too. This happens because when you fixate on something for a long time, the brain adapts to the stimulus, in this case adaptation to spinning motion. Other visual illusions are sometimes termed cognitive illusions. If you have ever seen an impossible triangle or some of the illustrations by the graphic artist M.C. Escher (1898–1970), you will know how difficult it can be to make sense of some pictures. Are babies fooled by visual illusions? Can they tell that something is wrong with what they are seeing? There is some evidence to suggest

The phenomenon of illusory contour—these lines give the illusion of forming a sphere.

that even with infants as young as two months, the answer may sometimes be that they can see that it is an illusion. Researchers have shown that infants of different ages can see an illusory contour such as the one shown above, as long as the illusion is stationary.

little further interest in the stimulus, they are shown a new stimulus, B. If the infants' interests revive in response to stimulus B, this indicates that the infants can discriminate between the two stimuli. Experiments of this type have been used to measure the development of visual attention and how effectively infants can discriminate between similar stimuli.

Visual evoked potentials
Preferential looking and habituation techniques observe the overt behavior of children to measure perceptual activity. By contrast, physiological measures such as visual evoked potentials (VEPs) measure electrical activity in infants' brains. Whenever nerve cells are active, they produce small electrical currents known as potentials. The electrical activity can be measured by placing electrodes on an infant's head over the area of the brain that is responsible for vision. As the infant looks at the stimuli, changes in electrical activity are recorded on a computer.

From the readings it is possible to create images showing the area of the infants' brain that is responsible for vision, which show that they can discriminate stimuli.

Although all three of these techniques are reliable, the most scientifically robust findings are those in which two or more of the procedures support each other.

Visual acuity
In order to understand how the visual system develops, it is important to discover what it is like at birth. Visual acuity is the ability to see fine detail. Investigating visual acuity in the newborn is one of the most important measures of early visual development. For example, it is easy for adults to read the text in a book from quite close up; but if they hold the book further away, it becomes more difficult for them to distinguish one letter from another.

This child has electrodes on his head and is undergoing psychological tests. The electrodes pick up electrical currents, called potentials, that are produced when nerve cells are active. Visual evoked potentials (VEPs) are produced when an infant looks at stimuli. By measuring this electrical activity, researchers have shown that infants can distinguish between different kinds of stimuli.

A test for visual acuity. One circle is gray, and the other is striped. If the baby's visual acuity is good, he will focus for longer on the striped circle (see p. 46).

Opticians test people's visual acuity by asking them to read a line of letters from different distances. If a person can read the letters at a distance of 20 feet (6m) but no farther, when normally adults can read the same line of letters from 60 feet (18m), then the person is said to have 20/60 vision. In other words, that person's visual acuity is only one-third as good as that of a normally sighted adult. Thus it is fairly

EXPERIMENT

VISUAL CLIFF

As much as a third of the brain is used for vision. Seeing is much more complicated than simply having eyes to form images of the world around us: We must also understand (perceive) this information. For example, when we walk to the edge of a cliff, we can see that it is a long way to the ground. We easily perceive this depth. But do infants see depth at birth, or do they learn how to see the world in three dimensions? According to psychologist J. J. Gibson, this type of perception is not learned. He claimed that there are a number of unchanging properties in the visual world that we can perceive immediately and without effort. His wife, E. J. Gibson, a child psychologist, disagreed and thought that children must learn to see depth in the visual world around them.

To put these hypotheses to the test, E. J. Gibson asked whether her infant son would stop at a significant drop, or whether he would fall off. Rather than putting her child in danger, she came up with a safe experiment to test her theories. In the "visual cliff" experiment an infant is placed on the middle of a glass tabletop. Half of the tabletop rests on a solid tiled box, but the other half stands over a drop to the tiled floor. The aim of the experiment is to see whether infants will avoid crawling over the "cliff." If they do, then this suggests that they can perceive depth without having to learn about it. E. J. Gibson tried this experiment not just with babies, but with young animals as well.

Almost all animals, as soon as they are capable of independent movement, avoided the visual cliff. Goats avoid it from the day they are born. Rats are blind at birth but avoid the cliff as soon as they can see (four weeks). Human infants refuse to crawl over the "cliff" from about seven months of age. Because infants younger than this cannot crawl, it was thought until fairly recently that they did not mind being placed on the transparent table. However, it has since been found that when three-month-

Do children perceive depth at birth, or do they have to learn that the world is three-dimensional? Here the child is very unsure of the depth of the water, and his father holds him to prevent him from falling in.

old infants are placed on the part of the table above the apparent drop, their heart rate increases, and they open their eyes wide, as if they are scared. Below this age infants cannot see very clearly. Therefore it is difficult to test depth perception from birth until the child is three months old. However, the results of the visual cliff experiment do suggest that depth perception is not learned in the way that E. J. Gibson believed.

Although results from different studies vary, there is general agreement that infants' visual acuity increases rapidly during the first six months of life. One potential reason for these changes is the development of the eye itself. At birth the cone cells on the retina have only short outer segments and so do not catch many photons of light. Because they are loosely packed, these cells cannot transmit fine-grained information. Yet even though the infant's perceptions are not fully developed, they are probably different from those of people with cataracts or other forms of blurry vision.

AUTISTIC CHILDREN

To understand normal perceptual development, many researchers have looked at how perception can develop differently. Autism is a rare developmental disorder (*see* Vol. 6, pp. 68–91). Children with autism have difficulty understanding the thoughts and feelings of others. They do not engage in play with other children. They often appear withdrawn or aloof. There is also evidence of perceptually based differences. People with autism are usually able to complete visual tasks—such as picking out an image hidden among a collection of shapes—more quickly than nonsufferers. In other words, they are better at recognizing objects. This may be because autistics' cognitive processing has developed differently from that of normal people, but it may also be a result of differences at an earlier perceptual level.

It is fairly common for people with autism to show a lack of coordination. There is evidence that the area of the brain concerned with motor coordination may not work as well in people with autism. This might explain the ill-coordinated movements and posture seen in some sufferers. The disparity between motor coordination skills and object recognition performance may indicate that some visual-processing mechanisms in the autistic brain are impaired.

There is evidence to suggest that one part of the human brain—the ventral stream—is used for recognizing faces and objects, and that a different part—the dorsal stream—is used for determining the spatial location of objects and processing information necessary for visual motor tasks.

In order to see if either of these parts of the brain is responsible for the perceptual difficulties seen in autism, researchers have proposed two different tasks. The first one measures motion coherence thresholds—that is, how we know where an object is and where it is going. Participants have to decide where on the screen a pattern of squares is moving among a lot of randomly moving squares. This has been used to test dorsal stream function. The other task is known as form coherence: how we perceive and recognize what an object is. Here, participants have to see if they can detect an area of aligned parts among a large number of randomly positioned parts. This measure tests the function of the ventral stream area of the brain and whether or not it is associated with perceptual difficulties seen with autism.

To see whether children with autism have problems processing motion, Janine Spencer tested children with autism on both form- and motion-coherence tasks. Their results were compared with those of nonsuffering children and adults in a control group. Spencer found that children with autism were much worse at perceiving motion than normal children. However, there was no difference in the way the two groups of children perceived form coherence. Spencer's study, which was conducted in 2000, seems to demonstrate that children with autism show a particular deficit in tasks that involve the dorsal stream. It seems to be separate from their ability to use similar visual information in tasks that require ventral stream processing. The results suggest that the perceptual abnormalities in children with autism cannot be explained fully in terms of cognitive processing.

This is a static diagram of a test that measures motion coherence and perceptual abnormalities in autistic children, who are asked to identify dots on screen that are moving in a different direction from the majority.

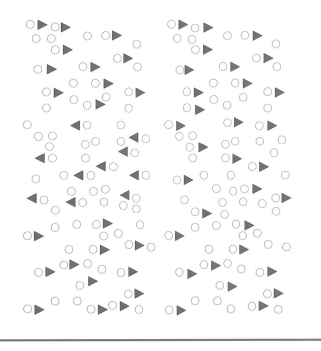

easy to test visual acuity in adults. Of course, infants cannot read, so researchers have had to come up with different ways of testing this faculty. Visual acuity in young children can be measured by VEPs (*see* p. 43) or by using preferential looking techniques (*see* pp. 41–44).

Contrast sensitivity

The other main way of assessing early visual acuity is by testing infants' contrast sensitivity—that is, their ability to differentiate an object from its background. Depending on the size of an object and how well it is lighted, it is usually possible to distinguish it from its background as long as the difference in brightness between the object and its background is greater than one percent. Contrast sensitivity is normally measured by getting people to look at spatial gratings. These are grids that have parallel bars with a series of gaps between them. They test the ability to discern what is behind the bars. The distance between the

bars and the brightness (luminance) of both the grating itself and the object behind it can be varied in the test conditions in order to establish the limits of people's sensitivity.

To understand how tests with gratings work, imagine a line of railings. If you are close to them, it is possible to see what is behind them through the gaps. When you move farther away, it becomes harder to see the difference between the railings and background. The size and number of

> "Researchers have shown that infants as young as 2 to 3 months are able to discriminate a variety of facial expression contrasts."
> — Barrera and Maurer, 1981

spaces between the railings will determine how easily you can see the contrast. If the railings are close together, or you are far away, you will not see the contrast.

Contrast sensitivity tests measure a person's ability to differentiate objects from their backgrounds. They can be compared to these railings. The closer you are, the easier it is to see what is going on in the background. As you move farther away, or if the railings are closer together, then it is more difficult to distinguish between the railings and the background.

ENVIRONMENTAL ISSUES

There is plentiful evidence to suggest that people are born with the ability to see. Does this mean that the environment is not important for perceptual development? Between the 1950s and the late 1970s numerous experiments were conducted on animals to try and answer this question.

One experiment involved covering up the eyes of newborn chimpanzees or keeping them in a darkened room. Researchers found that by the age of seven months the chimps' vision had permanently weakened, and after 16 months they were virtually blind because the retina and the optic nerve stopped working. Chimpanzees kept in a partially darkened environment seemed to suffer no such deterioration of the retina, but still had difficulty recognizing objects. As a result of this research, scientists wondered if there is a critical period in which visual perception develops.

One of the most efficient ways to perceive depth is through the use of binocular vision. Binocular vision is where the image of an object falls on corresponding points of the retinas in both eyes, and the image is merged into a single perception. However, in 1963 scientists David Hubel and Torsten Weisel covered up one eye of a number of kittens as soon as they were born for two to three months. When the bandages were removed, they found that the kittens had very poor vision in the eye that had been covered. Furthermore, it was found that they no longer had binocular vision. This would suggest that there is a critical period in which kittens can develop binocular vision.

More recent research suggests that this critical period for visual development is from three weeks to three months. In monkeys this critical period goes on until they are 18 months old. Is there also a critical period for the development of binocular vision in human infants? Of course, similar tests could not be carried out on infants since their sight might be permanently impaired.

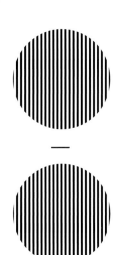

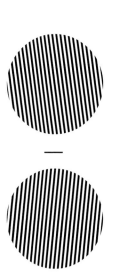

Many children have a squint when they are young, which affects their binocular vision. In 1975 a group of researchers did an experiment with a number of adults who had a squint during childhood that was later corrected. The level of binocular vision was measured using a visual illusion known as the tilt-after-effect. The participants were asked to cover one eye and look between the tilted images with the other eye. They were then instructed to look with the eye that had been covered up between the two nontilted images. The amount of slant that was perceived when looking between the vertical images (after-effect) with the eye that had been covered up was used as a measure of binocular vision. The more slant, the better the binocular vision. This effect—known as interocular transfer—is caused by an adaptation of the direction-selection cells in the brain's visual cortex.

Interocular transfer was near normal in the participants who had their squint corrected between 14 and 30 months of age. However, those who had their squint corrected between the ages of four years and 20 years did not shown any signs of interocular transfer. These results suggest that there may be a critical period for developing binocular vision in humans as well as in animals.

The tilt-after-effect is an experiment to measure binocular vision. People are asked to look at the line between the images on the right for a while with one eye covered. They then have to look at the line between the images on the left with the eye that has been covered. The degree to which the vertical lines appear to slant is used as a measure of binocular vision.

Depth perception

By about eight to nine months of age infants begin to crawl, and for the first time they are able to explore their environment on their own. They are able to move themselves around objects such as furniture and can reach out and grab things. That suggests that they can perceive depth and the distance between objects (*see* box p. 44). When we look at an object, the image projected onto the retina at the back of the eye is flat. It is also constantly changing. Young infants are able to maneuver in their environment because, like adults, they perceive a world that is steady and has three dimensions (length, breadth, and depth). In other words, when we look around us, we can see that things are not flat—they have depth. To be able to see the world in depth has numerous advantages. Think, for example, how many times we would trip if we could not see that the edge of the curb was higher than the street. Being able to see in depth helps us recognize objects. How could we get into a car if we perceived it as being flat? Luckily, there are a number of visual clues that help us see the world in three dimensions.

One of the most important aids to seeing in depth is stereoscopic vision. Depth perception based on stereoscopic vision depends on having a slightly different image received by each eye, and having two eyes that point in the same direction. When we look at something that is near us, we can see it with both eyes. This is known as crossed disparity. Hold up your finger directly in front of your nose, and look at it. Your eyes will move together so they can both see it. However, when you look at faraway objects, your eyes diverge, so you see a different image in each eye. This is known as uncrossed disparity.

In the visual cortex (the area of the brain concerned with vision) there are cells that respond to crossed disparity. There are also cells that respond to uncrossed disparity and sense objects that are far away. Look at an object in the distance. Now close your left eye and look at it. If you now close your right eye, and look at the same object with your left eye, it will appear to have moved. This ability to see two different images allows us to see in depth. It is known as stereopsis.

Stereoscopic vision tends to occur in animals that are predators. Having the ability to look at something and see it in depth allows predators, such as lions or eagles, to judge where their prey is in space and accurately target it. Animals that are preyed on, such as rabbits or hens, have a much better field of view. Because their eyes are placed on either side of their

Predators such as the lion have closely spaced forward-facing eyes, enabling them to track their prey at a close distance. This gives them good binocular vision. Prey animals such as hares, on the other hand, have eyes on either side of their head so they can see all around them and are aware of approaching predators.

head, they can see virtually all around them. Of course, this has advantages. It is very difficult to approach such an animal without it seeing you. However, rabbits and other animals that do not have stereoscopic vision have difficulty in seeing things in depth nearby. If you watch a hen eating, for example, you will notice that it continuously pecks at the ground to pick up food.

We know from behavioral tests and from visual evoked potentials (*see* p. 43) that human infants start to show sensitivity to stereopsis (stereoscopic vision) from as early as 11 to 13 weeks. However, stereopsis is not the only function that enables us to see depth. If we close one eye, the world does not look flat. One of the other functions that help us see the world in three dimensions is known as motion parallax. It makes objects farther away seem to move more slowly. For instance, when you sit on a train and look out of

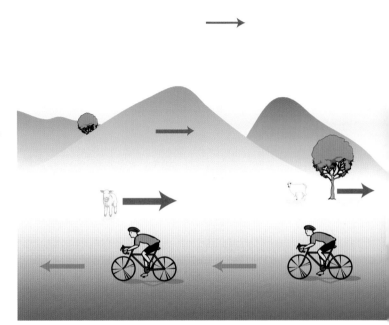

> *"Many of the visual cues used in perceiving depth or relative distance require only one eye; they are called monocular cues."*
> — *Dr. Ronald W. Mayer, 2002*

the window, the nearest objects are a rapidly moving blur, while trees in the distance glide by sedately, and the farthest objects (such as the Moon) even seem to move in the same direction as you.

The perception of depth through the observation of motion is a very complicated process. But we know that infants can tell the difference between directions of motion as early as seven weeks, and this starts to show up on visual evoked potentials from 10 weeks. After that young children gradually develop sensitivity to a range of speeds.

The texture of an object helps us perceive depth. Almost all natural surfaces are textured, and in many instances texture is a better cue to depth than motion. Texture means any pattern on an

object or surface—it could be anything from pebbles on a beach to patterns on wallpaper. The brain assumes that the pebbles are much the same size. Therefore, those that look smaller must be farther away. If we stand on a rocky beach, the pebbles seem to get smaller and smaller as we look toward the horizon.

For an infant to use such clues is a tall order. Infants can see differences in patterns from a very early age. In fact, they have the ability to detect the orientation of lines from birth and can separate areas with different texture patterns from about 12 weeks of age. But learning to understand what it is about objects that changes with distance requires a much higher level of processing, and consequently we might expect it to appear at a much later stage of development. Yet we know that from as early as two months an infant's heart rate will increase if it is placed on a glass platform above a drop (*see* box p. 44). When psychologists test infants' ability to avoid large drops, such as staircases, they always include clear texture patterns to indicate depth because they

Motion parallax enables us to see the world in depth. The **BLUE** arrows indicate the direction of the cyclist's movement. As the cyclist moves forward, objects are displaced and seem to move in relation to her. The rate of displacement is shown by the thickness of the **RED** arrows—the thicker arrows indicate that the closer objects appear to move more quickly than the distant ones.

know the children will recognize them. Although infants can perceive objects in three dimensions, researchers are interested in knowing the extent to which infant perception of depth is like that of adults. Do they see an object as separate from its background? Is the projection of a two-dimensional image onto the retina perceived as a three-dimensional image, as in adult vision? A variety of research methods such as habituation and visual acuity are used to test what a child can see and to monitor activity in the visual cortex. One area of study that scientists have been working on to answer these questions is object perception.

Psychological tests suggest that infants are able to use visual clues to perceive depth and to avoid a large drop such as this staircase at as young as 12 weeks of age (see box on p. 44).

Object perception

When you look around a room, you can see many different objects: chair, fireplace, lamp, rug, and so on. As an adult it is easy to see that a lamp is distinct from its background by using clues in the environment such as shape, texture, and color. In 1954 psychologist Jean Piaget (1896–1980) found that infants do not use these same clues. When his son Laurent was six months and 22 days old, Piaget held out a box of matches to him. However, just as the child was about to grasp them, Piaget placed the matches on a book. Rather than try to grab for the matches, his son reached for the book. Piaget suggested that when the two objects were stationary, Laurent could not perceive the boundary between them and treated them as a single object. Many subsequent experiments have provided support for Piaget's claims. So now scientists are trying to work out how and when object perception develops.

How do we divide the world into distinct objects? First, we must be able to see where one object ends and another begins. For example, when you see someone with a glass in his hand, you must be able to see that the glass is a separate object from the hand. Second, object perception involves being able to perceive that an object is the same as one you have seen before. Most objects rest on other objects. When we look at an object, we can never see all of it at one time. Objects are also frequently hidden by other ones moving in front of them. So we need to be able to recognize an object even though some of it is not visible—that means using incomplete information to decide whether the object in front of us is one that we have seen before. Although as adults we can solve these problems easily, it is not a simple procedure.

It is possible that people perceive objects according to a set of general rules. One suggestion comes from Gestalt psychology (*see* Vol. 1, pp. 46–51), which proposes that people will naturally try to organize what they perceive—even

COMPUTER VISION

For many years computer scientists and psychologists have been trying to figure out how to make computers operate intelligently. Most of the work in artificial intelligence (AI) (*see* Vol. 2, pp. 140–163) has involved trying to get computers to "think" in the same way as people. Early on, computer scientists realized that to get visual information into a computer, they would have to figure out how to process the information received by a camera.

This has proved to be exceptionally difficult. Most visual perception is so rapid and automatic that we don't even think about it. We don't even think that there is any "process" involved. We simply believe that we perceive the environment and objects in it directly.

But when computer scientists connected a video camera to a computer, they found out how difficult it is to write a program enabling the computer to recognize objects or navigate in an environment. We now know that as much as a third of the cerebral cortex helps with the processing of information. We also know that the brain is an exceptionally powerful computing device. So what is all this brainpower doing?

Computer scientist David Marr (1945–1980) made great strides in figuring out how the brain processes visual information. He also showed how computer programs could process similar information and understand the brain. Marr's first principle was to separate the computer from the program it was running. Second, he showed that the theory behind any particular stage of visual processing could be implemented with a number of different algorithms (mathematical formulas or processes) or computer programs.

When we look at a cup, we instantly recognize it whether it is red, blue, or yellow, upside down or the right way up, in full view or partly hidden by another object. In order to do this, our brain runs through several stages of processing. They include finding the edges of the object, calculating that it is in depth and not flat, and also that it matches our idea of what a cup is.

Marr broke down each of these stages of processing into three levels. The first level involves the theoretical steps of the process. The second level works out a program or algorithm that can achieve it. Finally, the third level is to work out the practical implementation of a system to achieve the theoretical steps in level one. The system is either a computer or a brain.

How does this relate to visual development? A number of computer vision systems are based on learning algorithms. They are computer programs that change with experience. While they are inspired by the neural networks in our brain, they do not acquire new information and change the way they work in the same way that the human brain develops. But there are interesting parallels, and computer vision researchers are increasingly looking to the neurosciences for inspiration.

So we can gradually figure out the brain processes underlying visual perception, and how they can be implemented on a computer. Does this mean that a computer could see? That depends on what we mean by seeing. If seeing is the ability to use visual information to accomplish tasks, then the answer is yes. If seeing is awareness of the visual environment, or consciousness, the answer is no one yet knows for sure.

---

meaningless arrangements of unfamiliar shapes—into the simplest, most regular units they can. As adults it is possible that we may recognize an object before we have seen all of it; for example, if we see a car from one side, we assume that the other side has two wheels as well. However, this implies that we have some previously acquired knowledge of what the object is. Infants do not have this information since most objects are unfamiliar. Studies of infants' object perception must therefore find ways of separating visual perception from any knowledge-based interpretation.

Motion and visual occlusion

How do infants perceive the wholeness and boundaries of an object when they can see only part of it? In 1983, using a preferential looking technique, psychologists Philip Kelman and Elizabeth Spelke showed four-month-old infants an object of which the top and bottom were visible, but the center was covered by another, closer object. The infants were shown this display over and over again. They were then shown two new stimuli. One was a complete object, and the other was two fragments of an object. As with all preferential looking experiments, the infants were expected to look longer at the stimuli they believed to be novel. If they perceived the partially covered (occluded) object as one continuous object, they would look more at the fragmented stimuli. However, if they perceived the occluded object as two separate objects, they would look longer at the complete stimuli. The diagram opposite shows what these stimuli looked like.

Kelman and Spelke found that when the visible parts of an occluded object moved together behind what was obscuring them, infants perceived them as a single, continuous object, as an adult would. Unlike adults, however, if the occluded object did not move, the findings imply that the infants perceive two

> "Occlusion often renders the sensory information defining an object incomplete, yet we normally perceive continuous 3-D forms."
> — Guttman and Sekuler, 1995

separate objects. These findings provide further evidence that infants can use motion as a clue to whether an occluded object is a single unit, but they cannot draw the same inferences from stationary objects.

Motion also seems to influence three- to five-month-old infants' perceptions of object boundaries. In one study infants perceived two overlapping objects as distinct if they moved independently of each other even if they sometimes touched each other while in motion. Yet stationary, overlapping objects were not perceived as separate even if they differed in color, texture, or shape. So we know that infants can perceive objects as separate from clues provided by their movement. But how do they perceive the identity of an object over successive intermittent encounters?

In a series of experiments designed to answer this question, four-month-old infants were shown two objects moving in sequence behind a large block. In one test

center–occluded object

complete object

fragmented object

Three views of the same object. Experiments on four-month-old infants suggest they can deduce that a partially covered object is a single unit when it is moving, but unlike adults, not when it is stationary.

both objects moved in and out of view at a constant speed. In others the objects were moved in such a way as to suggest that their speed was changing abruptly while they were behind the block. However, no matter what the apparent speed or jerkiness of the objects' movement, if the infants saw one object move behind the block at the start, they expected one object to come out again at the end of the sequence. These findings suggest that infants are not influenced by the apparent smoothness of object motion. Given that young infants have little or no knowledge of objects, it can be inferred that perceiving them might be an innate brain process rather than an acquired skill.

Face perception

Faces play an important part in human social interaction. We can show we are happy or angry simply by changing our facial expressions. It is easy to recognize people simply by looking at their faces. In fact, we do not even have to see the whole faces of people we know in order to be able to recognize them. Infants soon learn to distinguish their mother's face from others. From as early as two weeks of age they can watch an adult's face and imitate certain gestures such as sticking out the tongue. Such findings have led researchers to ask whether infants have an innate tendency to look for facelike stimuli.

Many researchers believe that young infants' ability to track faces casts significant light on the development of the brain. Although there is a lot of evidence to suggest that it takes infants about three months to learn the layout of facial features, some studies seem to indicate that infants can track facelike stimuli in the first 10 minutes of life. At between four and six weeks old, however, the preferential tracking of faces decreases rapidly. It returns only during the third month of life. This may show that newborns process faces using a different part of the brain from that which they will use for the same operation in later life. If this supposition is correct, it would appear that the cortex (outer layer) of the brain has matured by the time the infant is three months old. Before that other parts of the brain are used for identification.

It has also been suggested that the newborn's tendency to attend to faces might be a way of exposing and directing the developing cortex to important visual stimuli. After a while the cortical system gains sufficient experience with faces to continue to pick up more and more information about them. So there would

How do we recognize faces? This is recognizable as the face of George W. Bush even though most of the features have been obscured.

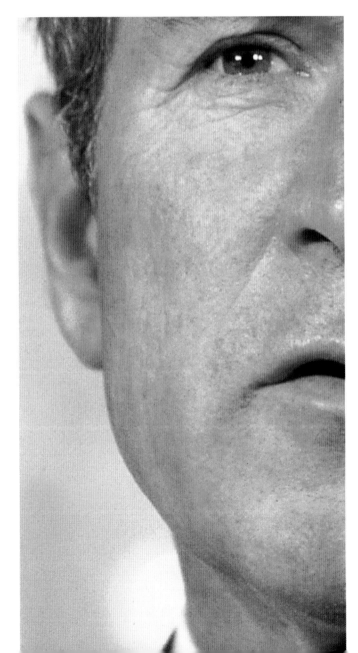

seem to be three factors that enable the human brain to learn about faces. First, the newborn has an innate tendency to focus on facelike patterns. Second, there are a large number of faces in the environment for the infant to look at. And third, parts of the brain become active whenever a face is seen. Together, these factors ensure that the brain becomes specialized to attend to faces.

Externality effect
How do infants recognize familiar faces? Research undertaken in the 1980s by Ian Bushnell suggests that newborns can discriminate between two similar faces on the basis of hair, eyes, and mouth. However, if a swimming cap is placed over the two heads on display, infants cannot tell the difference between them until they are about three months old.

The inability to tell the difference between changes in features if a border is placed around them is a product of what is known as the externality effect. Bushnell and his team found that the externality effect is reduced if the face has a dynamic expression, such as a smile. With older children this is not so important. Evidence of the externality effect can be seen in other species. In 1974 scientist Nick Humphrey studied the externality effect in Helen, a monkey whose visual cortex had been removed. Helen normally had no problem picking up raisins, but could not pick up a raisin with a ring around it. Psychologists have suggested that the externality effect may illustrate the limitation of newborns' attention capacities.

Emotional expressions
As we have seen, infants can imitate others' facial expressions from a very early age—as little as two days after birth. Yet although they can make happy and sad faces, they are not smiling or turning down their mouths in expressions of emotion. So when do infants learn to modify their behavior as a result of other people's facial expressions?

Research suggests that infants can begin to notice the difference in facial expressions at between four and ten months. They can also see the difference between smiling and laughing expressions. Noticing the difference between expressions is not the same, however, as understanding what they mean. Expressions of emotion are often accompanied by vocalization. For example, a wide-open mouth and eyes may express shock. They are frequently accompanied by a sharp intake of breath. We know that infants can discriminate the vocal sounds of happiness and sadness by three to four months of age and can match them with the appropriate facial expressions. However, what is less clear is whether infants realize that a smiling face and contented sounds mean that the person is "happy."

Social referencing

One way to measure when infants actually understand the meaning of an expression is to observe whether they can adapt their behavior on the basis of other people's emotions. This is known as social referencing. Social referencing can be thought of as the ability to communicate using expressions. For example, parents often communicate disapproval of an action to their children simply by looking at them or by raising an eyebrow. Whatever the expression is, children quickly learn what the look means.

In one relevant social referencing experiment infants and adults are put in an unfamiliar situation. A new toy is brought in. The experimenter tells the adult to make a particular facial expression such as one that conveys happiness or fear. The infant's response to this expression is measured. By about 12 months of age infants can match their behavior to the emotional expression. So if the mother shows fear when the toy is brought in, the infants avoid it. On the other hand, if the mother's expression is happy, they will approach the toy. Thus although infants can discriminate between faces from

between four and 10 months, they do not seem able to act on other people's expressions until they are about 12 months of age. There are two possible explanations for this. It may be that infants can discriminate between different expressions of emotion before they have learned what they mean. Alternatively, infants may learn the meaning of these expressions before they realize that people use them as a means of modifying the infant's behavior. It is by attending to other people's facial expressions that infants learn more subtle information about what facial expressions mean and how to act on them. A history of associating a particular expression with a certain outcome also contributes to learning subtle information about the meanings of facial expressions.

Visual attention

So far we have looked at the development of different aspects of visual processing. Researchers have been able to learn a great deal about how and when these processes develop. However, much of our understanding of perceptual development has come from measuring infants' attention to visual displays or actions. What do we mean by attention? Whenever we read a book or watch television, we are able to concentrate on what we want to look at. The ability to attend to something for as long as we want is known as "sustained attention."

In order to attend to an object or event, we have to be alert. This is the first step in developing the ability to attend to things. Researchers have studied the development of achieving rather than maintaining an alert state in infants. During the first month of life infants are in an alert state for less than 20 percent of the time and sleep for 75 percent of the time. During the first three months of life the distribution between alert and asleep states changes dramatically. By the age of three months infants' periods of alertness become more frequent. In young infants before two to three months old the alert state is achieved mainly by external stimulation—for example, by stroking their faces. However, from 12 weeks of age the ability to maintain attention rather than simply attain it begins to develop.

Attention involves selecting particular objects or events to focus on. Over the last 20 years researchers have found that one distinct form of attention is the ability to select and focus on objects no matter where they are located in the visual field.

If an object is moved slowly and at a constant speed in one direction in front of a newborn infant, it can follow it with its eyes. However, if the object changes direction or speeds up, then it is no longer able to follow it. This is known as smooth pursuit. It is different from saccadic eye movements, in which the eyes shift abruptly from one location to another. In smooth pursuit the eyes move in an unbroken progression from one location to another.

> *"A running controversy among scientists studying visual perception centers on the neural basis for our powers to pick out figure from background."*
> — *Julia Karow, 2000*

By three to four months of age infants display more smooth pursuit and are able to focus on and track faster-moving objects. Of course, another important aspect of attention is being able to stop tracking an object when you want to.

During the 1960s and 1970s researchers noticed that before two months of age infants would fixate on an object for long periods. They took this as evidence that these prolonged fixations meant that infants were not really processing what they were looking at. In other words, they believed that infants were not controlling how long they looked at it. More recently it has been suggested that young infants are unable to disengage their eyes easily. They may be processing the object, but they have difficulty in moving their eyes away from it. This phenomenon is sometimes termed sticky fixation.

The ability to disengage attention has been measured using overlap-gap tests. In these experiments an object is placed directly in front of an infant's eye. Other target objects are then placed so that they overlap the central object, touch it, or are nearby but with a gap in between. The researcher then measures the length of time it takes the infants to look at the peripheral targets. Like adults, infants have been fastest in shifting their attention when there is a gap, and they are slowest when there is an overlap of the central object and the target objects. This type of study shows that young infants are able to disengage their attention from one object to another. This ability develops rapidly in the first four months of life.

So far we have seen that from a very early age infants are able to follow and attend to objects in their visual field. Attention is the ability to choose where, when, and on what we focus and for how long. The aim of preferential looking studies with infants is to see if they can compare and distinguish between a familiar and novel stimulus. That involves the infant voluntarily shifting its attention from one stimulus to the other. The ability to shift attention between different stimuli seems to increase with age. At three months infants can shift their attention, but they do it far less frequently than four-month-olds.

To test the extent to which an infant can choose not to attend to something, an attractive display is shown while a peripheral stimulus is placed to one side of its field of vision so that it cannot look at it without taking its eyes off the main object. Researchers found that infants could learn not to look at the peripheral target under these conditions. In fact, six-month-old infants are able to delay looking at the peripheral target for up to five seconds in order to look at an attractive display in a different location. This suggests that by four to six months of age infants are able to control where they look and where they do not look.

Other research has shown that there are three periods of development of visual attention during infancy. From birth until about two months of age infants become more and more alert and aware of what is going on around them. From two or three months until about six months there is rapid development in spatial orientation. The third period begins from about five to six months onward. It is at this stage that infants are able for the first time to control their attention.

AUDITORY PERCEPTION

So far we have looked at visual perception. As adults, using our eyes to determine what is in the world around us seems to be of primary importance—no other sense seems to contribute as much to our perception. Yet newborns can hear much better than they can see, and therefore it is likely that, for them, auditory perception is at least as important as sight.

One of the first sounds that infants hear is their mother's voice. Research carried out in the early 1980s showed that infants could discriminate their mother's voice from that of a stranger within one to two days of birth. Are they very quick learners, or might infants be able to recognize their mother's voice while still in the womb?

To answer this question, psychologists ran another study in which they asked pregnant women to read a story aloud to their unborn child twice a day for the last six weeks of pregnancy. When the newborns were two days old, they were read the old story and a new one. The infants sucked more on a teat when they heard the old story than when they heard the new one, even if the mother was not reading it. This indicates that infants are able to experience and learn some things before they are born (*see* pp. 6–23).

There is evidence to suggest that infants distinguish between phonemes (speech sounds) in the same way as adults. For example, the words "park" and "bark" are almost identical and are distinguished only by a single phoneme. Being able to perceive sounds in this way is known as

categorical perception because each sound belongs to only one category.

In 1983 psychologist Patricia Kuhl tested children as young as 18 weeks of age to see if they could distinguish contrasting vowel sounds. The subjects of her experiment looked at two identical faces that silently articulated different vowel sounds—"ee" as in "reef" and "o" as in "bob"—while only one of those sounds was played through a speaker. The infants looked significantly longer at the faces that were making the mouth shape compatible with the sound. This result tends to confirm what had long been believed— that people are born with some genetically endowed mechanism for registering speechlike sounds. It is this ability to differentiate phonemes that enables children to quickly learn their "mother tongue" (the language to which they are most exposed in infancy).

Different nationalities often have difficulties with certain sounds in foreign languages. For example, adult English speakers may find the "rolled r" in French and Italian difficult. The Japanese find it particularly hard to distinguish between

Mother and daughter reading a book together. It is thought that infants hear and learn their mother's voice even before they are born. People are probably also born with some sort of genetically inherited mechanism for recognizing speechlike sounds.

"r" and "l" in English. Yet Japanese infants have no problem perceiving the difference between these two consonants. So when do infants lose this ability to discriminate between all existing speech sounds?

In 1984 Janet Werker and Richard Tees found that between the ages of six to eight months infants born of English-speaking parents could discriminate contrasting consonants in Hindi. By the time they were 12 months old, however, these same infants failed to discriminate between the same sounds. Yet infants of Hindi-speaking parents did not lose the ability to discriminate these consonant sounds. This suggests that people are born with some innate mechanism for learning language. Early on infants can discriminate between all of the speech sounds in the world. However, without exposure to these sounds in the environment infants will lose this ability and be able to distinguish only between relevant speech sounds in the language they hear around them.

INTERSENSORY INTEGRATION

In this chapter we have observed the development of visual and auditory perception. However, on a daily basis we integrate both visual and auditory information in order to get around our environment. For example, when you see your dog running in from the garden, you can hear it panting at the same time. We reach out to pick up a telephone when we hear it ring. We use our intersensory perception in many ways. We can communicate effectively by making an "uh huh" sound or simply by raising our eyebrows. If we are familiar with an object through one sense—for example, by seeing it daily—we can often recognize it by touch alone. For adults intersensory perception is an everyday occurrence. But when do infants learn to integrate information from their visual, auditory, and other senses?

In 1984 Elizabeth Spelke showed four-month-old infants two animated cartoon films simultaneously on separate screens. Each film had a soundtrack associated with it. While the infants were watching the films, one of the soundtracks was played on a loudspeaker placed centrally between the two screens. Spelke found that the infants would turn and look significantly longer at a film when the corresponding soundtrack was being played. This suggests that by four months

> **"Processes closely associated with the appearance of consciousness, such as information integration and dissemination, appear to operate unconsciously."**
> **— Max Velmans, 1999**

of age infants are learning to integrate and coordinate sensory information from different sources. Over the next few years these infants will learn to explore and interact with their environment. They will be able to communicate with other people and learn from their experiences. They will be able to do all these things because they were born with perceptual abilities.

Research into how much infant perception is innate or inborn, and how much is learned in the first few years of life, continues to fascinate cognitive psychologists. The problem of not being able to communicate fully with infants remains a major barrier, however. As psychologists attempt to learn more and measure infant perception with greater accuracy, further, ever-more ingenious tests are being created to help them.

CONNECTIONS

Stages of Development

Young, inquiring minds experiment with their new environment

Two of the most important theories of intellectual, or cognitive, development in children—how a child's thinking changes and develops from infancy to adulthood—were proposed by the Russian psychologist Lev Vygotsky and the Swiss psychologist Jean Piaget. Both believed that intellectual development occurred in stages. While Vygotsky saw children as "apprentices" who learn from more experienced individuals, Piaget regarded children as "inquiring scientists" who learn by experimenting with their environment. Piaget's work in particular has been hugely influential.

Psychologists studying how the mind develops agree that there are two fundamental questions to address: "What" develops, and "how" does it develop. Although identifying "what" changes is crucial, knowing "how" the changes take place is also important if we are to fully understand mental development.

The diagrams below show some possible approaches to the problem of how children's minds develop. In the first one the horizontal line identifies a child's age between 0 and 10. The vertical line identifies performance on some tasks (for example, solving a problem), with scores ranging from 0 (very poor) to 100 (perfect). The three dots show the child's performance at ages two, five, and eight.

At the age of two, it was low. At five, it was better, but not as good as at eight, when it was quite high. Clearly there has been development, but how has it occurred? What assumptions would you apply to fill the gaps between the three dots to predict performance at ages three or seven?

You might assume that development is the mere accumulation of experiences over time. In that case you would fill the gaps by drawing a line through all three dots, as shown in the next diagram. This is an example of continuous linear changes. It is linear because the line is straight, and continuous because the line is unbroken. Your theory of development would suggest that experiences add up, so over time children get better at tasks.

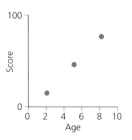

Data for a child tested at intervals over a period of years: The horizontal scale shows the child's age, and the vertical scale represents the child's score on a set of specific tasks.

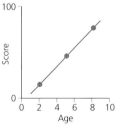

Continuous linear change: Development is a linear process—experiences are accumulated over time, and the child performs the tasks better, scoring higher.

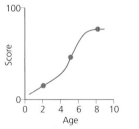

Continuous nonlinear change: As the child's accumulating experiences interact with one another, there is a period of accelerating development, before it reaches a plateau.

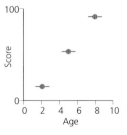

Discontinuous development: The child's mind is relatively stable for long periods of time, but there are sudden, periodic changes that increase performance.

If you assume that development is the accumulation of experiences, and that these experiences interact with one another to create even richer knowledge, you might fill in the gaps as in the third diagram. This is an example of continuous nonlinear change. It is continuous because the line is unbroken, but nonlinear because, unlike a straight line, it changes direction. In this example the changes are initially small, then increase dramatically around the age of five, and finally level off around the age of eight. Your theory of development, in that case, suggests that experiences add up and interact, so at a critical age there is substantial change when experiences have reached a crucial level. Past this level additional experiences do not contribute much more change.

An alternative to continuous theories is to suggest that development involves discontinuous changes. The last diagram is an example of discontinuous development because, instead of a single unbroken line, several horizontal lines called "plateaus" fill the gaps. The logic for this explanation is that the child's mind is relatively stable for long periods. At intervals, however, there are sudden changes that increase performance. Although the accumulation of experiences over time may trigger these changes, experience itself is not reflected in performance measures.

The two most important theories in developmental psychology assume discontinuous changes such as those shown in the last diagram. They are the theories of Lev Vygotsky (1896–1934) and Jean Piaget (1896–1980). Both men believed cognitive development was discontinuous but progressed in definite stages. They differed in their premises, however, and each tells a different story about cognitive growth.

VYGOTSKY'S DEVELOPMENTAL THEORY

During Vygotsky's youth his country underwent the Russian Revolution, which applied the theories of Marxism. Marxism was developed by the German

KEY POINTS

- Piaget and Vygotsky are major contributors to the study of cognitive development.
- Both psychologists tried to answer the question: "How does a child acquire a functional representation of the world?"
- They started with different assumptions about development. Vygotsky was influenced by Marxist ideology, while Piaget was influenced by self-organizing systems he studied as a biologist.
- Developmental psychologists have usually contrasted the two theories, stressing how Piaget ignored the social dimension, or how Vygotsky ignored the child's individual efforts to construct an understanding of the world.
- Both psychologists devised new research methods, identified novel phenomena, and more importantly, showed that in some respects, cognitive development is discontinuous.
- Recently, some researchers have stressed the complementary nature of both theories rather than presenting the contrasts. Piaget did not ignore the importance of the child's culture, nor did Vygotsky ignore the child's role as active participant.
- A definitive answer to the question of how cognitive development takes place remains to be found. But the stage theories of Piaget and Vygotsky, as well as the ideas of those who followed them, have stressed the issue of discontinuities in cognitive development.

philosophers Karl Marx (1818–1883) and Friedrich Engels (1820–1895), and is a political doctrine that stresses three important points: Activity generates thinking, development advances by dialectical exchanges (exchanges that force individuals to think about their thinking),

> *"Any function in the child's cultural development appears twice, or on two planes. First it appears on the social plane, and then on the psychological plane."*
> — *Lev Vygotsky, 1978*

and development is a historical process within a culture. As a scholar, Vygotsky tried to apply Marxist ideology to psychology. Vygotsky's theory can be described as the implementation or translation of Marxist political theory into psychological theory and terms.

Vygotsky's stage model

Vygotsky proposed that any mental function, such as thought or language, appears twice in the course of development. The first time, a mental function appears outside the child. That is when

> "Thought is not merely expressed in words; it comes into existence through them."
> — Lev Vygotsky, 1986

children are presented with cultural tools, such as words or problem-solving strategies. When they initially use a function, the tool is not quite theirs yet; it is "borrowed." Over a period of time, however, they will use the tool over and over and again. Through routine and practice they will gradually internalize the tool and make it their own. To internalize

The first stage of language development was defined by Vygotsky as primitive. Before the age of two years old a baby learns to identify the word "milk" with the white liquid he is given to satisfy hunger, but it does not have any independent meaning in the baby's mind.

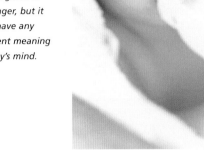

something is to incorporate it within the self, either consciously or subconsciously, as a guiding principle. That is achieved through learning.

The stage model proposed by Vygotsky charts the progression of this process of internalization, of making a cultural tool ones own. Because he believed that language and thinking start off as separate mental activities, Vygotsky proposed different stages for them.

The development of language

According to Vygotsky, language goes through four stages of development. From birth to about the age of two children are in the primitive stage of language. The essential quality of primitive language is its lack of intellectual function (that is, it does not involve thinking). Language begins with emotional releases, such as crying or cooing. They are followed by sounds for social reactions, such as laughter. In the primitive stage the first words emerge as substitutes for objects or desires. For example, children say "daddy" when their fathers walk into the room or "milk" when they see milk and because they are hungry. The words are merely a conditioned response. Children learn that the white liquid they drink is associated

A MARXIST THEORY OF DEVELOPMENT

KEY POINTS

The main points of Vygotsky's theory were:
• If action creates thought, then cognitive development is the progressive internalization of activity.
• Development is a constant stream of exchanges between the child and its environment. Each exchange provides opportunities to modify the child's thinking. When children notice a discrepancy between their thinking and their environment, they can adapt their thinking and develop. This exchange is said to be dialectic, since contradictions between what children think and what they experience force them to find a more adaptive form of thinking.
• In order to understand the development of children, it is necessary to consider the culture in which they live. Culture not only poses specific demands (that is, what the child is expected to do) but also offers the cognitive tools that help the child meet those demands. The sort of tools Vygotsky had in mind were numbers, maps, algebra, works of art, and most important of all, language.
• Thinking and language develop through various stages. Although they are initially independent and develop separately, they ultimately combine to form verbal thought, the most sophisticated form of thinking.

with the sound "milk," but the word has no meaning in their minds yet—they would not know what milk was without seeing it first.

The second stage of language development happens at about the age of two and is termed naive psychology. Children at this stage show a remarkable increase in vocabulary, mostly because they actively ask to be told the names of things. Words are no longer conditioned, and children begin to understand the symbolic value of words and what it is that they represent. This stage is called naive because although children make grammatically correct sentences, they do not yet understand the underlying structure of language.

The third stage of language development is called egocentric speech and emerges around the age of four. It is called egocentric because most of the speech of children at this stage is not addressed to anyone else. Rather, children perform monologues with themselves, especially during play. Children playing will often use different tones of voice as they "act out" different ideas.

For Vygotsky this form of speech marked the emergence of an important new intellectual tool: Speech influences children's thinking, which in turn influences their speech. The interaction between speech and thinking marks the emergence of verbal thought. The advantage of verbal thought is that it allows the child to plan a solution in the course of solving a problem. You can hear children using verbal thought when they tackle tricky tasks, such as tying shoes. Adults sometimes even revert to this stage by "thinking out loud" when they are faced with a difficult problem.

The fourth and final stage of a person's language development is the ingrowth stage. At this stage the child develops an internalized form of egocentric speech. The sounds of speech are replaced by mental symbols that serve a similar purpose to verbal thought or problem solving. At the same time, the functions of thinking and language become inseparable. Thinking becomes a form of inner speech, and at the same time inner language develops into a form of thinking.

The development of thought

Vygotsky believed that the development of thinking goes through three distinct stages. In the first stage children think in unorganized categories.

According to Vygotsky, it is during the second stage of his theory of thought development that children are able to "think in complexes," that is, to be able to group objects according to shape, size, or color.

The representations children initially form are trial-and-error groupings; objects and events are combined in a random manner. Progressively, the child begins to notice that some events happen at the same time as others. Thought is a social or cultural event—for example, the child begins to associate the appearance of a parent with being cuddled. By the end of the first stage, however, categories are still unorganized. The difference is that by the end of this stage children are dissatisfied with their categories. This causes frustration that motivates the changes that bring forth the next stage.

The second stage in thought development is termed "thinking in complexes." For Vygotsky a complex is a coherent basis for categorizing objects or events. At first, complexes are based on any relationship children notice between objects or events—color, for example, or shape. They then begin to use collection complexes based on contrasts rather than similarity. For example, if they are asked to group cutlery, they will put a table setting of a fork, a knife, and a spoon in

> *"The child begins to perceive the world not only through its eyes but also through its speech."*
> — *Lev Vygotsky, 1978*

each set rather than putting all the forks or knives together.

During the second stage of thought development the complexes grow more complicated but are still based on perceivable features of objects and events. It is only in the third stage, conceptual

THE ZONE OF PROXIMAL DEVELOPMENT

Vygotsky was interested in the way development could be stimulated, and he raised the following problem: Suppose there are two children perform identically on a test; have they achieved the same level of development?

The answer, Vygotsky found, is "no." Imagine Peter and Robert, who are both eight years old. They both take a problem-solving test, and their mental age is calculated to be eight years for each of them. We could conclude that Peter and Robert are equally developed and leave it at that. But suppose Peter and Robert are tested again, this time with an adult to help them. The adult doesn't give them the answer, but helps them identify the important features of the problem. With adult help Peter

achieves a mental age of nine, while Robert achieves a mental age of eleven. Now it is obvious that the two children have not achieved the same level of development. Robert is more advanced than Peter.

From tests like this Vygotsky made a crucial distinction between actual development (what the child can do on her own) and potential development (what the child could do with the help of someone with more expertise). The diagram shows this difference. Although Peter and Robert achieve similar performances on their own, Robert benefits substantially more from the help of an expert. The term that Vygotsky gave to this area between the actual and the potential level of development was the "zone of proximal development" (ZPD).

Vygotsky suggested that development takes place by stimulation of the ZPD. That is, children develop when they are stimulated beyond their current level of performance. ZPD has an upper limit, though. Stimulating both children with problems suitable for 10-year-olds will only benefit Robert. But stimulating both children with problems for a 12-year-old would benefit neither. To promote development, stimulation must exceed the child's current development level, but less than the child's potential level of development.

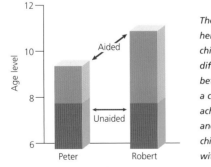

The ZPD, shown here in two children, is the difference between what a child can achieve alone and what a child can achieve with help.

thinking, that objects and events can be represented based on abstract properties, such as being able to recognize a shape or pattern in a series of dots or identify a face in a Picasso painting. At this third stage children analyze and synthesize information in more sophisticated ways. Language plays an important role in this achievement. Children have already learned to combine language with thinking in the first stage, and in the second stage language and thinking are closely tied together. Words can guide or shape thinking, and the results of thought can be communicated and expressed through language.

The role of play and tutors

According to Vygotsky, play is one of the two most important ways to stimulate development. As explained earlier, children use egocentric speech during play. Speech allows them to guide their activities and also helps them internalize speech and make it a sophisticated mental tool. For Vygotsky, playing takes place in the ZPD (*see* box p. 62) and involves activities that go beyond children's current levels of development and toward their potential level. The child also experiments in novel ways with the other tools provided by culture. During play children learn to use the mental tools that are not yet internalized. This learning promotes development.

The other important way in which development can be stimulated is through joint activity with a more developed person, such as an older child or an adult. Children at the same level of development cannot stimulate one another through the ZPD. Although they can do it when they are playing together, it is a trial-and-error process because they have yet to learn the tools that will take them beyond their current level of development.

Older children and adults, on the other hand, have usually mastered (and internalized) the tools that lie within younger children's ZPD. It is thus easier for them to provide the sort of

LEV SEMYONOVITCH VYGOTSKY

BIOGRAPHY

1896 Vygotsky is born on November 5 in Orscha, Belorussia (former Soviet Union).

1917 Graduates in law from Moscow University and Shanviavsky People University. Reads widely in linguistics, sociology, philosophy, and the arts, as well as psychology.

1921 First publications on psychology appear.

1924 For the next ten years until his death Vygotsky begins systematic studies in psychology with colleagues Alexander Luria and Alexei Leontiev. At the same time, he continues a medical practice in his home town in Belorussia.

1931 Joins the new Department of Psychology of the Ukrainian Psychoneurological Institute at Kharkov, which was then the capital of Ukraine.

1934 Vygotsky's career is cut short by his death from tuberculosis on June 11 in Moscow at the age of 37. *Thought and Language* is published shortly after Vygotsky's death. Initially suppressed by the government for political reasons, it later influences Russian education.

1950s It was not until the late 1950s that Vygotsky's works became known worldwide. Since then, they have had a profound influence on educationalists in the western world.

stimulation that will help younger children progress from their current level of development and develop new skills that they will eventually internalize.

Consider babies who have yet to learn words. They babble, coo, and react to

> *"All the higher functions originate as actual relationships between individuals."*
> — *Lev Vygotsky, 1978*

speech sounds from others. They are almost ready to utter their first words. Other babies of the same language level cannot help them utter words because these tools are also beyond their current level of speech development. The best that could happen is that the babies will coo and babble together. However, older children who have mastered word utterance could provide the right sort of stimulation

Major assumptions in Piaget's work were:

• Infants are not endowed with an innate (inborn) knowledge about anything. They are born with only a few basic reflexes, but these primitive reflexes are all that is needed to construct the mind.

• Children actively create their construct of the world by interacting with their environment. They are not empty containers waiting to be filled, nor are they passive observers. It is the activity of children, whether physical or intellectual, that modifies their thinking.

• Thinking is not a collection of individual abilities, but the organization of representations (see box p. 65) into a unified thought structure. Whatever children do reflects their current thought structure as they move through the various stages of development.

• Development involves important structural changes, and all children go through the same stages in the same order. These stages are associated with the progressively refined thought structures that children have the ability to construct over time.

for both babies. By stimulating younger babies' language within the ZPD, they could be helping them say their first words.

Evaluation of Vygotsky's work

Vygotsky raised awareness about two factors in intellectual development. In line with Marxist philosophy he stressed the influence of culture on development. Children are not raised in a void, but in a social environment that provides specific pressures as well as an array of cognitive tools, the most important being language.

Vygotsky also identified the important difference between actual development, as measured by performance tests, and potential development, as measured with aided performance. With this distinction Vygotsky proposed his notion of a "zone of proximal development." The ZPD is still an extremely useful concept today, especially in education. Researchers such as Barbara Rogoff have expanded Vygotsky's work substantially, giving rise to the "apprentice" theory of development.

Although Vygotsky's theory is clear, internally consistent, testable, and stimulating, it has some important limitations. First, it is limited with respect to the range of data it can explain. Vygotsky's work focused primarily on language and categorization skills. It is unclear how his stages of development might apply to other forms of thinking, such as problem-solving or logic. Second, it failed to specify mechanisms by which children develop from one stage to

another—there is more description than explanation in his theory.

Vygotsky died before he reached the age of 40. If he had lived longer, he might well have gone on to produce a broader and more comprehensive theory of developmental psychology.

PIAGET'S DEVELOPMENTAL THEORY

Jean Piaget (see box p. 65) was born in 1896, the same year as Vygotsky, but outlived his Russian contemporary by some 46 years. During his long career he formulated the most ambitious theory of intellectual development that has ever been devised. Initially trained as a biologist, Piaget soon became interested in the origins of knowledge and how children learn to define their world. The main question that his work addresses is "How do children come to know their world?"

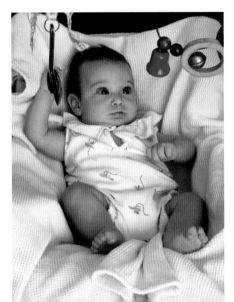

Piaget labeled the first period of cognitive development in a child's life the sensorimotor stage. It occurs between birth and two years. Newborn babies, like the one shown here, begin to develop an awareness of the world around them and to interact with the environment in which they live.

Piaget's stage model

Piaget's theory of cognitive development goes through four distinct stages. Each stage represents a particular organization of all thoughts in a unified mental structure, and each stage also applies to all possible cognitive activities—thoughts,

> *"Mental growth is an expanding upward spiral in which the same problems are attacked at successive levels but are resolved more completely and more successfully at each higher level."*
> — *Jean Piaget, 1954*

understanding, and so on. Therefore, whatever children do at any one time reflects their current stage of development.

Newborns begin to interact with their environment in what Piaget called the sensorimotor stage, which covers the period between birth and two years. The next stage is preoperational thought, which lasts from roughly two to seven years of age. Children at this stage acquire the ability to represent objects and events with symbols, but are incapable of logical thought. They achieve this ability at the

BIOGRAPHY

JEAN PIAGET

1896 Jean Piaget is born on August 9 in Neuchâtel, Switzerland.

1907 Piaget publishes his first scientific paper—a short note on his observation of an albino sparrow. Piaget is only 11! He goes on to publish many papers on mollusks during his teens. Because of his productivity people assume he is an established scientist. As a result, he is offered a position as curator at the Geneva Museum before he finishes high school.

1915 Piaget obtains his baccalaureate degree from the University of Neuchâtel and his doctorate in natural sciences three years later, from the same university.

1918 Piaget leaves Neuchâtel to gain training in psychology. He ends up at the Sorbonne, in Paris, and works with Alfred Binet on intelligence tests. He soon realizes that children's errors are more instructive than their IQ scores. Piaget

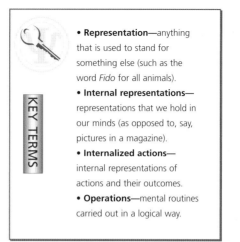

This photograph of Jean Piaget was taken about five years before he died. Piaget's development theory was a major influence on psychology.

develops the "clinical method" to assess children's thinking.

1921 Piaget becomes director of studies at the Jean-Jacques Rousseau Institute in Geneva, Switzerland.

1923 Valentine Châtenay and Jean Piaget marry. They have three children: Jacqueline (1925), Lucienne (1927), and Laurent (1931). The children's intellectual development from infancy provides Piaget with unique observations and evidence for his theory of development.

1955 Piaget sets up the International Center for Genetic Epistemology. He directs the center until his death.

1980 Piaget dies on September 16, aged 84. During his career he published more than 50 books and 500 articles, and was one of the most prolific researchers in psychology.

next stage, concrete operations. At this stage children can apply logical thought to their representations of the external world, but only in the presence of observable objects. This stage lasts from approximately 7 to 11 years. In the final stage, formal operations, children are able to apply logical thought to ideas, not just things. This can give rise to abstract representations, such as justice. The formal operations stage begins roughly around the age of 11 and is usually established by adulthood.

The ages associated with the various stages are only given as a rough indication of the developmental timeline. Each child is different and will go through the various stages at his or her own pace. Piaget also identified various substages within these four main stages of development.

The sensorimotor stage

This stage lasts from birth until two years. Piaget believed that children are born with only a few innate (inborn) reflexes, and that these reflexes provide the building blocks of intelligence. In the sensorimotor stage children experience these reflexes, apply them to the environment (which includes themselves and others), and modify them as a function of experience. Although the sensorimotor stage is the

---

OBJECT PERMANENCE

According to Piaget's theory infants are not born with an understanding that objects exist independently of their own selves. Initially, they perceive objects as an extension of their own bodies and their actions. For example, a red ball "exists" because the child "wants" to see it. If the ball or another attractive object is suddenly removed from sight, young infants will continue to look at the location where the interesting object was. It is as if the child wishes to enjoy the sight of the object for longer and expects to see it by staring at the place where it was last seen.

To an infant at this stage an object ceases to exist if it can no longer be seen. "Out of sight, out of mind," as the saying goes. A true object concept requires the belief that an object has a continued existence independent of the actions of the infant. Before infants believe that objects continue to exist when they can't be seen, they won't search for them when they disappear from sight. By substage three (see p. 68), however, infants will expect a complete object on the basis of seeing a part of it. If an attractive object is hidden under a blanket, they will try and retrieve it if only part of it is visible. In substage four (see p. 68) infants search for objects hidden completely out of sight.

However, if an object is hidden in a new location, substage four infants are likely to search in previous locations even if they saw the object hidden at the new location. This limitation is resolved at substage 5 (see p. 68), but these infants do not master so-called "invisible displacements." For example, imagine three boxes labeled A, B, and C. An adult hides a small toy in her hand, puts her hand in box A, then in box C, and then shows her hand to be empty. The toy has disappeared. An adult can figure out that it is either in box A or box C, but certainly not in box B. Only substage 6 infants will not look for the toy in box B. Younger infants are as likely to search box B as they are to search A and C.

A seven-year-old boy plays with his nine-month-old sister, who is sitting on their mother's lap. At substage four in Piaget's theory of development the girl learns that if she moves the blanket, she will find her brother.

shortest of the four stages, Piaget divided it into six substages. This is not surprising, because from birth until the age of two the child's brain goes through the most changes it will ever experience. Since cognitive abilities are associated with brain changes, it follows that much must go on in the first few years.

During the sensorimotor stage children make two crucial acquisitions: object permanence (*see* box p. 66) and representations. A representation is anything that is used to stand for something else. For example, when a child rides a stick as if it were a horse, the stick represents the concept of horse. In a similar way the word "horse" is a representation of the actual animal. The ability to think about absent objects and the ability to represent objects with other objects or words are both crucial for later development. The sensorimotor stage can be subdivided into six substages.

Substage one, the refinement of reflexes, occurs between birth and the age of one month. Newborns come into the world with a set of simple reflexes. They suck when objects are placed to their lips or in their mouths (the sucking reflex). If one of their cheeks is touched, they will turn their heads to that side (the rooting reflex). They close their fingers around objects that touch the palm of their hands (the grasping reflex). These reflexes serve useful purposes and are essential for the baby to survive. For example, the baby will benefit from turning toward its mother's nipples and sucking milk from them when they are in its mouth.

At first these reflexes are not sophisticated. The newborn will suck indiscriminately at a wide range of objects; a nipple or the tip of a finger will elicit the same response. But during babies' first month outside the womb their sucking becomes more discriminating. Similar changes take place with the grasping reflex, as newborns experience a variety of objects through touching.

By sampling the environment, infants develop behaviors that progressively become more adapted to the various forms of stimulation available. Although this is the most passive period of human life (one-month-old infants don't do all that much, and they sleep a lot), infants' active interactions with the environment prompt the adaptations that bring them to the next substage.

Substage two, the primary circular reactions substage, occurs between the ages of one to four months. The term "circular reactions" refers to the repetitive nature of behaviors in this substage. The earlier reflexes, having been well exercised, can now be combined into more complex behaviors that infants will repeat if they find them rewarding. For example, if infants grab a toy and succeed in bringing it to their mouths to suck, they will try to do it again (assuming that the toy is pleasant to suck).

Because the combination of reflexes is more complex than individual reflexes in isolation, most of these behaviors appear randomly. That is perhaps why infants try to repeat the exact sequence of behaviors that proved rewarding. Most combinations of behavior do not yield

This child is six months old. By the age of two he will have learned to differentiate between himself and other objects, and will also be able to think about his actions, rather than just grabbing the ball because it is an enjoyable thing to do.

positive results, and those that do are repeated with precision, which limits the range of behaviors infants will explore. Also, infants will only repeat actions that concern their own bodies. They are not yet interested in actions that affect objects in the surrounding environment. That will emerge in the next substage.

Substage three comprises secondary circular reactions, which happens at about four to eight months. As in the previous substage, interesting behaviors are repeated frequently. Now, however, the behaviors involve outcomes other than the infant's own body. For instance, infants may find throwing toys to the ground extremely interesting. They do it over and over again as toys are given back to them. The crucial distinction between the previous stage is that objects from the environment become the focus of interest.

Piaget did not believe that infants at this substage have formed genuine goals. Although they repeat interesting actions, he believed that their behaviors were not truly voluntary. Infants just did things that were possible (such as picking up and dropping a toy), circumstances permitting. This is different from hoping to be given a toy that they can then throw. There is no planning yet.

Substage four usually happens between 8 to 12 months, when infants develop coordination and extension of secondary reactions. In substage four infants show increasingly complex behaviors by combining two or more actions in order to achieve a desired goal. A simple example is the removal of an obstacle in order to retrieve another object. Two sequences of behavior (removal of the barrier and retrieval of the desired object) are coordinated into an efficient action chain. For Piaget this signaled the emergence of goal-directed behavior. Infants are now capable of performing some preliminary actions necessary for achieving desired outcomes and have developed a basic ability to plan.

Another important development is the emergence of object permanence (*see* box p. 66). When you close your hand around a small object in front of infants at substage four, they will not act as if the object has disappeared from the Earth. Instead, they will realize that the object is still there and look expectantly at your hand, waiting for it to appear again.

This is not full-blown object permanence yet. Infants at substage four still make errors when searching for hidden objects. A classic example is the A–not–B error. Suppose you have a toy and two boxes in which you could hide it. Before substage four infants would not search for the toy if it was completely out of sight. Infants at substage four will search for the toy in the box you hid it in. You could hide it two or three times in the same box (box A), and they would always retrieve it. After these few successful trials you put the toy in the other box (box B). Even if they have seen you hide the toy in box B, they will still continue to search for it in box A.

Piaget theorized that this is because the object is still closely tied with the infants' actions. Because they successfully retrieved it a few times in box A, they will try again at the successful location despite seeing that the object has been hidden somewhere else. Whatever they did before in box A was successful and resulted in the object being brought back, so they try the action again, expecting the same result. They know the object still exists, but have not yet learned that it exists independently of their actions.

Substage five begins around 12 to 18 months, when children develop tertiary circular reactions. As with previous circular reactions, they involve repetitive behaviors, but also involve experimenting with objects to explore their properties. For instance, rather than merely throwing toys, infants will observe how different toys behave when thrown. Or maybe an infant will shake the same rattle in different ways to produce different noises. Instead of repeating identical actions, infants perform similar actions repeatedly, varying their actions to produce different outcomes. For infants at this substage it is the novelty factor that is important.

The progression from primary to secondary and to tertiary circular reactions highlights the important developments taking place in infancy. Initially, infants are centered on behaviors that concern their bodies (primary reactions). Progressively, they become interested in outcomes that concern the environment (secondary reactions). By substage five they realize that their actions can be varied in order to generate new outcomes. To understand the world, one needs to experiment with it. This newfound way to interact with the world will provide infants with the sort of stimulation they need to develop further.

> *"The stage five baby shows even greater curiosity, anticipation, and purposive flexibility, which... contribute to a better understanding of object permanence, causal relations, and spatial displacements"*
> *— Margaret Boden, 1994*

Substage six: mental combinations and the emergence of representations, which happens at about 18 to 24 months of age. This last substage marks the end of the sensorimotor stage. According to Piaget, infant thinking during the first two years only involves action. Although infants start acquiring words around their first birthday, language is not yet used as a thinking tool. In substage 6, however, infants begin to internalize their actions. Here is an example. Piaget hid a small chain in a matchbox, leaving the box slightly open so that his daughter Lucienne could easily retrieve the chain. She could turn the box over, and the chain would fall out. Once Lucienne had done this a few times, Piaget hid the chain in the box and completely closed it before giving it back to her. After turning it over and failing to make the chain drop out, she looked at the box with great attention.

She then opened and closed her mouth—slightly at first, and then wider. It was as though Lucienne wanted to open the box, could not do it, and represented her thinking with mouth gestures. Lucienne's mouth openings referred to what she was hoping for—that the box should be opened—and not the actions she should do. The crucial point is that Lucienne internalized in her mind a desired outcome in her environment.

In substage six infants progressively internalize actions and sensations in the form of representations. They begin to think not through action but through representations of actions. This provides the grounds for the next stage of development, preoperational thought.

The preoperational stage

Despite the huge advances they have made in their first two years, young preoperational children are only just beginning to understand the world. During the preoperational stage, between two and seven years of age, continued development mainly involves substantial growth in representational ability—the ability to represent objects and events with symbols and signs.

Piaget stressed the difference between symbols and signs. Children use symbols as private representations. They are only meaningful to the child, not to other children or adults. For example, a child playing may use a special wood block to represent a house. Usually symbols are chosen that resemble the objects they represent. For instance, the child would not use a ball to represent a house, but a ball could be a good symbol for an apple. The personal nature of symbols limits their usefulness. Unless children explicitly tell you so, you cannot know for certain what the special wood block or ball, for example, stands for.

Signs, however, are representations shared by many people. Words are a good example of what Piaget called signs. Signs do not usually resemble the objects they refer to. For example, the word "house" has no resemblance to the structures we call houses. It is merely a combination of letters or sounds that people agree to use to refer to buildings where they live. Despite the lack of resemblance between signs and what they refer to, signs are much more powerful than symbols because they communicate meaning quickly and efficiently.

Switching from symbols to signs expands children's ability to obtain useful information from others. Piaget's notion of egocentric communication illustrates that the transition is slow and laborious, however. Piaget labeled preschoolers egocentric because they have difficulty taking other people's perspective, and not because they only care about themselves. Although preschoolers may use signs such as words, it doesn't follow that they use them in a way that will be meaningful to others. The following "conversation" is a typical example of how two preschoolers might use words:

Child 1: "My house is made of bricks."
Child 2: "I have a cat."
Child 1: "There are lots of windows in my house."
Child 2: "My cat loves fish."
Child 1: "My house has a door."

Each child utters meaningful sentences and takes its turn, but the children are not taking part in a conversation. They are engaging in two monologues: one about a house and the other about a cat.

Egocentrism can also be demonstrated by the three mountains test shown in the figure below. Three papier-mâché mountains with different sizes, shapes, colors, and features are arranged on a table. After the children to be tested have explored the model, they are seated on one side of it, and a doll is placed at a different location. The children are then shown pictures of different views of the mountains and asked to choose the one the doll can see.

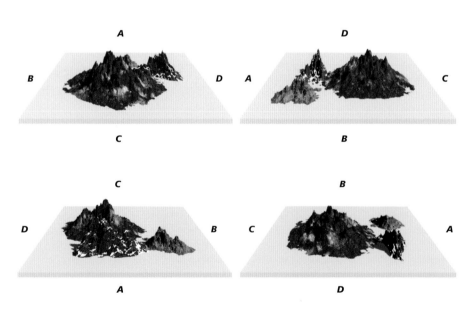

Figure 6. *The three mountains test. Three papier-mâché mountains, with different shapes, colors, and features, are arranged on a table. The sides of the table are labeled A, B, C, and D. The child being tested explores the model and is then seated on one side of it. A doll is then placed on one of the other sides. The child is shown a series of photographs and asked to choose the one that shows the mountains from the doll's point of view. The four possible viewpoints are shown above. This test is used to demonstrate egocentricity in preoperational children (two- to four-year-olds)*

Children in the early preoperational stage (two to four years of age) fail to recognize the correct picture; they always choose a picture showing what they themselves can see. Six-year-olds do better, but it isn't until children reach the age of seven or eight that they can "put themselves" in the doll's place.

Over the course of the preoperational period, and certainly by about the age of seven, children learn to see things from other people's viewpoints. This has many advantages, one being that it makes it possible for them to have meaningful conversations with other people.

Another limitation of preoperational children is their inability to represent transformations—changes in the physical arrangement of objects. If liquid is poured from a short, wide glass into a tall, narrow glass, preoperational children will typically think there is now more liquid in the tall glass. That is because they focus on a single dimension—height—and ignore an equally relevant dimension—width. The understanding that a quantity such as volume, number, or area can remain the same despite being arranged in different ways is called conservation. Conservation requires the ability to make what Piaget called compensations. A compensation would go like this: "The liquid is higher, but it is also less wide." This is a hallmark of operational thought that occurs in the concrete operations stage.

The concrete operations stage

This stage occurs between the ages of 7 and 11. By "operations" Piaget meant mental routines for processing information in a logical manner. They were lacking in the previous stage, hence the name preoperational. In this stage operations can form mental representations of how things work, but only in relation to observable phenomena, which is why it is called concrete, as opposed to abstract.

A conservation problem illustrates how concrete operations work. A child is asked whether two identical containers filled with

This six-year-old is carefully studying a Piaget conservation test. Conservation is the ability to recognize that two quantities remain the same however they are presented. In this case there is the same amount of liquid in the tall, thin glass as there is in the short, fat one. At the pre-operational stage of mental development children usually say there is more liquid in the tall, thin glass and do not take the width of the glass into account when making their calculations.

liquid contain equal quantities. If the child disagrees, the experimenter adds liquid appropriately until the child believes both containers hold equal amounts of liquid. The liquids are then poured into two other containers that differ in shape. One is taller and narrower, the other shorter

> *"Concrete operations are actions accompanied by an awareness on the part of the subject of the techniques and coordinations of his own behavior."*
> *— Piaget and Inhelder, 1958*

and wider. Preoperational children will focus on only one dimension (usually height, but sometimes width) and state that one of the new containers holds more liquid than the other. Children at the concrete operational stage, however, will say that both containers hold equal amounts of liquid. But in order to assess whether they really understand the problem, children must justify their answer. A typical justification concerns the identity of the liquids: "It's the same liquids. You didn't add or remove any." This answer shows that children understand that changes in appearance (taller and narrower versus shorter and wider) do not affect the quantity of the liquid. Another answer concerns the reversibility of the transformation: "If you poured them back, they would be the same." With this answer children show an understanding of the dynamics of transformations. What made one of the liquids taller and narrower could be reversed, suggesting that the amount of liquid remained the same. Finally, children may justify their answer with compensation: "The liquid is shorter but wider, so it's the same as before." This answer also shows an understanding of the dynamics of transformations. These children understand that a change in one dimension cannot be considered apart from a change in another, equally important dimension.

The ability to carry out concrete operations increases learning possibilities as children experiment with various object properties at the same time rather than merely exploring single properties. This richer cognitive functioning remains limited, however. For one thing, the operations only apply to observable properties. Abstract concepts such as gravity, justice, and truth still remain elusive.

Planning is also limited. When children experiment with more complex problems, they are not systematic; there is still a large element of trial-and-error, and they often repeat steps. These limitations disappear in the final stage of development, when children begin to think about their thinking: in other words, when they begin

The French philosopher René Descartes had a profound influence on western philosophy. His most famous saying, " I think, therefore I am," recognizes the importance of thought, and the awareness of thinking, as a crucial feature of human existence. The ability to think about thought marks the final stage of Piaget's development theory.

to apply operations on their operations—or formal operations—the most sophisticated form of thinking.

Formal operations
Perhaps the most defining feature of human intelligence is the ability to think about oneself. For the French philosopher René Descartes (1596–1650) all truths stem from the realization that one is thinking. His famous sentence *Cogito ergo sum* ("I think, therefore I am") implies that one is aware of the thinking ("I know that I'm thinking, therefore I know that I am").

The ability to think about one's thoughts is often called metacognition, meaning cognition about cognition. It is the most sophisticated form of thinking and marks the final stage in Piaget's theory of development. With formal operations, from about the age of 11 years onward children (and adults) are able to think about possible events and not just actual events, as is the case with children at the concrete operational stage. This is a significant change. If you can think about the various possible ways to solve a problem, it becomes much easier to plan how you will carry out a task. If you are not bound to the immediately perceptible world, you can entertain some abstract concepts such as justice, freedom, and so forth. One area where formal operations are useful is science. Piaget and his colleagues used various scientific experiments to assess formal thinking. A typical task is the chemical

PIAGET'S STAGES OF DEVELOPMENT

Stage	Age	Major changes
Sensorimotor (divided into six stages)	Birth to 2 years	• shift from own body to external world • emergence of symbols • object permanence
Preoperational	2 years to 7 years	• emergence of signs • focus on single dimensions • egocentric thought
Concrete operations	7 years to 11 years	• emergence of mental operations • acquisition of conservation • limited planning
Formal operations	11 years onwards	• abstract thought • effective planning • metacognition

combination problem. Children are first shown four containers, each holding a different substance. They are then shown a fifth container that holds an unknown combination of any of the four substances. When a special chemical is added to the combination, the result is a yellow substance. The children's task is to identify how some or all of the four substances were combined to produce the yellow result. They are allowed to mix them as they want, as many times as they want. They can test their combinations at any time by adding the special chemical.

Children at the concrete operational stage do not plan a logical and efficient approach to the problem. They try some combinations, leave out others, often repeat previous combinations, and usually stop as soon as one of their combinations turns yellow. On the other hand, children at the formal operational stage plan their testing by figuring out in advance all the possible combinations. They test them all systematically and do not stop at the first yellow result. This proves fruitful since there are two ways to obtain a yellow result in Piaget's experiment. It is therefore impossible to tell which of the

A
B
C
D
AB
AC
AD
BC
BD
CD
ABC
ABD
ACD
BCD
ABCD

The colors of the four chemicals and all their possible combinations in Piaget's chemical combination problem, devised to test formal operational thought.

two possible combinations they were initially shown. Unlike children at the concrete operational stage, who are certain they found the solution (because they stopped at the first yellow result), children at the formal stage have narrowed the possibilities down to two solutions.

The illustration shows the possible combinations children can try on the chemical combination problem. In order for the combination to turn yellow when the special chemical is added, the combination must contain substances A and B. When substance C is present, the combination cannot turn yellow. Substance D is neutral and has no effect. Therefore, the unknown combination children were first shown could have been AB or ABD. Although they can't find the exact answer to the question "What was the initial combination?" children at the formal stage were able to uncover the underlying structure of the experiment. That is a sophisticated achievement.

Although the formal operations stage marks the end of development in Piaget's theory, it does not mark the end of thinking. In fact, the opposite is true—because children and adults are no longer bound to the immediately perceptible world, an infinity of thoughts can be entertained. Children have come a long way from the initial sensorimotor stage in the first two years of their lives. Remember the infants seeing the red ball as an extension of their own actions and because they "think" they want to see it? From this extremely simple form of thinking, bound to the actions of the infants, has emerged a use of the imagination and a form of thinking so sophisticated that adults can only speculate about what infants think.

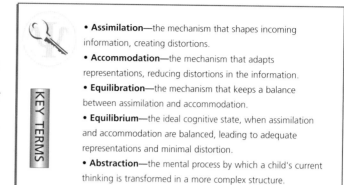

KEY TERMS

- **Assimilation**—the mechanism that shapes incoming information, creating distortions.
- **Accommodation**—the mechanism that adapts representations, reducing distortions in the information.
- **Equilibration**—the mechanism that keeps a balance between assimilation and accommodation.
- **Equilibrium**—the ideal cognitive state, when assimilation and accommodation are balanced, leading to adequate representations and minimal distortion.
- **Abstraction**—the mental process by which a child's current thinking is transformed in a more complex structure.

Mechanisms of change

Piaget, unlike Vygotsky, proposed that all the changes during development are controlled by a small set of mechanisms. By "mechanisms" he did not mean pieces of machinery but processes for achieving particular results. According to Piaget, the basic mechanisms that adapt a child's cognitive structure are assimilation, accommodation, equilibration, and abstraction (*see* box above). Piaget called the first three mechanisms (assimilation, accommodation, and equilibration) functional invariants because they

accomplish the same functions over the whole course of development and are never modified or changed by experience.

Assimilation

When children receive information, it is deformed to fit their cognitive structure—a process Piaget called assimilation. As an

This young child may call all animals by the same name as the family pet. Piaget called the mechanism used to shape incoming information assimilation. This mechanism can create distortions. They are adapted using accommodation, which enables the child to recognize that not all four-legged animals are called Fido.

analogy, imagine what happens to water when you pour it into a glass. The liquid takes the form of the glass, while the glass remains unchanged. This, in essence, is what happens in assimilation. Information comes in and is forced to take the shape of the child's current thought structure. In the process it becomes distorted. For example, imagine a child raised in a family that owns a dog called Fido. One day at the park the child sees another dog and calls it Fido. The new dog was assimilated by the child to the representation of the family's pet dog.

> *"Assimilation and accommodation are obviously opposed to one another . . . it is precisely the role of mental life in general and of intelligence in particular to intercoordinate them."*
> — *Jean Piaget, 1954*

Imagine that the child then sees a cat and calls that Fido, too. The child has assimilated information into a thought structure in which the word "Fido" represents all cats and dogs, and possibly a wide array of other small, four-legged, furry animals. Children need to modify their representational structure to distinguish between different dogs, between dogs and cats, and between other animals. The mechanism that allows this to happen is accommodation.

Accommodation

Suppose you pour water into a balloon. The water will modify the balloon, stretching it. At the same time, the water will take the shape of the balloon. The water and the balloon dynamically shape one another. This, in essence, is accommodation, the mechanism that "stretches" the thought structure so it can accommodate new information. As with assimilation, too much accommodation may not prove ideal. For instance, it would be pointless for children to learn the individual name of every animal they encounter. Better to have a few general categories, such as dog and cat, and then a few specific examples like Fido the family pet, Brutus the growling hound at the end of the street, and Tom the neighbor's cat.

Equilibrium

The changes that take place at any given stage are an effort to produce a state of equilibrium. Children are in a state of equilibrium when their current thought structure is able to deal with most new experiences. Equilibration, the process by which equilibrium is achieved, strikes a balance between assimilation and accommodation. The process of equilibration allows children's performance to improve. It evaluates the level of distortion generated by assimilation and requests the necessary amount of accommodation to minimize these distortions. Over time the cognitive structure stabilizes in an ideal state, which marks the end of a stage.

The ideal state for young children is not necessarily the same as it is for an older child. Children at the preoperational stage carrying out the conservation-of-liquids task say that the taller glass contains more water. An adult points out that it is also narrower, while the short glass is wider. They say, "Yes, but that one is taller, so it has more." They are perfectly happy with this explanation—not understanding the relationship between height and width—

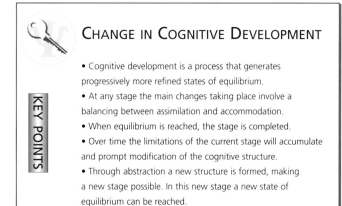

CHANGE IN COGNITIVE DEVELOPMENT

KEY POINTS

• Cognitive development is a process that generates progressively more refined states of equilibrium.

• At any stage the main changes taking place involve a balancing between assimilation and accommodation.

• When equilibrium is reached, the stage is completed.

• Over time the limitations of the current stage will accumulate and prompt modification of the cognitive structure.

• Through abstraction a new structure is formed, making a new stage possible. In this new stage a new state of equilibrium can be reached.

and cannot see the relevance of your comment. Further accommodations will not help them, so they are in equilibrium and happy about their understanding of the world. Over time, however, the limitations of their thought structure mean that they fail to solve a variety of similar problems. The accumulation of failures will create what Piaget called a disequilibrium. It will prompt the structural changes that allow the children to move to the next stage.

Abstraction

The progression from one stage to another is made possible through the mechanism of abstraction. Abstraction creates a new cognitive structure that is based on the previous structure, but which attempts, in the process, to correct the limitations that caused disequilibrium in the previous structure. The old structure is assimilated in the new one, which accommodates it in order to correct its previous limitations. However, equilibration ensures that an ideal balance between assimilation and accommodation takes place during this complex process.

Evaluation of Piaget's theory

Piaget made major contributions to the study of child development. On the subject of child testing he argued that children should be provided with the opportunity to justify their behavior. Like Vygotsky, he thought that performance scores provided limited information. Piaget's focus was on

> *"Life is a continuous creation of increasingly complex forms and a progressive balancing of these forms with the environment."*
> — *Jean Piaget, 1963*

children's errors, which offer a clearer insight into the underlying thought processes. On the research front Piaget devised a wide range of ingenious tasks to study children's reasoning errors. His experiments on object permanence and conservation are classics, and they are easily replicable. Try the conservation-of-liquids task with a four-year-old, and you

---

FOCUS ON

SOME ALTERNATIVES TO PIAGET'S THEORY

Domain-specific theories Some scientists reject Piaget's notion that children's mental skills develop in a single cognitive structure. Instead, they believe that different skills develop in different mental "domains." Researchers have suggested different domains for language, visual perception, mathematical understanding, and so on. Different domains may develop independently of one another—in stages, according to some researchers, continuously, according to others. Domain-specific approaches to stages of development have been put forward by the U.S. psychologist Susan Carey and the British psychologist Annette Karmiloff-Smith.

Constructivist theory The U.S. psychologist Jerome Bruner proposed that learning is an active social process in which children use their current knowledge to construct new ideas or concepts. Unlike Piaget, Bruner suggested that children's development is accelerated by

giving them tasks they are capable of accomplishing, rather than tasks that are beyond them. They build on success, not failure. In tackling new tasks, children use the information they already have to help them go beyond the information given.

Information-processing theories Information-processing theorists use the computer as a model for cognitive development. Like computers, children take in information (the input), encode and store it, and then respond to it by behaviors (the output).

Information-processing theorists such as J. Pascual-Leone at York University, Toronto, and R. Case at the University of Toronto, Canada, approach development mainly by studying children's memory. The more complex a problem, the more memory space is required. Young children have limited memory space. As they develop, the amount of memory space increases.

will find that you obtain the same results as Piaget. Most of his tasks still generate substantial research.

Although Piaget's theory has been a major influence, it has also been severely criticized by psychologists. That is not surprising because it was such an ambitious theory. Many researchers find the definitions of Piaget's mechanisms of change too vague to be of practical use. For many psychologists it isn't clear what assimilation and accommodation are, and equilibration and abstraction prove even more puzzling.

A more severe blow to Piaget's theory is the discovery that some abilities within a stage do not develop at the same rate. For Piaget thinking is organized in a unified mental structure. If this were so, all children would solve all conservation problems at the same age; however, some

Some children can solve conservation problems at six years old, while others are not able to complete these tasks until they are ten years old. Here, colored blocks are used to test a child's skills in area conservation.

conservation problems can be solved as early as six years of age, while other problems are only solved later, at around 10 years of age.

Many researchers have rejected part or all of Piaget's theory. Alternative theories (*see* box p. 76) challenge some of Piaget's ideas, such as his notion of a unified cognitive structure. However, despite these well-founded criticisms, Piaget's theory remains the most ambitious attempt to explain how children's thinking develops.

CONNECTIONS

- Infant Cognition: pp. 24-39
- Perceptual Development: pp. 40-57
- Cognitive Psychology: Volume 1, pp. 104-117
- Perception: Volume 2, pp. 62-85

Memory Development

"I am not young enough to know everything"

Oscar Wilde

Knowing your own identity is something you take for granted. But have you ever wondered how you know who you are? Does it ever amaze you that this information is always in your memory? Do you sometimes wonder how you came to know yourself? Do young infants know who they are? What is in their memories? How does memory develop?

That you can even understand this sentence as you read it depends on your memory. All sentences would be meaningless if we did not remember their beginnings when we reached their ends. Not only that, we must also remember the meanings of the words in the sentence. Reading depends absolutely on memory, and so, too, do nearly all aspects of human functioning and awareness.

IMPLICIT AND EXPLICIT MEMORIES

In everyday speech memory usually means two related things: having information in storage and being able to retrieve it. But, as psychologist Endel Tulving (born 1927) has pointed out, you cannot always find what you know you have. The allegory of the unfortunate centipede illustrates this well. A scientist asked a centipede to explain how it could walk so elegantly

Endel Tulving's main area of research was the brain and how memory works. He defined two types of memory: semantic (consisting of abstract ideas and facts) and episodic (consisting of personal experiences). His case studies provided strong evidence that different parts of the brain are involved in these two different processes.

with its many legs. The centipede tried to explain which leg went where, but could not describe the complicated business of walking. In the end it became hopelessly confused and wound up tying many of its legs in horrible knots. Although it clearly knew how to walk or had implicit knowledge of what to do, it could not make this knowledge explicit, that is, describe it to someone else.

Infants' memories are like the centipede's knowledge of walking: implicit rather than explicit. A human baby cannot deliberately retrieve memories and verbalize them. By definition preverbal infants put nothing into words. This poses

KEY POINTS

- There are three main types of memory storage: sensory (or echoic) memory, short-term (or working memory), and long-term memory.
- Infant memory is linked to development of brain structures.
- There are three main stages in the development of infant memory: fleeting memories (birth to three months), recognition of the familiar (three to eight months), and more abstract remembering (eight months to one year).
- From two to six years children learn at a great rate, particularly language, but their memory is less reliable and more suggestible than that of older children and adults.
- Memory improves in older children as they learn memory strategies and gain more knowledge.

	Sensory Memory	Short-Term Memory	Long-Term Memory
Alternate names	Echoic	Working	None
Duration	Less than one second	Less than 20 seconds	Permanent, indefinite
Stability	Fleeting	Easily disrupted	Not easily disrupted
Capacity	Limited	Limited (7 ± 2 items)	Unlimited
General characteristics	Momentary, unconscious impression, a passing sensation or association	What we are actively paying attention to, immediate consciousness	All of our knowledge, explicit (can be put into words) and implicit (skills)

This table shows the three main types of memory storage. Short-term memory and long-term memory are relatively easy for researchers to measure. Sensory memory is of a more subjective and transitory nature and is, therefore, more difficult to quantify. Measuring memory development in infants before they have learned to talk is another challenge psychologists face.

some problems for psychologists studying infant development. But as we will see, there are a number of clever ways of investigating implicit infant memories.

Many adult memories are also implicit. That is not usually because we have not learned the words for them. For some memories there are simply no words. For example, take riding a bicycle. You cannot learn this skill by being told how to stay upright on it. Nor can you tell someone else how to ride once you've learned. In the end, knowing how to cycle is implicit in your body but cannot be made explicit.

TYPES OF MEMORY
Psychologists recognize three main kinds of memory storage: sensory memory, short-term memory (also termed working memory), and long-term memory.

Sensory memory describes the effects of stimulation on senses such as vision, hearing, touch, taste, and smell. Research shows that this type of memory might be available to us even when we aren't paying attention and after the stimulation is finished. Some researchers call this kind of memory echoic because it is as if the

memory remains as an echo.

When you pay attention to a stimulus—that is, when you become conscious of it—it becomes part of short-term memory. Short-term memory is what we are immediately aware of at any given time. Keeping things in mind for a short period is necessary for thinking and understanding. That is why short-term memory is often known as working memory. For example, as we saw earlier, understanding this sentence requires remembering something about the

Learning to ride a bike uses implicit rather than explicit memory. This means that this girl will be able to learn by doing, but she will not be able to describe or explain exactly what she is doing to another person.

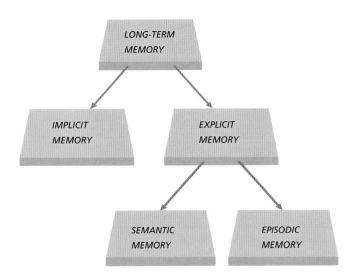

beginning when you reach the end; it relies on working memory. Short-term memory is severely limited: Its effects last for seconds (usually fewer than 20), and in adults it is limited to about 7 items.

"The lizard's name is Adolphus." If this sentence were very important to you and you desperately wanted to remember it, you might reread it and repeat it to yourself several times. This process is known as rehearsing. Alternatively, you might make a mental link between some Adolphus you know and this lizard, a process termed elaborating. Or you might think of some other meaningful way of remembering the sentence by organizing it with other items of information you possess. Rehearsing, elaborating, and organizing are the three most important strategies we have for bringing information from short-term to long-term memory. Psychologists use the term encoding to describe how information is processed to become part of long-term memory.

Long-term memory contains our relatively permanent information about the world. It includes everything we know about ourselves, about others, and about things. It represents the relatively permanent or long-term effects of all the

Characteristics of long-term memory.

A dog will appear to be asleep but will be wide awake as soon as there is the hint of a walk or some food. This is the orienting response. It also occurs in people, but the signs are different.

experiences we have had. Some of this information is explicit: It can be put into words. And some of it is implicit: It cannot be put into words. Implicit memory (*see* p. 78) is also called nondeclarative memory because it consists of memories that are nonverbalizable, for example, skills such as walking or tying shoelaces. There are two types of explicit memory, and they seem to involve different parts of the brain. Semantic memory consists of abstract information like the facts you learn at school such as addition or multiplication. Episodic memory consists of the memories that make up your recollection of your personal experiences.

Our long-term memories are extremely important to our sense of who we are. All of our skills, our habits, our competence, our very identity reside in long-term memory. Patients who suffer memory loss, as happens with Alzheimer's disease, for example, may eventually lose even the most basic competence required for the tasks of daily life (*see* table p. 79).

Memory in infants

Because young infants cannot put their memories into words, investigators have devised ways of studying how experiences affect them, and what they remember. One of the most important of them is by measuring something known as the orienting response. The orienting response in people is similar to that in a dozing dog. The animal may seem to be asleep, but its ears will twitch if the noise of something that interests it becomes audible—a passing car or a bird it might like to chase. The orienting response prepares the animal to interpret and respond to a new source of stimulation. In a sense, it's a response that orients the animal.

People, too, make an orienting response when there is new stimulation. While our ears don't prick up noticeably, other changes take place: Our heart rate slows down, our pupils increase in size, and our skin becomes more conductive to electricity as a result of very subtle increases in perspiration. Each of these changes is very small, but each can be measured with the right instruments.

Young infants also make orienting responses. New stimulation causes measurable changes in heart rate and sometimes physical movements such as turning the head. The usefulness of this for the psychologist who is interested in the infant's memory lies in the fact that whenever a stimulus is no longer novel—in other words, when it has been learned and is therefore remembered—the orienting response stops happening.

In one study infants less than 24 hours old were exposed to the sound of a single word. At first they turned toward the word every time they heard it. But after a while they stopped turning. They had gotten used (habituated) to the word; it was no longer novel. But when the same word was presented to them a day later, they again turned toward it. This time, however, they habituated much more rapidly than a second group of similar-aged infants who had not heard the word before. This provides evidence that newborns are able to learn and remember.

Imitation

Infants' ability to imitate provides another way of studying memory. The argument is that if infants imitate an action, that is evidence that they can remember it. In a number of studies people bend over infants' cribs and purse their lips, stick out their tongues, or blink their eyes. In some studies investigators report that within an hour of birth some infants respond by blinking, sticking out their tongues, or pursing their lips. But in these studies of imitation in the newborn it is not entirely clear that infants are actually imitating. It is possible that sticking out the tongue and pursing the lips are simply reflexive (automatic) behaviors brought about by the closeness of the person. This idea is supported by the fact that newborns do not seem to be able to imitate any other

more complex behaviors. Nor do they continue to imitate when the person has left. But by the age of 9 to 12 months infants are able to imitate people who are no longer present. According to Jean Piaget, deferred imitation is clear evidence of the fact that the child has the ability to remember, that is, to represent mentally.

At 16 months old this child can imitate his mother and continues to do so even when she is no longer there. This suggests that he has the ability to remember expressions.

CONTROLLED BEHAVIORS

With older infants it is possible to study memory by looking at behaviors that the infant can control. In an early study Piaget tied one end of a piece of string around his infant son's big toe and the other to a mobile hanging over the crib, so that every time the child moved his foot, the mobile moved. The first foot movements, Piaget explained, are general movements that have nothing to do with the mobile. But very soon infants learn the connection between foot movements and movements of the mobile and move their feet very vigorously in order to make them happen.

Now suppose you wanted to test a monkey's memory. How might you do so? Given that monkeys and young infants are nonverbal, could the same procedures be applied? Research suggests that the answer might be yes. The most common approach to testing the memory of a monkey is what is termed "the delayed nonmatch to sample procedure," in which the investigator shows an infant monkey

> *"Live as long as you may, the first twenty years are the longest half of your life."*
> — *Robert Southey, 1774–1843*

(or a human infant) a sample object—say, a small box. When the infants reach for the box, a reward is presented. The box is then taken away and later presented again, along with a second, different object—say, a teddy bear. Now the infants are rewarded only if they reach for the new object. The procedure continues for a number of trials with a variety of novel objects being paired with the original object. The infants are rewarded only when they reach for the novel object, not the original one.

The delayed nonmatch to sample task is not easy to perform. It requires at least three capabilities: learning and remembering a rule (the new object is always the one that is rewarded),

remembering which object is familiar in order to identify the new one, and being able to reach in an intended direction. Infant monkeys do not usually accomplish these three tasks until they are at least four months old. And human infants, who develop more slowly than apes, rarely perform very well until they are at least a year old. At the age of one they require many trials before they learn. Even at the age of five or six years their typical performance is far worse than normal adult humans.

A-not-B

The A-not-B experiment gives an indication of the age at which infants develop short-term memory. If you show an object—say, a ring—to an adult and then hide it under a pillow (which we will call pillow A) while they are watching, they will have no difficulty reaching for and retrieving it. Neither would four- or five-month-old infants.

Now suppose that after you have hidden the ring under pillow A, you remove it and slip it under a second pillow (which we will call pillow B) right next to it, again in full view of both an adult and an infant. The adult will reach immediately under pillow B and find the ring, but the infant, who has witnessed the same sequence of events, reaches for A, not B (hence the name of this demonstration). It is not until after the age of eight months or so that infants reliably reach toward B—and then only if the object has just been hidden. If there is a delay of as little as 8 or 10 seconds between hiding the object and letting the infant retrieve it, very few infants less than a year old will correctly reach for it under pillow B.

The A-not-B problem provides a useful test of memory. The infant has to be able to remember where the object was hidden in order to be able to reach out for it. The task tests the infant's short-term memory and can also provide evidence about the relationship between changes in the brain and memory development.

K.C.'s Motorcycle

A patient of the psychologist Endel Tulving (see p. 78) identified only as K.C. went to the psychologist as part of his rehabilitation after an accident during which he missed a sharp curve while riding his motorcycle, hit a tree, and ended up with serious brain damage. He was 30 years old at the time of his accident. Despite his injuries, K.C. continued to

Studies on victims of road accidents with head damage or brain injury provide strong evidence that different parts of the brain produce different types of memory.

be a bright, alert, and quite normal young man—or so it seemed to the casual observer. He appeared to remember everything he had ever learned. He knew how to play chess, where he lived, what he owned, multiplication tables, and a host of other abstract facts, the sorts of things that make up what we define as semantic memory or abstract information (see p. 80).

But Tulving soon discovered that although K.C.'s semantic memory was intact, his episodic memory or recollection of personal experiences (also called autobiographical memory) seemed to have vanished completely. For example, although K.C. was absolutely certain that his parents had a cottage, and although he knew exactly where it was and everything that was in it, he could not remember a single time that he had ever been there in the past. Similarly, although he knew how to play chess, he had no specific memory of the time, place, or people present when he had played a match.

The case of K.C. provides strong evidence that different parts of the brain are involved in semantic (abstract) and episodic (autobiographical) memory.

EARLY BRAIN DEVELOPMENT

There are significant developments in areas of the brain during the first few months of life. Following a major growth spurt in the brain during the last few months before birth, the newborn's head is about one-quarter the size of the rest of the body; in adults the ratio is closer to about one-tenth (see pp. 6–23). The infant's brain continues to grow very rapidly during the first two years of life, a phenomenon referred to as brain proliferation. This growth does not involve the production of new brain cells so much as the growth of protective coatings over them and the development of a vast number of connections between existing nerve cells. In fact, the brain of a two-year-old may contain more potential connections than it ever will again. That is because many of the billions of connections that are not used eventually disappear—a process that is known as neural (nerve cell) pruning.

The infant's relatively large brain consists of three main parts (like the adult brain): the brain stem (at the lower rear of the brain, like an extension of the spinal cord); the cerebellum, which is also at the lower rear of the brain, behind the brain stem; and the cerebrum, which is the wrinkled, grayish-looking mass that you

"For the first year or two of life outside the womb, our brains are in the most pliable, impressionable, and receptive state they will ever be in."
— David J. Darling, 1996

would see if a human skull were opened from the top (see Vol. 2, pp. 21–39).

The brain stem and other lower parts of the brain are more highly developed and functional in the infant—and in the fetus—than are the structures of the cerebrum. That is because the brain stem is closely involved in physiological activities such as breathing, heart functioning, and digestion. Hence it is essential for physical survival. The cerebrum is more concerned with activity of the senses, movement, and balance. Some of its most important functions relate to thinking, language, and speech.

Much of the information we have about the relationship between brain and memory comes from three sources. Advances in technology have meant that studies can be carried out showing computer-enhanced, real-time images of the brain in action. A second area of investigation uses the brains of animals, especially nonhuman primates; the effect of surgically altering the animal's brain is recorded. Finally, psychologists study people with brain injuries. Among other things, these studies seem to demonstrate conclusively that different parts of the brain are involved in different kinds of memories (see box on p. 83).

Not surprisingly, an infant's memory appears to be closely tied to the development and functioning of different parts of the brain. Charles Nelson, professor of developmental psychology at the University of Minnesota, suggests that the infant's first memories, which cannot be put into words and are therefore said to be implicit (he uses the term preexplicit), depend on lower brain structures such as the brain stem and the cerebellum. These structures, as we saw, are the most highly developed at birth. The infant's more explicit memories begin to appear toward the end of the first year of life. These memories are more dependent on the structures of the cerebrum.

Memory in young infants

Within a few days of birth infants are able to recognize their mother's voice as well as her smell. Evidence of this comes from studies that have found that infants turn more readily toward the sound of their mother's voice than anyone else's. Similarly, they react more positively to smells associated with their mothers than

to smells associated with others. But while this is clear evidence of memory, it may be memory of information acquired before birth rather than from postnatal learning. We do know that the ear of the unborn child is fully formed and functional some months before birth.

Yet even within a day of birth infants can learn and remember new things. Recall the habituation study described earlier, in which infants less than a day old heard a single word being repeated until they stopped reacting to it. When these same infants heard the word again the next day, they habituated to it far more rapidly than they had the previous day. That is clear evidence of a kind of implicit memory—a memory that cannot be put into words but that affects behavior.

The infant's first implicit memories are

> "...Much that people forget about their early childhood influences their responses later in life. In this sense there may truly be an unconscious...."
> —Nora S. Newcombe et al., 2001

fleeting recollections, not long remembered—unless, of course, there are reminders between learning and being asked to remember. For example, infants can quite easily learn an association between a puff of air and a musical tone. A puff of air blown into infants' eyes causes them to blink. If the puff of air is blown into their eyes a number of times, and if it is always preceded by the distinctive sound of a single piano note, the infants will quickly learn to blink whenever they hear the note. They will continue to react in this way even when there is no longer a puff of air directed at their eyes. This is a simple example of a kind of learning known as conditioning (see Vol. 1, pp. 74–89).

The interesting thing about this kind of learning in early infancy is that the infants may show evidence of remembering. In this instance infants continued to blink in response to the tone on the following day, for a half-dozen days afterward, or sometimes even longer. However, if there are no reminders later—that is, if the puff of air never again follows the note—the infants will quickly stop blinking in response to the sound.

Recent studies by Carolyn Rovee-Collier and her colleagues at Rutgers University in New Jersey also demonstrate that infants can learn and remember. The studies are based on the Piaget experiment with three-month-old infants and mobiles (*see* p. 82). When investigators place infants back in their cribs a week after they have learned to make the mobile move by kicking, they very quickly start to kick again. They clearly remember what they learned. But just as in the eye-blink conditioning studies, their memories are shortlived. If these infants are not placed back in the crib with the mobile until two weeks after the initial learning, they kick no more than infants who have never before seen the mobiles. They appear to remember nothing of what they learned.

Another series of experiments, which used reminders, shows that infants do in fact remember the connection between kicking and the mobile moving. In these studies the investigator placed the infants back in their cribs two weeks after the initial training but did not attach their feet to the mobile. Instead, the investigator jiggled the mobiles while the infants lay briefly in their cribs. Then a day later the investigator again placed the infants in the cribs, but this time attached their ankles to the mobiles. This time the infants kicked as vigorously as they had done two weeks earlier, indicating that they did remember.

Changes in infant memory

Child psychologist Marion Perlmutter describes three stages in the development of infant memories. The first spans the first three months of the infant's life. As we have seen, during this period infant memories appear to result mainly from the repeated pairing of events: mother and voice or smell, mobile and foot movement. These memories represent a very simple kind of learning. And most strikingly, the young infant's memory during these months is often fleeting and highly impermanent. Infants simply do not remember as long as adults. Memory during this period seems to be largely a matter of neurons firing when a new stimulus is presented and then stopping when the stimulus becomes more familiar.

The second stage in infant memory development begins at the age of about three months. It is marked by two things: recognition of familiar objects and events, and the beginnings of intentional behaviors. As infants grow older, objects and events become progressively more familiar. As a result the time needed for habituation (the process of becoming familiar and disinterested) to these more familiar objects and events continues to shorten. This is evidence that the infants are learning and remembering, and, as a result, can recognize things that are familiar. Soon infants begin to look and search actively for objects and people. This shows not only that their memories are

Phase	Characteristics
First (before 3 months)	Memory is fleeting, often lasting only a few hours or days. Evidence of memory is provided by habituation (the infant stops looking, or the orienting response disappears). With repeated learning, the habituation period becomes shorter.
Second (beginning at about 3 months)	Longer-term memory is now evident in the infant's recognition of things and of people. There is growing evidence of intention in the infant's behaviors.
Third (by 8 months)	The infant's memories are now more abstract and more symbolic. Infants can pay attention and deliberately try to remember.

Marion Perlmutter defined three stages of infant memory development. The first is a very simple form of learning. At the end of the third stage infants learn how to speak, so they can represent their memories with words.

becoming more permanent but also that their behaviors are being guided more by intention. Repeatedly reaching for a recognized object or person is proof of intentional or directed behaviors, as opposed to behaviors that are primarily accidental or random.

During the third of Perlmutter's stages, which begins at the age of about eight months, infants' memories have become more like those of adults. They are more abstract and symbolic. Very soon, of course, infants will have words with which to represent objects and events. Infants can now pay attention and try to remember things (see table p. 85). There is a vast difference between the memory of a week-old infant who has a fleeting recollection of a smell or a sound and that of a one-year-old. The one-year-old can not only readily recognize members of the family such as their mother or father or the family pet, but can also associate each of them, and dozens of other things, with a whole repertoire of remembered feelings and impressions—perhaps even words. All of these things are learned during that first busy year of life. However, there is still an enormous difference between the one-year-old's memory and that of a normal adult (see box p. 89).

Infants' worlds

William James (1842–1910), one of the early pioneers of psychology, described the young infant's world as a "blooming, buzzing mass of confusion." He thought that the infant's senses did not function very well during the first weeks and months of life. As a result, the infant would not see or hear anything very clearly; everything would be blurred and confused. James was at least partly wrong: We now know that most of the infant's senses function very well from birth or shortly thereafter. James may have been partly right, however, about the infant's world being confusing and uncertain because, as Piaget later pointed out, infants often act as though they do not realize that objects are permanent and

real. It is as if they do not understand that things continue to exist even when they are not actually looking at them or tasting them. The infant's world, says Piaget, is "a world of the here and now." Thus five-month-old infants will reach for an attractive object that is placed on a table in front of them but will stop doing so the moment a cushion is thrown over it.

"Out of sight, out of mind," claimed Piaget, who used this procedure to illustrate the infant's lack of what he termed the object concept—the realization that objects are real and permanent, that they continue to exist even when they are beyond range of the infant's senses. The young infant is unable to think of objects that are not immediately present, explained Piaget. It is as though the infant does not remember objects that are absent.

Other researchers disagree. They suggest that the young infant's failure to reach for an object that has just been hidden does not prove that the infant does not yet understand the permanence of objects. It may simply be that infants are unable to form the intention of reaching for the object. Or even if they intend to reach for the object, they may not yet be able to coordinate all the activities that are required to do so successfully—looking, reaching in the right direction, and grasping. Or they may simply be too tired or too unmotivated to reach at just that moment (see box p. 89).

MEMORY AND ACTION

When an infant reaches for an object that has just been hidden, it is at least partly the infant's memory that guides this action. The infant needs to remember where the object is to reach for it.

There are two factors closely related to how well the infant performs the A-not-B task. One is the infant's age. Few six-month-olds perform it successfully; few eighteen-month-olds get it wrong. There are clear improvements with age.

The other factor is the time lapse involved. The longer the delay between

TWO IMPOSSIBLE SITUATIONS

Psychologists have devised tests to measure memory in young infants. Piaget's hidden objects task tests the infant's understanding of the permanence and realness of objects. Infants must be able to remember objects even when they can't see them. The task also requires that infants be able to form and carry out the intention to reach. What if the task were made easier? Would we discover something different about the minds of infants?

Yes, we would, suggests Renée Baillargeon, professor of psychology at the University of Illinois, and her associates. In one of their studies a solid screen rotates slowly back and forth in front of an infant. Then, while the screen is flat in front of the infant, a tall, sturdy box is placed in its path. The screen begins rotating again but has to stop when it strikes the box. It then reverses its direction and repeats the movement again. The infant shows no surprise, almost as though understanding, and expecting, that when the box is placed in the way of the screen, the screen will be forced to stop.

But next, while the screen is in motion, the experimenters remove the box through a hidden trapdoor, and the screen continues to rotate through where the box should be. This seems to astonish many of the infants, who stare at this impossible situation as though trying to understand what happened.

In a related study a long carrot moves on a track across the infant's field of view until it disappears behind a screen. Then a shorter carrot follows the long carrot until it, too, disappears behind the screen.

Now a second screen is substituted for the first. This screen has a window cut into its top half so that, as the carrots pass behind it, the tall one will be visible although the short one will not. As expected, infants show no surprise when they don't see the short carrot behind this second screen. But again, when the experimenters pull the long carrot down so that the infants can't see it, infants as young as three and a half months stare significantly longer at this impossible event.

Baillargeon concludes that even at this age infants know that objects are solid, that they continue to exist when they cannot be seen, and that two of them cannot occupy the same space at the same time.

This experiment suggests even very young infants appear to have a short-term memory of objects and also that they understand something about their permanence and about some of the laws of physics that govern their movements and positions in space. But it will nevertheless be some months before infants begin to look for hidden objects, even when someone has hidden them before their very eyes.

the hiding and the opportunity to reach, the more likely the infant is to reach incorrectly for A rather than B. For example, few nine-month-old infants make the A-not-B error after a delay of three seconds or less. But if the delay is seven seconds or more, most are mistaken.

As the developmental psychologist Adele Diamond points out, improved performance of the A-not-B task is evidence of the infant's increasing ability to let intentions rather than habits guide behavior. Also, the A-not-B task provides evidence of improvements in short-term memory, especially when there is a time lapse between the hiding of the object at B and the opportunity for the infant to reach for it. The fact that older infants can tolerate longer delays before making the A-not-B error is strong evidence that they have longer-lasting short-term memories. It may also be evidence of increasing maturity of parts of the cerebrum.

Young infants, as we saw, soon learn to recognize their mother's voice or face. And

> *"If you're like most people, you probably can remember your high school prom, but not your third birthday or when your younger brother was born."*
> — *Brian Weaver, 2001*

although in the beginning their memories for new learning are short-lived, sometimes lasting no more than a few hours or days, they very soon learn to recognize familiar places and things. By the time they reach the age of two, they will have learned an overwhelming assortment of different things: the identities of people and animals, how to walk, the locations of hundreds of very important objects, hundreds of words, and all sorts of complex rules for putting them together. All this happens during the first two years of life.

Incidental mnemonics

During the preschool period (between ages two and six) children learn at an amazing rate. This is especially evident in the acquisition of language, where there is an enormous growth in vocabulary. This vocabulary spurt begins toward the last half of the infant's second year of life and continues into the preschool period. So good are children at learning words during this period that very often only one or two exposures to a new word are sufficient to ensure that they will be able to remember and use that particular word during the rest of their lives.

Nevertheless, there are some important differences between the memories of preschoolers and those of older children and adults. Most noticeably, preschoolers do not deliberately and systematically use the powerful memory strategies that older children and adults use: organizing, rehearsing, and elaborating. It is as though they still know little about remembering. They have not yet developed notions of themselves as learners and rememberers, and they have not figured out that there are certain strategies that can make it a lot easier to remember.

According to Henry Wellman of the University of Michigan, the strategies used by preschoolers are incidental rather than deliberate. He calls them incidental mnemonics. Mnemonics are principles or tricks that make it easier to remember. Because incidental mnemonics are not deliberate, they are not really strategies. One of the most common incidental strategies used by preschoolers is that they might pay more attention.

Although many preschoolers seem able to use strategies for remembering, very few do so spontaneously. For example, when Wellman asked three-year-olds to bury a toy in a large sandbox, only about one in five thought of marking the spot so they could find it later, even though they were asked if there was anything else they wanted to do before leaving. However, half of a second group who were instructed to try to remember where the toy was hidden used the simple strategy of marking the spot. Significantly, even among the group who knew they should remember the location of the toy, half used no apparent strategy to do so and remembered no better than if they had not been asked to remember at all.

Memory reliability

Imagine that there is a group of three- to five-year-olds playing in a schoolroom when suddenly a tall, red-haired, bearded stranger wearing a green cloak bursts in

> *"Since the time of Freud, scientists have sought the roots of adult memory in the infancy period."*
> — *Carolyn Rovee-Collier, 1999*

and, right in front of the children, steals the teacher's purse! Now suppose you did exactly the same thing with a group of eleven-year-olds and again with a group of adolescents and another of adults. Later, you ask each of these groups of witnesses to describe the thief. And then you bring all these eyewitnesses to view a lineup that includes him.

How well do you suppose the preschoolers will fare? How many will remember the color of the thief's hair, that he wore a green cloak, that he was tall and bearded? How many will point confidently to the thief?

Now suppose you put a twist in the proceedings and don't include the thief in your lineup. Will your preschoolers shake their heads and say, "No, the bad guy is not here!" or will they finger some poor innocent? Will the older children and adults fare better?

INFANTILE AMNESIA

FOCUS ON

By the age of two the infant's long-term memory is nothing short of astonishing compared to what it was earlier in the first year of life. For example, by now most infants have learned a huge number of words, and they will remember most of these words for the rest of their lives. But it is also true that they will be able to tell you nothing about any of their personal experiences throughout infancy and even through most of the early preschool period.

This curious phenomenon, which psychologists label infantile amnesia, is so powerful that when researchers showed 9- and 10-year-old children photographs of their classmates from their early preschool years (up to age four), they were unable to recognize them. And these were classmates they had seen every day a mere half-dozen years earlier. Yet when adults were shown photographs of their elementary school classmates, they recognized more than 90 percent of them. It made no difference that they had not seen some of them once since elementary school. Nor did it make any difference that many of these adults had been out of school for more than half a century.

It is important to note, however, that although we appear to have little explicit memory of events that occurred before age five, we may nevertheless have some implicit memories of them. In one study psychologist Laraine McDonough showed that even a year after learning some novel behaviors, two-year-olds can still recall them. In this study recall was assessed by how the children acted when shown the objects that had been used for the novel behaviors a year earlier. Hence their memories,

This lady can recognize and name most of her high-school companions from many years ago. At the age of ten, however, she would not have been able to remember the preschoolers she was with every day.

though not explicit, were evident in their behaviors. There is little doubt that these same infants could not have told you anything about these experiences 10 years later.

No one knows for certain why we are subject to infantile amnesia. One theory is that structures of the brain involved in long-term, autobiographical (episodic) memory are not sufficiently developed during this period. Another theory is that the child has not yet developed the kinds of memory strategies that are required. Yet another theory is that the infant does not have a sufficiently strong sense of self with which to associate autobiographical memories.

These are important questions because preschoolers are often witnesses to crimes or, sadly, sometimes their victims. And they are often asked by courts of law to remember who did what, where, and when. How reliable are their memories?

Hundreds of studies have examined this question, many using procedures similar to the one with the bearded man. The conclusions, seem clear (*see* box p. 90): preschoolers do not remember as accurately and in as much detail as older children and adults. Furthermore, they are very trusting of adults such as interviewers, judges, lawyers, and politicians. They are anxious to please,

THE RELIABILITY OF CHILD WITNESSES

How can you, a devious and clever prosecutor, make a child remember and help you nail your prime suspect, the one you absolutely know did it?

Well, you should ask leading questions such as "Did the man have a beard?" rather than open-ended questions like "Tell me what the man looked like." You should ask your leading question repeatedly and on different days, and you should include the answers you want in other questions you ask. For example, you might ask, "Was the bearded thief wearing a green cloak?" rather than "What was the thief wearing?" It might not hurt if you also use a little emotional coercion and inducement with your preschool witnesses. Try saying things like: "You'll feel a lot better if you tell me what he did to you," or "That man has done a lot of bad things, and you can help us get him!"

Using these methods, you may well be highly successful not only in getting your preschool witnesses to remember, but also to misremember and wrongly accuse someone. You may be guilty of planting false memories—memories for things that never happened. This is especially true when considered in the light of the following research findings about preschoolers, which question the reliability of child witnesses giving evidence to a court of law:

• They are less likely than older children and adults to correctly identify a guilty person.

• They are more likely than older children or adults to mistakenly identify an innocent person as being guilty.

• They can be made, by the power of suggestion, to remember events that never occurred.

• When asked to imagine something, they may later report the imagined event as though it actually happened.

• The reliability of memories for events that occurred during the period of infantile amnesia, that is, the early preschool years, is highly suspect.

• Preschoolers have a "yes" response bias. They are more likely to say that something happened rather than that it didn't or even to admit that they do not know.

• When preschoolers are asked to guess repeatedly, they become progressively more certain of their guesses, often ending up totally confident that the guess is the truth.

A police officer talking to a young child witness in a housing project in Seattle, Washington. Questioning children can be difficult since they are vulnerable to suggestions from interviewers or other adults and can produce unreliable evidence.

eager to follow wherever leading questions take them, and they can be made to remember things that never happened. Some children are remarkably resistant to misleading suggestions. When questioned by a sensitive and neutral interviewer, many children have remarkably good recall for significant events, but it isn't always possible for courts to determine how reliable a child witness is.

Memory in older children

As we have seen, young preschoolers do not often deliberately use strategies to improve their ability to remember. Interestingly, however, when researchers asked the mothers of four-year-olds to help their children learn and remember different things (like the names of cartoon characters or the locations of animals in a zoo), most of the mothers spontaneously used strategies with their children. The commonest strategy was simple rehearsal—repeating for the children and having them repeat back. But mothers also use other strategies. If the dog in the book the mother is reading is called "Patches," the mother points out the black patch over its eye; if the doll is named "Twiggy," the mother points out the doll's twiglike limbs.

Children may learn to use memory strategies partly from these sorts of social interactions, especially from parents and older siblings. It is clear that children become better memorizers as they age at least partly because they make more and better use of strategies. For example, groups of four-, seven-, and eleven-year-old children were shown pictures under one of two sets of instructions: "Look at these pictures" or "Remember these pictures." Four-year-olds behaved the same way under both sets of conditions. When seven- and eleven-year-olds were told to remember, they deliberately used strategies to improve their recall.

The evidence indicates that memory improves quite steadily from infancy through the preschool period until about age seven. After that improvements are less noticeable. But at all ages there can be marked individual differences in how well different children remember.

Improvements in memory are clearly related to children's increasing use of strategies such as organizing and rehearsing. They are also closely linked to increasing familiarity with things and events. In studies in which children are shown photographs depicting different scenes, the more familiar the children are with the scenes, the better they can remember details from the pictures. For example, investigators in one study showed a group of eight- and nine-year-olds an assortment of soccer pictures and

> *"When I was younger I could remember anything, whether it happened or not; but I am getting old, and soon I shall remember only the latter."*
> — *Mark Twain, 1835–1910*

then asked questions about them. Children who were soccer players did significantly better than children who were not. In much the same way many chess masters can easily replace all the pieces in a half-played chess match after examining the board for just a few moments. A novice player, by contrast, might be hard pressed to replace more than a few pieces correctly.

Improving memory

We have seen that memory improves with increasing use of strategies and with increasing knowledge. Thus the more children know about history, for example, the easier it becomes for them to remember new historical facts.

Research has shown that it is also possible to increase the capacity of memory by teaching specific strategies or sometimes simply by making children aware of how important and effective such strategies can be. Thus certain school-based programs have been designed to teach children general

FLASHBULB MEMORY

If we dredge around in our memories, most of us can find at least one of what is termed a flashbulb memory. A flashbulb memory is an unusually vivid recollection of the exact time and place that we heard about something highly dramatic, important, or emotional. These memories result from a single event and are typically extraordinarily clear recollections of what we were doing at the time, how we felt, and what happened next. In the United States many people have flashbulb memories related to the assassination of President John F. Kennedy in 1963. In Britain and elsewhere many people have similar memories relating to the death of Princess Diana in 1997.

Flashbulb memories are very common; eidetic images, which are exact, photolike recollections (also termed photographic memory), are not. Many of us, when we remember something, say, "I can see it in my mind." In fact, very few of us see a clear mental image of what we remember. But there are a small number of individuals who actually do see with their mind's eye an image so distinct that they can examine it and answer extremely detailed questions about it. An individual so gifted might, for example, look at the painting below by Pieter Breughel and remember every detail exactly.

Eidetic images appear to be more common in younger children than in adults. However, they are seldom a real advantage in school because they usually fade within minutes. Seldom are they available for even an hour. But there are rare cases of individuals whose eidetic images last indefinitely. One such case is that of S., a patient of psychologist Alexander Romanovich Luria (1902–1977).

S. was a journalist. His employer sent him to Luria because he never needed to take notes, but remembered everything he was told. On May 10, 1939, Luria presented S. with an array of 50 numbers. S. initially spent three minutes studying the table and then reproduced it flawlessly in 40 seconds. When asked, he could easily recite any of the four-digit numbers that appeared in the first 12 rows as well as the two-digit numbers in the last row, and he could read off the columns vertically as well as diagonally. Not only that, but he could probably have recalled the table of numbers perfectly at any time in the future. Luria once asked S. to recall a list of words that he had shown him 16 years earlier. S. took a few moments to recollect. He closed his eyes, explains Luria, and then commented, "Yes, yes… That was the series you gave me once when we were in your apartment… You were sitting at the table and I in the rocking chair… You were wearing a gray suit… 'Now, then,' I can see you saying." And then he recited the list without error. Unfortunately, his excellent memory caused him problems in everyday life. His mind was such a jumble of information, sounds, and sights that he had trouble following an ordinary conversation.

Eidetic recollection of an image is more commonly known as photographic memory. Most people can recall only a few details when looking at this picture by Pieter Breughel, but some remember every detail clearly. Eidetic images usually fade after a few minutes, but in rare cases the person preserves the memory for years.

methods of organizing material, how to elaborate using mental imagery, or simply how to rehearse information so that they commit it to memory.

Memory strategies

There are also several specific memory strategies, such as rhymes and sayings, which are sometimes known as mnemonic devices. Examples include the verse "Thirty days hath September" for remembering the length of each month and "*my very earthy mother just served us nine pizzas*," which is a mnemonic for the first letters of all the planets in our solar system from the Sun outward.

Other powerful memory strategies make extensive use of visual imagery. They are strategies that ask the memorizer to form highly vivid mental images. Such images can often be recalled far more easily than words or ideas. One example of a visual imagery system is the loci system. The word loci is the plural of the Latin *locus*, meaning "place." This mnemonic system requires the formation of a link between items on a list and a series of familiar places. For example, in order to remember all the things you want to put in your knapsack for a camping trip, you might visualize everything you need in a different room of your house. Imagine a tube of insect repellent on the kitchen table; in the bathroom, your hatchet hanging from the mirror; in the hallway, a roll of toilet paper; in the bedroom, the lunch your mother packed.

Another powerful mnemonic device is the link system, which requires the memorizer to form a visual connection between the first item on a list and some other familiar and easily remembered item. Then a visual link is formed between the first item and the second, between the

second and the third, and so on. For example, this strategy might be used to memorize the following grocery list: bread, dog food, ketchup, sausages, and broccoli. Visualize, if you will, a loaf of bread hanging over the edge of a shopping basket. In the basket next to the bread is a dog. The dog has a large, ketchup-covered sausage in its mouth and a bizarre-looking tuft of broccoli growing from its left ear. These are just a few of the techniques that you can use to help improve your ability to remember.

FUTURE CHALLENGES

Psychologists have devised a range of experimental techniques to measure the memory capabilities of children who have not developed language skills. The next challenge is to hone these techniques in an effort to answer questions such as "Do infants know who they are?" and "How does memory develop?"

Researchers have shown that the development of memory in infants is closely linked to the growth of their brain structures, and that it occurs in three stages, beginning with fleeting memories and impressions (before three months),

> *"Just as eating against one's will is injurious to health, so study without a liking for it spoils the memory, and it retains nothing...."*
> — *Leonardo da Vinci, about 1500*

progressing to an ability to recognize familiar things (three to eight months), and culminating in more abstract remembering (after eight months). Memory improves in older children as they gain more knowledge and develop memory-improving strategies.

 CONNECTIONS

- Behaviorism: Volume 1, pp. 74–89
- Biology of the Brain: Volume 2, pp. 20–39

- The Mind: Volume 2, pp. 40–61
- Language Processing: Volume 3, pp. 114–135
- Fetal Development: pp. 6–23
- Infant Cognition: pp. 24–39

Development of Problem Solving

"A problem well stated is a problem half solved."

Charles Kettering

Problem solving is a term used by psychologists to describe the ability of an individual to deal with a situation of some complexity that demands initiative and mental agility if a certain goal is to be reached. Although some animals can solve problems, the ability to solve complex problems is widely supposed to be one of the things that distinguishes humans from other creatures. The reasoning processes that people bring to problem solving are of great interest to psychologists and cast light on the nature of intelligence.

Problem solving is a means of finding a way to achieve an objective that is not immediately attainable. As children pass through the preschool and school years, they become increasingly able to solve complex problems. Some psychologists suggest that these skills develop in distinct stages, while others claim that they

KEY TERMS

• **Deductive reasoning**—the rigorous proof of a statement (a conclusion) from one or more given statements (premises). For example: All men are mortal; Caesar is a man; therefore Caesar is mortal. Some logicians regard all valid reasoning as deductive in form and reject inductive reasoning (see below) as a possible alternative.

• **Inductive reasoning**—a method of inferring the whole from a part or parts, the general from one or more particulars. For example: All the red-headed people I have ever known have gone bald by the age of 40; therefore all red-headed people go bald by that age. Inductive reasoning may lead to the right conclusions, but it is unreliable because its methodology is not rigorously scientific.

Playing with a Rubik's cube is fun and shows that people have a capacity for problem-solving. It is not, however, a task that can be used to measure intelligence or to study how individuals develop problem-solving skills.

develop in a more gradual or organic way. To test these ideas, researchers have devised various experimental tasks that shed light on the mechanisms involved in problem solving. These tasks require the use of analogy, logical reasoning, planning, and representation—all methods of advancing toward a conclusion by looking at an object or a concept in terms of something else. New and more "child-friendly" experiments show that some problem-solving skills develop earlier in life than psychologists previously suspected.

People's abilities to solve problems far exceed those of other animal species. Indeed, people often get pleasure from problem solving for its own sake. Take, for example, Rubik's cube, which became a worldwide craze in the 1980s. The cube is made up of small tiles of six different colors that can be rotated into different positions. The challenge is to rotate layers of tiles until each side of the cube has only a single color. The number of combinations is so great that if you had a cube for every possible combination, you could cover the entire surface of Earth. Yet some people can solve Rubik's cube in less than 30 seconds.

> *"Young children are far more competent problem solvers than they had been given credit for. The key to revealing these competencies has been simplifying problems by eliminating…difficulty extraneous to the process being examined."*
> —*Robert Siegler, 1998*

Rubik's cube captures the essence of a problem, but it is not a good test of problem-solving skills in children (or most adults, for that matter) because it is too complicated. To assess children's problem-solving abilities, researchers must devise tests that are taken from within their subjects' normal environment and experience. The experimental tasks should also be designed to show what processes children use to solve problems, and how these processes develop over time.

TWO THEORIES OF DEVELOPMENT

According to Swiss psychologist Jean Piaget (1896–1980) (*see* pp. 58–77), children's problem-solving abilities develop in clearly defined stages. Their skills are not underdeveloped versions of adult thinking, but are different in nature and both reflect and are appropriate to the stage of development they have reached. Children have their own strategies and will solve certain types of problem only when they are ready to do so. However, some information-processing theorists disagree with Piaget's theories and regard

problem-solving development as a more gradual and continuous process linked to increasing powers of memory. They focus on how children represent problems, the processes they use to solve them, and the way these processes change as the children's memories improve. Robert Siegler of Carnegie-Mellon University argued that as children develop, they encode aspects of problems that they previously ignored. This enables them to develop increasingly complex rules.

The balance beam problem

Siegler's approach is neatly demonstrated by an experiment he devised to examine how children aged between 5 and 17 years use various rules to solve a balance beam problem (*see* diagram p. 96). Although he found that in general the older the children, the more complex the mental processes they used to arrive at their

KEY POINTS

- In order for researchers to assess problem-solving skills, tasks should be presented so that children clearly understand the goal of the task.
- By the age of about three children can use mental representations of real objects to help them solve problems.
- Although young children tend to act before they think, even infants as young as 12 months sometimes use planning to help them achieve their goals. Planning may involve breaking down a problem into one or more parts or subgoals in order to reach the ultimate objective.
- Between early infancy and the age of about three or four children develop an understanding of the principles of cause and effect.
- Analogical reasoning (using a solution to a familiar problem to solve a new one) develops in infancy and generally improves with age.
- Four-year-old children can solve some simple problems by deductive reasoning (reaching a logical conclusion by reasoning from the information given). Four-year-olds can also reason about rules, especially if the rules are realistic.
- Recent research challenges the traditional view that children younger than seven cannot understand that a given number of objects remains the same however they are arranged.
- As children develop advanced problem-solving skills, they do not automatically stop using less-advanced skills.

answers, this generalization did not always hold good. The balance beam task measures ability to use information about the relationship between weight and distance. Each child is shown a beam balanced on a fulcrum (the support on which a lever turns). Along the beam are a number of pegs. At first the beam is prevented from moving by wooden blocks placed underneath both of its ends. The researcher then places a number of weights on a peg on either side of the fulcrum and asks the child to predict how the beam will behave if the supporting blocks are removed. For example, if three weights are placed on one arm of the beam eight inches from the fulcrum, and six weights are placed on the other side four inches from the fulcrum, the beam will balance. If both sets of weights are placed the same distance from the fulcrum, the side with six weights will go down. But how do the children figure out these problems?

Using different combinations of weights placed at various distances on either side of the fulcrum, Siegler created six types of balance problem. He suggested that whatever the problem, children would seek a solution by applying one of the following rules:

Rule 1: If the weights are the same on both sides of the fulcrum, the children predict that the beam will balance. If the weights are different, they predict that the side with more weight will go down.

Rule 2: If there are more weights on one side of the fulcrum than the other, the children predict that that side will go down. If there are equal weights on both sides, they predict that the side on which the weights are farther from the fulcrum will go down.

Rule 3: If the weights and the distance from the fulcrum are the same on both sides, the children predict that the beam will balance. If either the weights or the distances from the fulcrum are unequal, they predict that the side with the greater weight or distance will go down. If one side has more weight and the other side more distance, they do not know which side will go down and have to guess.

Rule 4: If the weights on one side of the balance beam are heavier and those on the other side are farther away from the fulcrum, the children calculate the torque (that is, weight multiplied by distance) for each side. On this basis they are able to predict that the side with the greater torque will go down.

Problem	Answer	Percentage of correct responses using rules			
		Rule 1	Rule 2	Rule 3	Rule 4
	Balance	100	100	100	100
	Left down	100	100	100	100
	Left down	0	100	100	100
	Balance	100	100	33	100
	Right down	0	0	33	100
	Right down	0	0	33	100

Diagram showing the percentage of correct answers given by children to problems requiring them to predict whether or not a beam will balance. Thirty-three percent is chance responding—in other words, the number of times a child might give the right answer purely by luck, without using any reasoning.

Siegler found that there was a developmental trend in the use of these different rules. Rule 1 is the simplest and so should be the easiest for a child to apply. It was the rule most often used by the five-year-olds. Rules 2, 3, and 4 are successively more complex and harder to apply because they require more knowledge and greater powers of memory. Most nine-year-olds used Rules 2 or 3, while most 13- to 17-year-olds used Rule 3. Although Rule 4 is the only rule that is accurate for all types of problem, Siegler was surprised to find that it was used by fewer than 20 percent of the 16- and 17-year-olds, even though they had learned about balance scales in science courses at school.

One fundamental aspect of problem solving is the ability to use symbols such as mental images, language, and numbers to represent real objects. Although Piaget thought that children could not use representations before the age of about 18 months, subsequent research has shown that even infants under one year of age may use gestures to stand for various objects or events.

The scale of the problem

Nevertheless, older infants and children are much better at using symbols to help them solve problems. This was convincingly demonstrated in an experiment conducted in 1987 by Judy Deloache, professor of psychology at the University of Virginia. In the first part of the experiment Deloache asked two- and three-year-old children to search for a toy in a scale model of a room. Later the children were taken into a life-size room just like the model they had seen. When asked to find the toy, the three-year-olds

Toddlers such as this one make no discernible distinction between reality and fantasy, toy railroads and prototype trains. But by about the age of three children can understand that a symbol or model can represent a real object or situation.

> *"Children are…highly attuned to the response of their listeners, eager to be good storytellers, driven to tell about what matters to them."*
> —*Susan Engel, 2000*

were successful in more than 70 percent of trials because they tended to look where they had found the toy in the scale model. Two-year-olds were successful in only about 20 percent of trials. The difference could not be explained in terms of poorer memory among the two-year-olds because when both age groups went back to the scale model, they were equally successful at locating the toy. It seems that two-year-olds have difficulty in understanding that a scale model can represent a life-size room, but that by age three this understanding has developed.

Preschool children still have difficulty using symbols and numbers that do not refer to real objects. Many experiments have shown that children between the ages of three and five can solve simple arithmetical problems if the numbers are small and related to real things. They may have no difficulty with questions such as:

"If there are three children in a candy store, and two go out, how many children are left in the shop?" But very few children of this age who solved the problem could give the correct answer to: "What does one and two make?" For them the concrete is easy, the abstract impossible.

PLANNING

Planning is another important aspect of problem solving, especially for complex and unfamiliar situations. It is the method by which children can avoid the frustrations and wasted time involved in trial and error. However, planning can be quite demanding and carries the risk that the effort may be wasted if the child fails to execute the plan correctly, or if the problem turns out to be too difficult to solve. Another drawback is that planning requires inhibiting the tendency to act immediately, yet the ability to inhibit action is something that develops slowly over the course of childhood. Also, children are sometimes rescued from the consequences of lack of planning, as, for example, when a parent steps in to help.

Despite these complications, it seems that children often do plan from a very early age. Consider the following experiment with two groups of 12-month-old infants carried

Asked to put both these items into the larger saucepan without touching the contents, this one-year-old tries to figure out which of the containers needs to be tipped—a subgoal on the route to his ultimate objective.

out by Peter Willatts of the University of Dundee, Scotland. Each group was seated at a table. On the table was a small barrier, and beyond that was a cloth. For one group of infants one end of a length of string was placed on the cloth, and the other end was attached to a toy at the far end of the table. The setup for the other group of infants was almost identical, except that in this case the string was not attached to the toy.

The children in the first group tended to remove the barrier, pull the cloth toward them, grab the string, and pull it to reach the toy. Children in the second group tended to play with the barrier, were slower to reach for the cloth, and did not pull the string. Their actions suggest they realized the string was not attached and could not help them reach the toy.

Goals and subgoals

Successful task completion in the first group involves comparing the current state with the goal state and finding the action that will bring the two together—pulling the string to get the toy. Because the string is initially out of the children's reach, the children set the subgoal of bringing it closer; that is achieved by moving the cloth. Yet even this action is not immediately possible because of the barrier, so the removal of the barrier becomes another of the children's subgoals.

The setting of goals and subgoals in order to reduce the difference between the current state and the goal state is a form of planning known as means-ends analysis (*see* Vol. 3, pp. 136–163). Willatts found that the rudiments of means-ends analysis are present in children as young as four months old.

MONKEY CANS

In the standard version of the Tower of Hanoi puzzle (*see* Vol. 1, pp. 104–117) there are three pegs. On the first peg are 64 disks of decreasing sizes, with the largest at the bottom and the smallest at the top. The other two pegs are empty. The task is to move all the disks until they are in the same arrangement on the third peg. They can be moved only one at a time, and a larger disk cannot be placed on top of a smaller one.

Children aged five and six have difficulty with this version of the task. Part of their problem seems to be that they forget the basic rules, such as the rule that larger disks cannot go on top of smaller disks.

In 1981 David Klahr and Mitch Robinson of Carnegie-Mellon University developed a version of the Tower of Hanoi better suited to children in which the rings were replaced with cans of different sizes, and the rule was that smaller cans could not be placed over larger cans. To make the task fun, it was described in the form of a story about monkeys, hence the name "Monkey Cans." The cans represented a mommy, a daddy, and a baby monkey who can jump from tree to tree. The "monkeys" the children were asked to move were described as copycat monkeys who want to be in the same arrangement as the other monkeys.

To help the children keep in mind the goal of the task, the desired arrangement of cans and pegs was set up in front of them. Instead of actually moving the cans, the children had to tell the researchers their sequence of moves. In this way the researchers could establish the extent to which the children planned their moves. The researchers also varied the number of cans and where they were placed at the start of the task.

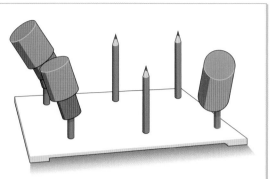

The front row of pegs is the model that the children are asked to reproduce on the back row without placing smaller cans over larger ones.

Depending on the number of cans and their initial arrangement, successful completion of the task involved between one and seven moves.

Klahr and Robinson found that most four-year-olds were able to find the best solution to two-move puzzles, but not to more complicated problems. Five- and six-year-olds were good on four-move problems, and most six-year-olds could solve six-move problems.

Although all the children showed evidence of subgoal use, it was much more marked among the older children. Younger children often made illegal moves and lost track of their objectives. Despite this, it seems that the difference in abilities shown by the younger and older children is simply one of degree: Young children try to plan ahead, but sometimes forget the objectives, while older children are able to hold more information in mind and so can plan further ahead. This kind of gradual change is consistent with the information-processing view of problem solving.

As children grow up, the number and complexity of subgoals they can keep in mind increases along with their ability to resist the lure of short-term goals that divert them from longer-term objectives. These developments are associated with a greater ability to implement means-ends strategy. This has been illustrated in an experiment known as "Monkey Cans" (*see* box), a modified version of the Tower of Hanoi puzzle (*see* Vol. 1, pp. 104–117).

Problem solving often involves trying to understand what caused a particular event. In some situations it is easy to identify causes, as when one pool ball hits another, and the struck ball begins to move. But why do we assume that the first ball caused the second one to move? Could not the second ball have started moving for some other reason?

Causal judgments

Causal judgments are based on three main principles. The first is the assumption that when two events occur close to each other in time and space, the second has been caused by the first. This is known as the contiguity principle. The second is the idea, widely regarded as self-evident, that all causes happen before their effects—this is termed the precedence principle. Third, the covariation principle is based on the assumption that if a certain cause has produced a particular effect on a previous occasion, it will happen again.

Awareness of contiguity

Modern research has shown that even in the first year of life babies are sensitive to contiguity in time and space. Six- to ten-month-old infants spend longer looking at scenes that violate the contiguity principle than at scenes that are consistent with it. In one experiment infants were shown a film of a moving object hitting a stationary object and the second object starting to move. They then watched a sequence in which the second object started to move before the first one had reached it. Finally, they saw a sequence in which the second object did not start to move until three-quarters of a second after the first object hit it. The fact that the infants paid more attention to the two "violation" sequences suggests that they were surprised by them.

The precedence principle (cause precedes effect) seems to be in place with most children by about age three. In a 1979 experiment Merry Bullock and Rochel Gelman of the University of Pennsylvania used a "jack-in-the-box" device to investigate whether children understood that causes cannot occur after their effects. The apparatus consisted of a box with small openings at either end through which a marble could be dropped into a tunnel. In the middle of the box was an opening through which the jack could jump. The experiment consisted of the researcher dropping a marble down one end of the tunnel, the jack appearing, and the researcher then dropping a marble down the other end of the tunnel. It did not actually matter which tunnel the marbles were dropped into: The jack always appeared after the first marble was dropped and before the second one. In fact, the experimenter pressed a hidden pedal in order to make the jack appear, but the children did not know that. All the five-year-olds were able to figure out the relationship between the first marble being dropped and the jack jumping, compared to 88 percent of the four-year-olds and 75 percent of the three-year-olds.

HYPOTHESIS TESTING IN CHILDREN

CASE STUDY

Although the basic mechanisms of causal thinking seem to be in place at a relatively early age, children do not perform well when there are several variables involved. To do so requires the ability to systematically test a hypothesis. This is the cornerstone of scientific method.

Deanna Kuhn and her colleagues at Columbia University devised a study in which children and adults had to discover which types of foods were associated with "catching a cold." Pictorial information showed the variation of certain types of food with the development of colds in children. In one example apples and French fries were associated with colds, while several other products on show were not. When questioned about whether particular foods or drinks made any difference to the incidence of colds in children, only 30 percent of

responses from 11-year-olds were made on the basis of the evidence. Adults achieved the same scores as 14-year-olds, with only 50 percent of responses in each group consistent with the evidence. Many errors were made whereby a single instance of a food being associated with colds led participants to infer a connection that did not necessarily exist.

Other researchers have used tasks in which participants do not have a strong prior belief about the relationship between events and their causes (such as with "catching a cold"). With straightforward tasks children as young as six can understand how evidence relates to a task. Nevertheless, where many potential variables are involved, children and adults have difficulty in making accurate causal judgments.

When we need to discover which of several possible causes is the true cause of an effect, we must observe which of the possible causes occurs regularly and predictably with the effect. This ability—which is known as the covariation principle—also seems to develop by three or four years of age. In a 1975 study Thomas Shultz and Roslyn Mendelson of McGill University, Montreal, Canada, showed children a box with two levers and a light that sometimes came on when one or both levers were pulled. Sometimes only Lever 1 was pulled (the light came on), sometimes both levers were pulled (the light came on), and sometimes only Lever 2 was pulled (no light). Most three- to four-year-olds were able to figure out that Lever 1 caused the light to come on.

Children seem to be less sensitive to cause-and-effect relationships when they happen out of context. For example, when an effect does not occur until five seconds after the event that triggered it, five-year-olds rarely see the first event as the cause of the second. However, from eight years of age onward children do see such events as connected.

Use of analogy

Another problem-solving mechanism that develops in children rather than appears in a sudden flash of inspiration is the ability to reason analogically—using knowledge about past situations to deal with new ones. To do this, children need to find correspondences between the familiar and the new problems, enabling them to "match up" the two situations.

Research has shown that a rudimentary ability to reason analogically begins in infancy. In 1997 Z. Chen and colleagues at Carnegie-Mellon University used an experiment similar to that carried out by Peter Willatts (*see* p. 98) in which children tried to get hold of toys that were out of reach. Infants between 10 and 13 months were presented with a doll of Ernie from *Sesame Street* placed behind a barrier. The doll was attached to a string, and the end nearest the infant was lying on a cloth.

As in Willatts' experiment, the infants were required to remove the barrier, pull the cloth to bring the string closer, then pull on the string to bring Ernie within reach. After completing this task, with or without assistance, the infants were presented with two further problems involving cloths, boxes, and strings. Each of the new problems used two strings and two cloths, but only one pairing of cloth and string actually reached the doll. Although the basic structure of the new problems was similar to that of the original problem, the visual appearance was different—the color and size of the barrier, cloth, and string were varied. Also, children performed the task from a different position—if they had been seated for the first, they were made to stand for the second, and vice versa.

> *"Babies are acute observers and active players who make increasing use of their new skills to influence events and solve problems."*
> —*Peter Willatts, 1999*

On the initial task some of the 13-month-old infants figured out how to reach the Ernie doll without assistance. Those who did not were shown how by a parent. Once the older infants knew the solution, they were better able to transfer it to the new problems than were the 10-month-olds. Younger infants were able to solve the new problems only when the tests were made visually similar to the original task (for example, by using the same toy in all three problems).

Karen Singer Freeman of Purchase College, State University of New York, showed that two-year-old children can reason analogically without having seen another person solve the problem they are set. She devised problems involving the causal relations of stretching, fixing, opening, rolling, breaking, and attaching. In one test children were given a piece of elastic, a toy bird, and a model landscape with a tree at one end and a rock at the other. They were then asked if they could use these materials to make the bird fly.

Before attempting the problem, some, but not all, of the children had watched the experimenter stretch a rubber band between two poles to make a "bridge" across which she then rolled an orange. Of the children who had not seen this demonstration, only 6 percent thought of the stretching solution to the transfer problem. Of those who had seen the demonstration, 28 percent solved the new problem. And when these children were given a hint that the elastic needed to be used, 48 percent found the solution.

In a 1986 experiment Ann Brown and her colleagues at the University of Illinois showed that children are able to reason

The ins and outs of genies and bottles. Research has shown that children as young as three years old can perform fairly complex reasoning tasks if they are shown a way into the problems via analogy—for example, children told a story about a genie were shown toy props like this genie in a bottle.

about more complex analogies. Three- to five-year-old children were told a story about a genie who needed to transport his jewels across a wall and into a bottle. To do so, he rolled up his magic carpet to form a tube, placed one end of the tube over the bottle, and then rolled the jewels into it down the tube. The story was demonstrated using toy props, with a piece of paper representing the magic carpet. The scientists then tried to find out if the children could apply this model to a similar but slightly different problem.

> *"Psychological functioning is composed on multiple levels, with multiple levels of influence, and shifting patterns of dominance, depending on the situation."*
> —*Joseph Glick, 1998*

So, next the children were asked to think about an analogous situation. The Easter Bunny needed to deliver some eggs to children in time for Easter, but was running late. A friend had offered to help, but was on the other side of a river. The problem involved getting the eggs to the friend without getting them wet. The Easter Bunny was carrying a blanket, so the analogous solution was to roll the blanket up into a tube, and roll the eggs through it, just as the genie had done with his jewels. Some of the five-year-olds found the solution, but very few three-year-olds managed it.

In addition to hearing about both problems, some children were asked questions intended to help them establish goals to solve the problem. The questions were along the lines of: "Who has a problem?"; "What did the genie need to do?"; and "How does he solve his problem?" Irrespective of age, most of the children in this group successfully solved the analogous problem.

These studies show that children are often able to use analogies to solve problems, but that sometimes they first

VERBAL SYLLOGISM PROBLEMS

A syllogism is a form of reasoning in which a third proposition is formed from two initial ones. In 1984 J. Hawkins, R. D. Pea, J. Glick, and S. Scribner gave the following instructions to four- and five-year-old children:

"I am going to read you some little stories. Some of them are about make-believe animals and things, and some of them are about real animals and things. Some of the stories are going to sound sort of funny. I want you to pretend that everything the stories say is true."

Following an initial practice story, the problems were read one at a time to the children. The answers to the problems were either "Yes" or "No." Here are some examples of the problems used:

1. Bears have big teeth.
   Animals with big teeth can't read books.
   Can bears read books?
2. Rabbits never bite.
   Cuddly is a rabbit.
   Does Cuddly bite?
3. Glasses bounce when they fall.
   Everything that bounces is made of rubber.
   Are glasses made of rubber?
4. Every banga is purple.
   Purple animals always sneeze at people.
   Do bangas sneeze at people?
5. Pogs wear blue boots.
   Tom is a pog.
   Does Tom wear blue boots?
6. Merds laugh when they're happy.
   Animals that laugh don't like mushrooms.
   Do merds like mushrooms?

Children averaged 94 percent correct on congruent problems (questions based on what they know, such as 1 and 2), but only 13 percent correct on incongruent problems such as 3, which is contrary to what they know. On the fantasy problems (4–6), where previous knowledge could neither help nor hinder performance, children scored 73 percent on average.

need to have their attention drawn to the parallels. Adults also often fail to transfer the solution from one problem to another. Like children, they are more likely to spot an analogy when there are similarities in superficial characteristics (such as visual appearance) or when they are given a hint. Thus although analogical reasoning improves with age, the factors that contribute to successful or unsuccessful performance tend to be the same.

TYPES OF REASONING

To explore the use of reasoning, Kathleen Galotti at Carleton University, Ottawa, Canada, created the following problem:

All shakdees have three eyes.
Myro is a shakdee.
Does Myro have three eyes?

If you have reasoned correctly, you answered "Yes" (Myro does have three eyes). Yet you do not know what shakdees are, or even if it is true that they have three eyes. Your answer is based on deductive reasoning, which produces a conclusion that could be untrue in reality but follows logically from the information given (the premises). A deductively correct conclusion is true only if the premises are true. In other words, a deductively correct answer to a problem involves responding to the form of the argument rather than to its content.

By contrast, sometimes we use reason to reach conclusions that could be true but do not definitely follow from the stated premises. Consider the following problem:

Myro is a shakdee.
Myro has three eyes.
Do all shakdees have three eyes?

There is no definite answer to this question. Even if all shakdees do have three eyes, that conclusion cannot be drawn from the information provided. To answer "Yes" would be to make a generalization on the basis of a specific instance, a process known as induction or inductive reasoning.

Because deduction is concerned with the form of an argument rather than its content, it involves the kind of logical

Researchers compose reasoning problems based on the characteristics and behavior of animals such as cats, dogs, and hyenas to test the deductive reasoning skills of children. The results suggest that children can make deductions at about four or five years old.

thinking that Piaget believed did not develop in children until they were at least seven years old (*see* pp. 58–77). Some aspects of reasoning also involve metacognitive processes (thinking about thinking), an ability that does not develop until the age of 11 according to Piaget. However, J. Hawkins and his colleagues at Bank Street College, New York, found that children aged four and five years performed well on some deductive reasoning problems.

Congruent and incongruent
Some of these problems contained premises that were congruent (agreed) with the children's practical knowledge; others had premises that were incongruent (disagreed) with it. A third set of problems involved fantasy creatures and situations that bore no relation to any practical knowledge (*see* box p. 103).

Hawkins found that overall performance was highest among children who had been given the fantasy problems before the other types. In the light of these

findings could it be that this order of presentation suggested to children that they should ignore empirical knowledge (knowledge acquired by experience or observation) on subsequent problems? Further research suggests that this is probably the case. Brazilian researcher Maria Dias and Paul Harris from Harvard University gave four- and five-year-olds a series of reasoning problems that involved known facts ("All cats meow. Rex is a cat. Does Rex meow?"), unknown facts ("All hyenas laugh. Rex is a hyena. Does Rex laugh?"), or that contained premises that were contrary to fact ("All snow is black. Tom touches some snow. Is it black?"). One group of children received the problems in a "play" mode in which, for example, toy cats, dogs, and hyenas were presented, and the experimenter made the models meow, bark, or laugh as appropriate. A second group was simply told the premises and not given any toys or demonstrations. These children tended to answer correctly only on the "known facts" problems, while the children in the "play" group performed well on all three types of problem. To rule out the possibility that the toy animals acted as memory prompts for the children in the "play" group, a second experiment was then conducted in which the "play" group was simply told the premises but was asked to imagine that the experimenter was on another planet where everything was different. Again performance was very high with the children in this group— once they had been warned to expect the unexpected, it seemed that they were able to clear their minds of irrelevancies and cut straight to the heart of the question.

These studies indicate that children, although sensitive to the context of questioning and the content of the problem, can make deductions at an earlier age than predicted by Piaget.

Pragmatic reasoning schemas

Another task that has been widely used to investigate deductive reasoning in both children and adults is the selection task, first developed by Peter Wason in 1966 (*see* Vol. 1, pp. 134–143). In the original version participants were shown four partially obscured items of evidence and asked which of them they would need to look at more closely in order to test a rule. A typical version of the task involves testing the rule: "If there is a vowel on one side of a card, then there is an even number on the other side." The participants would then be shown four cards and told that each card has a letter on one side and a number on the other. The facing sides of the cards might be E, K, 4, and 7. To test the rule, you need to look for cards that could potentially show the rule to be false. In this case any card showing a vowel on one side and an odd number on the other would mean the rule is false. Therefore you should pick the two cards that show E and 7.

Only about 10 percent of people perform this task correctly. But when it is modified to involve a more realistic content, performance improves considerably. It is argued that such tasks

activate familiar knowledge structures in the mind—constructs of this type are known to psychologists as pragmatic reasoning schemas.

One type of schema is known as the permission schema, which is activated when we think about permission rules. Because children encounter many rules about what they may or may not do, they might be expected to reason about rules at quite an early age. In a 1989 experiment Paul Light of the Open University, England, gave a version of the task to six- and seven-year-olds. One of the rules he used was: "In this town the police say all trucks must be outside the center."

> *"People often reason... using abstract knowledge structures induced from ordinary life experiences, such as 'permissions,' 'obligations,' and 'causations.'"*
> —P. Cheng & K. Holyoak, 1985

That rule was intended to be realistic. The other rule used was intended to be arbitrary and stated: "In this game all mushrooms must be outside of the center of the board." Children were shown a game board with a brown center and a white surround. Pictures were used to represent trucks and mushrooms, and also cars and flowers. Two trucks (or mushrooms) and a car (or flower) were shown in the central area, and a truck (or mushroom) and three cars (or flowers) were shown in the surrounding area.

The children were then given various tasks. First, they were asked to move the pictures on the board so that they obeyed the rules. This involved moving the trucks or mushrooms out of the central area. Second, the experimenter moved a car or flower outside the center and asked if that disobeyed the rule (it didn't). Third, the children were asked to move a picture so that it did disobey the rule. Finally, children were presented with a version of the selection task. They were again shown the brown-and-white board and two cards face down so that the pictures on them could not be seen. One picture was in the central area, and the other was in the surrounding area. The children were asked which picture they would need to turn over to see whether the rule had been disobeyed. Once the picture had been turned over, they were asked if it disobeyed the rule. The other picture was also turned over, and the children were asked if that disobeyed the rule.

When the realistic rule about trucks was used, correct answers were given by 45 percent of six-year-olds and 77 percent of seven-year-olds. But when the arbitrary rule about mushrooms was used, correct answers were given by only 5 percent of the six-year-olds and 23 percent of the seven-year-olds.

> *"The clear implication is that when children violate a permission rule, they do so knowingly."*
> —Paul Harris & Maria Núñez, 1996

Light and his colleagues also showed that children who performed correctly in the pragmatic, realistic context were often able to transfer this ability effectively to abstract reasoning. Some of the children who had performed correctly were given an abstract version of the selection task involving squares and triangles ("All the triangles must be in the center"). Correct responses were given by 30 percent of the six-year-olds and 59 percent of the seven-year-olds.

Permission rules
Paul Harris of the University of Oxford, England, and Maria Núñez of the Universidad Autónoma de Madrid, Spain, showed that even three- and four-year-olds can engage in some basic reasoning about permission rules. Most children of this age were able to identify one picture from a set of four that showed a rule being broken. For example, the children were told about a girl named Sally who wants

to play outside. Sally's mother tells her: "If you play outside, you must put your coat on." The children were then shown a picture of Sally indoors with her coat on, a picture of Sally indoors without her coat on, a picture of Sally outdoors with her coat on, and a picture of Sally outdoors without her coat on. Most children correctly chose the last picture as the one in which the rule is being broken. They also gave a sensible answer to the question: "What is Sally doing that is naughty?"

Transitive inference
One of the most widely used tests of deductive reasoning in children is the transitive inference task. An example of a transitive inference problem is:

These two boys have been told to wear coats when they play outside. Psychologists have found that children can reason about basic permission rules from about the age of three.

Ann is taller than Brian.

Brian is taller than Clare.

Is Ann taller than Clare?

The correct answer is "Yes" (Ann is taller than Clare).

The size relations described in this problem are often represented as A > B > C (the symbol > means "is greater than"). In the problem above there are only three terms (Ann, Brian, and Clare). In experiments researchers use at least five terms in order to avoid the problem of "labeling." You can see that Ann is referred to as being taller than someone, while Clare is not referred to as being taller than anybody. Therefore children could answer the problem correctly by basing their response on the label attached to Ann rather than by making a transitive inference from the given data.

Now suppose the problem is:

Ann is taller than Brian.

Brian is taller than Clare.

Clare is taller than David.

David is taller than Elizabeth.

Is Brian taller than David?

Here an answer cannot be based on labeling because both Brian and David have the label "taller than" attached to them—to answer the question, a transitive inference has to be made.

Piaget claimed that logical reasoning does not start to develop until seven years of age, but much subsequent research has indicated that children can make transitive inferences before then.

Sticks to the point

The most illuminating study in this area was that carried out by the British researchers P. Bryant and T. Trabasso, who reported their findings in 1971. Instead of giving children verbal statements, they used five sticks of different lengths and colors. Stick A was (say) red and longer than Stick B, which was white; Stick B was longer than Stick C, which was blue; Stick C was longer than Stick D, which was green; and Stick D was longer than Stick E, which was yellow. During the training phase of this experiment the children were shown the sticks only in pairs—A and B, B and C, C and D, D and E. In the testing phase they were shown the sticks again, but this time they were not completely visible—they had been placed in a hole so that only their tops could be seen. The children were then asked which half of various pairs was taller or shorter. After the children had made their choice, the sticks would be removed so that they could see if they were right.

> "High success rates on these concrete 'if…then' forms is a problem for a Piagetian account of reasoning development."
> —Linden Ball, 2000

In the next phase of the experiment the children had to make their own judgments without any visual feedback—in other words, they were not shown whether their answers were right or wrong. The four- to six-year-old children who were tested all performed at above chance level on these transitive comparisons—in other words, they gave correct answers to more than half the questions. In particular, correct responses were given to the crucial B > D comparison by 78 percent of four-year-olds, 88 percent of five-year-olds, and 92 percent of six-year-olds.

Metacognition

Although children may be able to make deductive inferences, this does not necessarily mean they understand why the inference is correct. That kind of understanding requires metacognitive skill (the ability to think about thinking). Also, even children older than four may fail to distinguish between outcomes that are logically necessary and those that are empirically necessary. Given the statement that "Either the chip I am holding in my hand is blue or it is not blue," seven-year-olds often will not accept the statement as true until the experimenter has actually opened her hand. Just because children of

EXPERIMENT

EVIDENCE FOR TRANSITIVE REASONING IN YOUNG CHILDREN

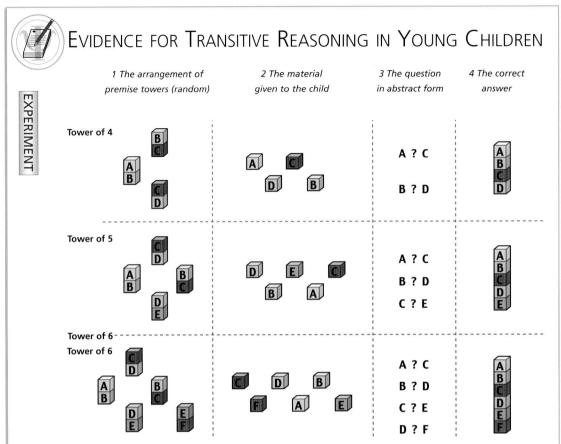

1 The arrangement of premise towers (random)

2 The material given to the child

3 The question in abstract form

4 The correct answer

Tower of 4

A ? C

B ? D

Tower of 5

A ? C

B ? D

C ? E

Tower of 6

Tower of 6

A ? C

B ? D

C ? E

D ? F

In 1990 Rosalind Pears and Peter Bryant of the University of Oxford, England, presented preschool children of various ages with completely visible premises as a way of reducing the memory load that would otherwise be needed to keep all the relevant information in mind. Children were presented with pairs of differently colored bricks in "little towers." Then, using single bricks, the children had to build a larger tower by adding bricks in the order that matched the relationships between the bricks in the little towers.

On some trials the children were asked to build a tower of four bricks (involving three premises). On others they had to build a tower of five bricks (four premises), and on a third set of trials they had to build a tower of six bricks (five premises). For example, if six little towers showed respectively yellow on top then blue beneath (YTB), blue on top then purple beneath (BTP), purple on top then green beneath (PTG), green on top then orange beneath (GTO), and finally orange on top then red beneath (OTR), the children had to build a tower with the order YTBTPTGTOTR.

Diagram representing the transitive inference task used by Pears and Bryant. Children are shown pairs of bricks (1); the children are then given single bricks to build a tower (2). Before building the tower, they are asked about the relative positions of bricks within the tower (3); the child builds the tower (4).

Before building the tower, the children were asked a series of questions requiring transitive inferences, such as: "Which will be the higher in the tower that you are going to build, the green brick or the blue one?" This question is equivalent to the B > D comparison in the Bryant and Trabasso experiment (*see* p. 107). A correct answer requires children to combine information from the BTP and PTG premises using a transitive inference. On the "tower of six" problem the C > E comparison (PTG/GTO) was also critical. Pears and Bryant found that children performed significantly above chance on two-thirds of the questions, and from this they concluded that the ability to make transitive inferences is in place at the age of four.

four and older respond differently to deductive and inductive problems does not mean that they understand the difference between the two.

In an effort to find out when such an understanding begins, Kathleen Galotti and her colleagues at Carleton University, Ottawa, Canada, conducted two experiments in which they gave children a series of deductive and inductive problems involving fantasy content. In addition to answering the problems, the children were asked to rate their confidence in their answers and to explain their responses. Irrespective of age, children tended to respond faster to deductive problems than to inductive ones. In terms of accuracy, however, children of kindergarten age (about four to five years old) were no more accurate on the deductive problems than on the inductive ones. By second grade (about six to seven years old) children were beginning to distinguish between deductive and inductive problems, but this became most clearly defined at fourth grade (about eight to nine years). At fourth grade children gave different responses to the two types of problem, and their confidence was somewhat higher for deductive problems.

Conservation tasks

Piaget believed that children should not be taught number concepts until they were ready to understand them. One of the ways in which he investigated children's understanding of numbers was through conservation tasks (*see* pp. 58–77). In one classic conservation task children were shown two identical rows of counters and asked if there were more counters in one of the rows or the same number in both. Next, the counters in one row were spaced out to make it longer than the other row. Piaget found that children under the age of seven said that the longer row had more counters than the other row. This supported his belief that children would not understand the conservation of number until the concrete operations stage (seven to eleven years).

But there is a problem with Piaget's conservation task. If someone asks you the same question twice, it usually means you should change your answer. That feeling may be particularly strong when the questioner is older than you and has just done something that appears to be important. To get around this difficulty, James McGarrigle and Margaret Donaldson from the University of Edinburgh, Scotland, developed a version of the task in which children were introduced to "naughty teddy." It was a teddy bear who, the children were told, would sometimes escape from his box to "mess up the toys" and "spoil the game." The first part of the task proceeded as before, with the children asked about the number of counters in two identical rows.

> *"What shows development across the ages studied is a refinement of sensitivity to different aspects of reasoning tasks."*
> —*Kathleen Galotti, Lloyd Komatsu, and Sara Voelz, 1997*

Then the naughty teddy suddenly appeared and altered the length of one of the rows. When questioned, most children as young as four and five told the researcher that there were still equal numbers of counters in both rows.

In 1995 Robert Siegler published a study that appeared to show that children's understanding of conservation develops gradually rather than as the result of them having passed through distinct developmental stages. His study involved five-year-olds who had all failed a standard conservation task. They were then given a series of different conservation tasks. One group of children was told whether their answers were correct or not. Members of another group were asked to explain their reasoning and then given feedback. A third group was given feedback and then asked by the experimenter: "How do you think I knew that?" Thus this last group of children had to explain the experimenter's reasoning. The performance of this group was better than that of the other two groups. It involved the realization that the relative lengths of the rows did not predict the number of objects within each row, while the type of transformation (adding or subtracting counters, as opposed to altering the length of rows) did.

Siegler found that children who could appreciate the importance of the type of transformation did not automatically reject the less-advanced forms of reasoning. Also, there were big differences in children's ability to benefit from having to explain the experimenter's thinking. Siegler argued that less- and more-advanced ways of thinking could therefore coexist, as opposed to children moving from one distinct stage to another.

Understanding class inclusion

Class inclusion is another kind of logical task that Piaget associated with the concrete operations stage. For example, think of a bunch of flowers that includes four red flowers and two white ones. In Piaget's experiments children would be shown the flowers and asked: "Are there more red flowers or more flowers here?" Children younger than six years of age tended to say that there were more red flowers. For Piaget this was evidence that they could not think simultaneously about the parts and the whole of an entity. In this example they could not think about the subset of red flowers and the entire set of flowers.

However, the problem with Piaget's method of presentation is that it seems to violate the normal conventions for communication. The question "Are there more red flowers or more flowers here?" sounds odd. A more natural way of asking the question might be to say: "Are there more red flowers, or are there more flowers in the bunch?" Several studies have shown that five- and six-year-olds (and three- and four-year-olds in one

experiment) can correctly answer class-inclusion problems when the question involves familiar collective terms such as "a bunch of flowers," "a class of children," or "a pile of blocks."

Family matters

Usha Goswami of the University of Cambridge, England, suggested that the word "family" is a particularly useful collective noun in this context. Most children are familiar with the term and know that a family is made up of parents and children. Goswami and her colleagues conducted an experiment with four- and five-year-old children who had all failed a standard class-inclusion task ("Are there

"Are there more red flowers or more flowers here?"—the form of words is so weird that any researcher using it is unlikely to elicit the desired response. The wording of questions is important when studying the class-inclusion skills of young children.

more red flowers or more flowers?"). The children were shown a family of toy mice (two large mice as parents and three smaller mice as children) or a family of yo-yos (two large yo-yos as parents and two small yo-yos as children). Next, the children were asked to construct families of two parents and three children from an assortment of toy animals or other types of toy. Following this task, the children were given four class-inclusion problems involving toy frogs, sheep, building blocks, and balloons. The collective nouns "group," "herd," "pile," and "bunch" were used for these problems. Another group of children who had not participated in the "create-a-family" task were given the same problems. The children who had engaged in creating families performed much better on the class-inclusion problems than those who had not.

Information processing

According to Piagetian theory, aspects of problem solving that require logical thought should not start to appear in children until seven years of age. Metacognitive understanding (thinking about thinking) should not appear until the age of 11. Yet subsequent research has indicated that the kind of abilities required for problem solving develop at an earlier age than Piaget predicted.

Information-processing theorists argue that the very idea of stages of development is wrong. They believe that development occurs more gradually. As children's working memory capacity expands, they are able to represent more information and think about more complex strategies for problem solving. There is also evidence from studies of conservation to suggest that less-advanced ways of thinking are not automatically dropped as more-advanced modes of thought are acquired—this is the clear implication of the final part of the balance beam problem (*see* p. 95).

The types of experimental tasks used by psychologists are crucial to an understanding of when children's abilities

develop. As experiments have become more refined, psychologists have been able to discover that certain abilities are present at earlier ages than had previously been believed. It should also be apparent that while adults outperform children on problem-solving tasks, the mistakes they make are often of the same kind as those made by their juniors. This seems to be consistent with a continuum of development rather than a series of stages.

The notion of a family is particularly useful for psychologists studying class inclusion in young children. Models of tigers and lions are being used here to test the class-inclusion skills of this five-year-old boy.

CONNECTIONS

- Beginnings of Scientific Psychology: Volume 1, pp. 30–39
- Cognitive Psychology: Volume 1, pp. 104–117
- Evolutionary Perspective: Volume 1, pp. 134–143
- The History of the Brain: Volume 2, pp. 6–19
- Memory Development: pp 78–93
- Abnormalities in Development: Volume 6, pp. 68–91

Emotional Development

Emotions are a key part of our overall development.

People are emotional. They experience spontaneous emotions (which are distinct from moods). Yet they differ from each other in the types of emotions they experience in different contexts and also in how they control these emotional reactions. How do these differences develop? And how does emotional development relate to children's cognitive and social development? What is the effect of parenting and child-rearing practices on the emotional development of children?

There are many different theories about the causes of emotional development and different accounts of its chronology. However, insofar as it is possible to generalize, the following landmarks are passed at roughly the following ages.

• **Birth to four months**
Babies show most of their emotions through crying—it is their only method of communication. They have at least three different cries that caregivers quickly learn to tell apart. The cry most often heard is the one that signals hunger. The other two cries signal anger and pain. Caregivers and parents who respond immediately to the infant's cries during the first year of life foster the development of a strong sense of trust. Other emotions present at this age are distress and disgust. Social smiling begins during this period, together with anger, surprise, and sadness.

• **Four to eight months**
Infants begin to express a wider range of emotions. Pleasure, happiness, fear, and frustration are shown through noises such as gurgles, coos, wails, and cries, and physical movements such as kicking, arm-waving, rocking, and smiling.

• **Eighteen months**
At around this age toddlers start to develop a sense of self. They recognize their image in a mirror as themselves and begin to become independent of their mothers or caregivers. Toddlers of around this age often have a broad range of emotional states. One minute they may be playing happily, the next lying on the floor crying. This behavior is widely regarded as a normal function of the toddler's developing sense of self.

• **Two years onward**
From this age most children are able to communicate their thoughts and feelings in words. This is both a simplifying and a complicating factor—while it enables them to make themselves understood more easily through explicit utterances, it introduces several other variables. They may, for example, say not what they really think but what they think others want to hear; alternatively, the words they use

These two boys may have different emotional reactions to the same wet weather. One is fascinated by watching it, but the other is frustrated since he is not able to play outside without getting wet. From two years old onward they will be able to express these feelings verbally.

THE IMPACT OF FREUD

Sigmund Freud (1856–1939) (see Vol.1, pp. 52–65) strongly influenced the theory of developmental psychology. He emphasized the importance of biological factors in the emergence of the "self" and personality, and believed that normal social and emotional development, as well as the various forms of mental illness, could be explained by examining the history of the individual's childhood. Over several decades, through his reading of other scientists and observation of his own patients he formulated a theory that was revolutionary because it emphasized strong biological drives and the role of unconscious processes in human behavior.

Freud proposed that people are propelled toward action by an internal force he called the libido. The libido is defined as psychic energy emanating from the id, which is the primitive instinct in the unconscious mind. According to this theory, when we are born, we are confused and unable to make any sense of the world. Therefore to be certain that we receive nourishment and care, we have several primary drives—hunger and thirst, for example—that compel us to seek out the things we need. In infancy we are driven by the id, the instinctual component of the self that seeks out pleasure and satisfaction and tries to minimize pain and fear. Obviously, infants can neither choose their parents nor control their environment, and thus the id easily becomes frustrated in its attempts to satisfy these needs. Freud believed that the ego then developed soon after birth to balance the drives of the id with the demands and constraints of the real world. Unlike the id, the ego is rational—it reasons about the world and makes sense of experiences. Once the child has grown older and learns the rules and morals of society, a third structure, the superego, is formed. The superego is the conscience that causes us to behave appropriately to live in an orderly society. Freud believed that once all three had developed, throughout life our conscious awareness of our experiences was a result of the ego balancing the demands of the id (pleasure) and the superego (morality). Normal development and mental health were results of the ego doing its job without the id or the superego taking control of the individual.

Freud's theory has been influential because of its emphasis on primacy—the notion that early experiences in life influence our subsequent development—and on the importance of the unconscious mind. Freud's ideas are still popular with some clinical psychologists today.

A bronze statue of Sigmund Freud. His ideas that early experiences are important in later life and his emphasis on the unconscious mind are still popular with psychologists.

cannot convey their true meaning accurately. Thus verbal skills are at the same time liberating and constraining, a paradox that may be observed throughout the rest of human life. Increasingly, emotions can be controlled or repressed and sometimes replaced by moods. A mood is a state of mind rather than a feeling and may last for a considerable period, unlike an emotion, which is by its nature is spontaneous and short-lived.

Children quickly learn to control or regulate their emotions. Much of this regulation, particularly in early childhood, occurs through social interaction with other people, especially parents, siblings,

The first day at school for this five-year-old. At school she will meet and be influenced by other children as well as teachers. She may be feeling fear or excitement at the prospect of starting school. The attitude of her mother will also influence how well she adapts to this major change in her life.

and peers. There are wide-ranging individual differences in temperament from infancy throughout the life span. In many animals a strong bond forms between mother and infant. In people this bond is a very complex system of flexible and enduring attachment relationships. Parents differ in the extent to which they love and accept their children, and the degree to which they try to control behaviors. These differences in parenting styles have important implications for the children's development.

Though these four stages are generally agreed to be the facts, there is little consensus about the validity of many theories of emotional development. However, they all cast interesting light on the complexities of emotional development, and students of psychology need to know something about them in order to organize their own thoughts and to formulate new ideas.

The development of emotions

The development of emotions in infancy and childhood is one of the key aspects of individuality and has been the focus of much research. Emotion is a feeling state that motivates the individual to carry out some sort of action. Emotions are not just language labels that we apply to these feeling states; they contain biological or physiological components—for example, anger and fear are associated with increases in heart rate and blood pressure. Thinking and perception are also involved in emotion. In order to become fearful or angry as a result of some event that has just occurred, we must first notice it, then decide what to do about it, and finally react. For example, if infants are exposed to a sudden banging of pots and pans while playing with a rattle, they will drop the toy and start crying because they are frightened. However, they may derive great pleasure from banging those same pots and pans with the rattle if that is part of a game in which sounds are expected.

> *"Knowledge about life is one thing; effective occupation of a place in life, with its dynamic currents passing through your being is another."*
> —*William James, 1890*

When do our emotions develop? Are they present at birth; and if so, in what ways do they change later? Much of the research into these questions has relied on observing infants' facial expressions following their exposure to some sort of stimulation that is known to arouse specific emotions in adults. Paul Ekman and others have conducted research in many cultures to demonstrate that children and adults around the world have the same facial expressions for the same emotions. So long as we assume that facial expressions reflect emotions in the same way among infants, we can identify the presence of these emotions in children at a very early age. In these studies infants are exposed to objects that are known to cause specific emotional reactions in older children and adults—for example, a sudden loud noise that startles adults or a gentle and interesting object that makes them smile and feel happy. If the children react similarly, then it is accepted that they are reacting emotionally to the stimulus.

Primary emotions

By six months of age infants are showing evidence of what are known as primary emotions—interest, happiness or joy, surprise, sadness, anger, fear, and disgust. Researchers disagree about the nature of the development of these distinct emotions. Some believe that they emerge over time from the basic emotions of contentment and distress. Others take the view that they are present from the beginning of life, but are not easily distinguished because infants' bodies are not yet sufficiently developed to display the conventionally recognized external signs. It is important to note that because researchers rely on the facial expressions of these emotions alone (a five-month-old is not able to say why she is crying), it is not possible to make any valid distinction between emotions as they are expressed and emotions as they are experienced. This is significant because, though all children are born with the basic capacities to experience a wide range of emotions, they can differ remarkably in the extent to which they show these emotions, the intensity of their emotional reactions, and their abilities to control their emotions.

Secondary emotions

More complex emotions emerge during the second year of life, arguably as a result of the child's developing sense of "self" and a growing understanding of the expectations of other people. They are known as secondary or social emotions. They include feelings such as shame, guilt, and embarrassment. They emerge at about the same time as children begin to show clear signs of self-awareness, and their language skills begin to expand. Individual differences are very important at this age as well. While some toddlers are very compliant because they are highly sensitive to these social emotions, other toddlers may barrel through the day with little regard for other people's expectations about appropriate behavior. These differences between us in fear, joy, and shame are the seeds of individuality.

ERIK ERIKSON

Erik Erikson (1902–1994) (see Vol. 1, pp. 52–65) was a psychoanalyst who believed that Freud had set down some important foundations—in particular, the separation of id, ego, and superego—but that he overemphasized sexuality and primitive drives at the expense of social and environmental influences on the individual. Freud's theories ended at young adulthood, as though the ego was somehow complete at this age, but Erikson asserted that the ego continued to develop throughout life.

Instead of placing the libido at the center of motivation as Freud had done, Erikson believed that as we develop, we face a series of developmental tasks that lead inevitably to psychosocial crises. These crises arise when we are faced with conscious and unconscious decisions about the directions our lives are taking.

These crises are universal (experienced by all individuals in all cultures) and can only be resolved through interaction between the ego and the outside world. Like Freud, Erikson believed that psychosocial development involved a balancing act between the biological needs of the individual and the demands of society. He organized these crises into a theory with eight stages: To progress to the next stage, the preceding crisis must be resolved.

The first stage is known as "trust or mistrust" and occurs during infancy. Infants must learn to depend on their caregivers. It is at this time that they form a strong and enduring emotional bond with the primary caregiver. The second stage is termed "autonomy or shame and doubt" (two to three years). During this crisis toddlers must become more independent and capable of controlling the world around them. They must also realize that they

should often show restraint and self-regulation of strong desires, or others will reject them. The third stage is "initiative or guilt" (three to six years). Here the crisis is caused by the development of ambition and independence from parents, and it must be resolved for the child to lead an independent life. The superego is formed at this stage.

The fourth stage is "industry or inferiority" (7 to 12 years). Children become absorbed by the activities that motivate and interest them. They learn new skills and gain knowledge, and must develop the desire to apply this knowledge in different settings in order to succeed in life. In the fifth stage, "identity or confusion" (12 to 18 years), adolescents must seek to identify their likes and dislikes, beliefs and behaviors, and morals. They must come to accept contradictions but maintain a clear sense of self.

The sixth stage is "intimacy or isolation" (18 through 20s). The young adult shifts attention away from establishing an identity as an individual toward forming long-lasting romantic relationships with other adults. The difficulty is finding a balance between the desire to be with others and to feel love, and the desire to be independent and free. Those who are able to find both love and independence resolve this crisis successfully. In the seventh stage—known as "generativity, stagnation, or self-absorption" (20s through 50s)—the adult must become able to consider the needs of peers, family members, and children. Finally, from the 50s onward "fulfilment or despair" arises when aging individuals are forced to contend with their own impending death and must also cope with physical decline. People are forced to look back over their lives and start drawing conclusions.

Crips gang, Los Angeles. During the transition from adolescence to adulthood people identify their beliefs, their likes or dislikes. They must learn to accept contradictions in others but maintain a sense of self. Erikson called this stage of development "identity or confusion."

Emotion regulation

Experiencing an emotion is only part of the puzzle. Once we begin experiencing an emotion, we need to be able to control it, either internally by using the mind or externally by changing the situation that caused it. Emotion regulation refers to a very broad class of behaviors and cognitions that people carry out to control their nervous systems when strong emotional reactions occur.

Emotions occur as part of our adaptation to a constantly changing environment. When we are frightened, we may experience rapid heartbeat and a churning stomach. But these physical feelings are only temporary—it would be intolerable if this level of fear were maintained for days or weeks at a time. To survive as a species we need these strong internal signals that motivate us to act. However, once the need for this strong

> *"Identity develops through all earlier stages; it begins way back when the child first recognizes his mother and...feels recognized by her...but he has to go through many stages until...the adolescent identity crisis."*
> —*Erik Erikson, 1967*

signal has passed, we also need a way of regulating these emotions so that we are not always passively responding to everything that happens around us. Without emotion regulation we would be unable to do anything but monitor our environments for the things that make us fearful.

Emotion regulation is one of the keys to understanding emotional as well as social and cognitive development in infancy and childhood. If our emotions are well-regulated, we are then able to enjoy social interactions with others, interactions in which we learn new and important skills. We are also able to learn language and learning skills that allow us to function in

complex societies. If our emotions are poorly regulated, it is very difficult to attend to and learn from these interactions with people and objects. Poorly regulated emotions are also central to the emergence of behavioral and emotional problems in childhood as well as in adolescence and adulthood.

Coregulation of emotions

Infants have few skills for regulating emotions, although they are not without some basic abilities in this regard. For example, some infants are able to soothe themselves if they become overstimulated by looking away or by sucking a thumb or fist. However, even with these rudimentary skills young children still rely on their mothers and fathers to help them regulate their emotional reactions; for example, parents can hold and soothe frightened infants. When infants show keen interest in an object, parents can hold it close to them so that they can see it and take it away when they start showing signs of being too stimulated. This shared regulation (coregulation) of emotions is a central component of the parent–child relationship throughout infancy and childhood, and over the

Well-regulated emotions enable people to enjoy social interactions with others. Developing emotion regulation in childhood is crucial to learning language and communication skills, which are essential in later life. Infants depend heavily on their parents to help them regulate their emotional reactions.

THE NEW YORK LONGITUDINAL STUDY

U.S. psychologists Alexander Thomas and Stella Chess were the first to study systematically the development of temperament in infancy and childhood. They conducted the New York Longitudinal Study, beginning in the 1950s, in which they examined temperament in a group of infants and followed them until they started school. They interviewed parents and then coded and scored their descriptions.

Through their research Chess and Thomas were able to identify nine attributes that were crucial for characterizing differences in infant and child temperament. They were: (1) activity level; (2) regularity of feeding, sleeping, and toilet schedule; (3) reactivity or response to the presentation of a new person (a stranger) or new object; (4) sensitivity to experiences in the environment; (5) adaptability, or the ability to adjust to sudden changes in the environment; (6) intensity of behaviors; (7) attention and the ability to persist with a task; (8) distractibility; and (9) overall mood (irritable, happy, sad, or withdrawn).

Thomas and Chess defined three groups of infants. The largest group, easy babies, are adaptive, well regulated, attentive, happy, and content, and not overly sensitive to changes in the environment, such as being moved to a new location or the removal of a toy. In contrast, difficult babies are far less adaptable. They are fussy and cry frequently, are difficult to soothe, and are not well regulated in their sleeping, eating, and toilet schedules. These infants tend to be very sensitive to changes in the environment, and their reactions to these changes are intense and frequent. Finally, slow-to-warm-up babies were not happy and content like easy babies, but were not intensely irritable like difficult babies. Instead, this last group showed low levels of energy and would often withdraw from new people or situations; and although they were often crying and fussy, these negative moods were generally mild. About one-third of the children in this study could not be classified because they did not show a clear pattern of behaviors and moods based on these nine attributes.

course of development the pair become better at regulating the child's emotions. As children acquire language skills, more of this coregulation of emotions occurs through spoken words. For example, eight-month-old infants who have become distressed by a stranger may be held and rocked by a parent for comfort, while two-year-olds in the same situation are more likely to respond to a parent holding their hand while saying, "It's okay, this is my friend Sally from work; she is really friendly. Do you want to say hello to her?"

When children start school, they are normally able to self-regulate most emotional reactions, although they continue to need some help. This may be provided by parents, teachers, or members of their peer group. Even as adults, most of us occasionally need to speak with a parent, sibling, or friend when a particular thought or situation makes us feel angry, sad, or fearful because confidantes such as family members help us regain control of those emotional reactions.

Individual temperament

Although children show typical patterns of development—for example, they start off unable to speak but gradually acquire language and eventually learn to read—there are wide variations in the types of behaviors and emotions that children feel in different situations. Just as adolescents and adults differ in their personalities, infants and young children are different from each other in their emotions, reactions to exciting or frightening events or situations (including other people), and sensitivity to environmental changes. These individual differences in emotions, attention, and reactivity have a strong biological basis and are defined collectively as differences in temperament.

The New York Longitudinal Study (*see* box) made an important contribution to research into temperament. Nevertheless, current research and theory on temperament do not emphasize these nine attributes in children, but instead describe the biological and brain systems that correspond to various aspects of attention, emotion, and physical movement as they change over the course of infancy, childhood, adolescence, and adulthood. Many researchers today prefer to examine how reactive children are, while also assessing their abilities to control or self-regulate these reactions.

The infant bond

Most developmental psychologists believe that to survive and develop normally, all children must form an enduring emotional bond with a parent or caregiver early in infancy. The concept of bonding between infants and their mothers was one that psychologists borrowed from ethology, the science of observing the natural behavior of different species of animals, including humans, in their own environments. Konrad Lorenz (1903–1989), one of the most influential ethologists, had a major effect on developmental psychology through his research into the nature of imprinting (bonding) in animals. One of his most famous studies involved examining the behavior of goslings. Like many other

> *"All attempts to arrive at a definition of life through straightforward characterization based on a single principle are doomed to failure."*
> —*Konrad Lorenz, 1996*

birds, geese form an intense bond with the first thing that they see moving when they are newly hatched. Most often that is the mother goose. This bond is essential to the goslings' survival because in order to avoid being eaten by predators, they must stay very close to the mother so that she can protect them.

Lorenz discovered that newly hatched goslings would even imprint on him if he was the first thing they saw moving; they would follow him around as though he was their mother. This innate, or inborn,

Konrad Lorenz combined an interest in zoology with his studies in psychology. This exploration of animal behavior led to the creation of modern ethology, or the comparative study of behavior in people and other animals. In 1973 he shared a Nobel Prize for his pioneering work.

ability to bond becomes less prominent and effective as time passes, suggesting that there is a critical or sensitive period in the development of geese for this imprinting to occur. Other researchers discovered similar bonding in mammals such as goats. This research raised a more important question—do human infants "bond" with their mothers; and if so, how important are those first crucial hours and days following birth? In a famous study John H. Kennell and Marshall H. Klaus tried to answer this question by conducting an experiment in which they allowed some mothers to have frequent

HARLOW'S STUDIES OF INFANT MONKEYS

Sigmund Freud believed that mother and infant formed a very close emotional bond during the latter's first year of life. He proposed that this bond was a result of what he termed drive reduction—that is, infants must satisfy their need for nourishment, and mothers meet this need, thereby creating a strong emotional link with their infants.

Harry Harlow, a researcher who studied human development by conducting research on monkeys, was the first to test this theory. In the 1950s he conducted a series

The psychologist Harry Harlow (1905–1981), who studied newborn Rhesus monkeys to examine the emotional bond between infants and mothers.

of experiments with newborn Rhesus monkeys raised without their mothers. Rhesus monkeys frequently cling to their mothers as infants.

These experiments involved several conditions that allowed Harlow to test whether it was the satisfaction of the need for food and drink or satisfaction of the need for touch and being held that led to the formation of this bond with the mother. Some of the infant monkeys were placed in cages where they had access to a wire model of a mother and a soft cloth model of a mother. In some conditions the infants were fed by the wire mother, and in others they were fed by the soft-cloth mother. The results of these experiments were very clear. The infant monkeys would spend virtually no time at all with the wire mother even when it was this model that fed them. Instead, they showed a strong preference for the soft-cloth mother, particularly when they became frightened. Harlow concluded that it was contact comfort, and not feeding, that promoted the formation of an attachment relationship between an infant and its mother.

physical contact with their newborn babies, while denying it to others. They concluded that physical contact in the first few days following birth was crucial to the formation of a strong emotional bond between mother and baby. However, the effects were not very strong, and other researchers were not able to replicate the same results. Thus the importance of bonding to the emotional development of human infants remains unclear.

Attachment theory

At about the same time as Lorenz was conducting his research, John Bowlby, a clinical psychologist in London, England, began formulating attachment theory. This theory had a great influence on developmental psychology during the latter half of the 20th century. Bowlby believed that the bonding that occurs between infants and parents was too complex to be explained as a simple imprinting process. Bowlby observed many infants and young children who had

been separated from either both of their parents or orphaned. He noticed from these clinical observations that many such children seemed to suffer from the lack of a close intimate relationship with a parent or some other adult caregiver. He

> *"Loss of a loved person is one of the most intensely painful experiences any human being can suffer."*
> —John Bowlby, 2000

therefore proposed that there is an innate attachment system that links the infant to just the mother. This attachment system, when functioning properly, is highly protective of infants, because they are able to stay close to the mother who can protect them from danger. In addition, Bowlby proposed that the mother or other attachment figure (the adult with whom the infant forms an attachment relationship) also promotes the healthy

THE SEASONS OF LIFE

Levinson termed the fourth and final period of life from 65 until death "late adulthood." It can be a time of great fulfilment, as is the case for this elderly couple who are enjoying relaxing on the beach. Aging individuals have to contemplate the limitations and successes in their lives and come to terms with the ambitions that have not been achieved.

In the 1970s Daniel J. Levinson proposed a theory that captures the ever-changing aspects of the social and emotional worlds of each individual, from birth to death. Rather than thinking of temperament, Levinson believed that in order to understand individuals, we must consider their life structures, that is, the types of choices that each person makes with respect to relationships, marriage, family, and occupation. His work provided a method by which an individual's life history can be elicited and expanded. His later work focused on interviews with women conducted between 1980 and 1982.

The human lifespan consists of constantly evolving relationships with others and with oneself. Levinson proposed four eras, each with a transitional period that lasts for several years. In the first stage, preadulthood (conception to 18 years of age), the primary task in development is to shift away from complete dependence on parents and caregivers toward self-reliance and autonomy. During the transition stage (17 to 22 years) the adolescent or young adult begins preparing to become an adult. At this time the young adult begins to nurture dreams about the future. In the second era, early adulthood (22 to 40 years), the individual enters into an energetic and aggressive period of life, pursuing dreams

and aspirations. This comes at a cost because it is also a period when difficult decisions have to be made that can cause both psychological and physical stress. It is followed by a midlife transition (40 to 45 years) in which adults become increasingly aware of the fact that they are running out of time in which to accomplish their goals. According to Levinson's theory, this is also an important time for separation from parents and other older adults on whom we have relied, and we come to fully realize who we are, and what we can contribute to others.

In the third era that Levinson describes, middle adulthood (45 to 60 years), people become less concerned with their own goals and aspirations as they shift their attention toward the welfare of others—such as aged parents and quickly growing children.

Following a transition period (60 to 65 years), the fourth and final era, late adulthood (65 to death) begins. In this period of life the goals become accepting and understanding our strengths and limitations. This is similar to Erikson's final stage of development, which could lead to either fulfilment or despair since the individual has to cope with increased health problems and reflect on life— and as death approaches, adults develop a detachment from life while maintaining strong ties to others.

development of the infant by allowing the baby to explore the world without getting into danger. This exploration of the world allows the baby's brain to develop rapidly through exposure to many different types of experiences and stimulation.

This attachment system is driven by infants' need for security. When frightened, infants cry or, if able, crawl or walk toward their mother, ideally the mother responds sensitively by soothing and calming them. Once infants are calm again, they can carry on exploring their surroundings, knowing that if they become frightened, the mother will be there to provide protection and safety. According to Bowlby, since babies need both a sense of security (so that they are not constantly afraid) and an ability to explore their environments, a healthy attachment relationship would require that mothers strike a balance between allowing infants to explore the world and making infants feel safe and secure without being overly protective. In unfamiliar surroundings infants with secure attachment relationships are able to use their caregivers as a secure base. They can explore new objects and new people; and when things become a little too frightening, they can move back toward their caregivers and be soothed until they feel ready to explore some more.

Bowlby believed that in time these experiences with mothers and other caregivers became part of an internal working model of relationships, a schema or "road map" of sorts that represents for the infant the trustworthiness of other people. The most important point from Bowlby's theory is that attachment in infancy sets the stage for development through the rest of their lives, because it will affect the quality of the children's social relationships with other people and also how they develop both socially and emotionally.

Infant attachment

U.S. psychology professor Mary Ainsworth (1913–1999) was a colleague of Bowlby. She traveled to various parts of the world and observed many aspects of his theory in practice. Ainsworth reasoned that nearly all infants are attached to their parents, but the quality of these attachments can vary enormously. She believed that it was important to consider why some infants and mothers seemed to develop a secure attachment relationship, while others did not. To understand this, Ainsworth conducted a classic study in which she used extensive and detailed observations of mothers and their infants at home. Ainsworth studied older infants (unlike the earlier studies of bonding between mothers and newborns) because Bowlby's theory emphasized that this was the time when attachment behaviors in infants were most apparent. In this research she noticed that while some of the mothers responded immediately and sensitively to their infants' crying and distress, other mothers would not do so— some ignored their children altogether. Convinced

This Bolivian mother and infant have clearly formed a strong and secure bond with each other. The researcher Mary Ainsworth studied attachment such as this between mothers and infants in Uganda and the United States, and other researchers continue to investigate this behavior in cultures around the world.

BOWLBY'S DEVELOPMENT STAGES

There has been a lot of research into the nature of the relationships between babies and the people who care for them. According to the British psychologist John Bowlby, the attachment relationship between parent and child is not inborn and does not emerge suddenly: It develops gradually over the first two years of life.

Early in infancy, prior to about six months of age, infants do not behave in a way that suggests they have a strong emotional bond with anyone. Strangers can enter the room and play with the infant happily, and the mother and father can leave the room and return without any apparent distress from the baby. Between six and eight months most infants start showing separation anxiety or distress when the mother leaves the infant alone, especially if the setting is unfamiliar. This is a clear indication that the infant is developing a strong preference for particular individuals, such as his parents. Babies form attachments for social reasons rather than for the satisfaction of physical needs such as food and warmth. The theory that infants form attachments purely to satisfy physical needs is based on the work of Sigmund Freud and is known as drive reduction theory. At about the same time of six to eight months or slightly later, most infants also develop a fear of strangers. The intensity of this fear reaction peaks, on average, at about 12 months of age, but there are wide-ranging differences in children's attitudes toward strangers—for example,

some infants retain this intense fear of strange individuals throughout their childhood, while others are so friendly toward strangers it is a great worry to their parents.

Bowlby described these changes as a series of stages in the first two years of life.

Stage 1: *Preattachment (0–2 months)*
Infants show no obvious preferences for caregivers and do not discriminate with whom they will interact.

Stage 2: *Attachment in the making (2–7 months)*
Infants begin showing clear signs of recognizing caregivers and siblings.

Stage 3: *Clear-cut attachment (7–24 months)*
At this stage children becomes distressed when they are separated from the mother or father and will be wary or show obvious signs of distress when around strangers. It is at this time that toddlers become skilled at communicating with caregivers and others in order to regain closeness and that feeling of security.

Stage 4: *Goal-corrected partnership (24 months onward)*
The relationship between children and caregivers becomes more balanced as children become aware of parent intentions and are capable of the verbal communication of needs.

that these differences were important, Ainsworth developed a laboratory procedure known as the Strange Situation that is still used today. The procedure set out to measure children's attachment relationships: infants' reactions to separations and reunions with their mothers, which provide information about the infants' security of attachment.

It involves a series of steps, each lasting about three minutes. They are: (1) mother and infant together in room with some toys; (2) stranger enters room and gradually starts to play with infant, mother leaves; (3) stranger and infant together in room; (4) first reunion: mother returns, stranger leaves; (5) mother leaves room, infant left alone; (6)

stranger returns to room, stranger and infant together; (7) second reunion: mother returns, stranger leaves.

Types of infant attachment
Ainsworth's research highlighted four types of infant attachment relationships. Secure infants, typically the largest group in any study, behave as though they are able to trust and rely on their caregivers when they are distressed. In the Strange Situation laboratory procedure these secure infants become very upset when the parent leaves the room and are comforted quickly when she returns. The parents of these secure infants hold and talk to the infant to soothe her, and within a minute or two the infant is calm and is

The social and emotional skills these children develop at kindergarten will depend in part on how their parents have treated them. Secure infants are comforted by their parents when they are distressed, and this lays the foundations for the development of supportive relationships with the children they meet when they are older.

able to begin exploring again. In contrast to these secure infants are two groups of insecure infants. Anxious ambivalent or resistant insecure infants, like the secure infants, show clear signs of distress when the parent leaves, but cannot be comforted when their parents return. These infants will often show signs of wanting to be held and comforted, but the parents'

> *"The thing that struck me most was how ACTIVE babies are and how much it is THEY who take the initiative. They are not passive little things to whom you do things ...they are the initiators of what happens to them."*
> —*Mary Ainsworth, 1994*

attempts to do so are met with resistance, and these infants are not able to be calmed. The second group, anxious avoidant insecure infants, often show few or no visible signs of distress when their parents leave or return; even if they do become upset when their parents leave, they seem to ignore the parents on their return. Finally, for disorganized infants

there is some concern that they have not formed any sort of organized attachment relationships. They may seem secure and insecure at different points in separation and reunion with their parents, and sometimes show bizarre behaviors such as suddenly freezing, going into trances, or rocking back and forth continually.

Numerous studies have demonstrated that secure infants are most likely to develop normally in their social and emotional skills. They have more supportive relationships with friends and peers, and they are best able to cope with difficulties at home and in school. It is also clear that becoming a securely attached infant and child depends, in part, on parenting. As Bowlby had proposed, secure infants are most likely to have parents who are very sensitive and responsive to their children's needs.

Attachment in adulthood

More recently, attachment theorists such as Mary Main have expanded the focus of this research to include attachment in adolescence and adulthood. They found that adults have internal working models of relationships based on their childhood relationships. Just as in childhood, those adults who believe that other people are trustworthy and supportive are the most likely to have satisfying relationships and to be healthy in their own development.

Secure, autonomous adults are those who have clear memories of their childhood experiences regardless of whether they are happy or unhappy memories. These secure adults have close and meaningful relationships with friends and romantic partners and are able to get the social support they need from these important individuals. This category corresponds with the secure attachment classification found in infancy. These adults are the happiest, have the most satisfying relationships with others, and the best mental health.

Dismissive adults are those who, when recalling memories of past and current relationships with their parents, seem more autonomous and independent and minimize the importance of their relationships with parents and other people. This corresponds with the anxious avoidant attachment classification in infancy.

Enmeshed or preoccupied adults are anxious about their past and current relationships with their parents. They report having unresolved concerns about problems in these relationships and sometimes are so preoccupied by these concerns that they may interfere with their ability to interact with others. This category corresponds with the anxious ambivalent or resistant insecure attachment classification in infancy.

Disorganized adults are individuals who do not seem to have a structured attachment system. They have unclear memories of their pasts and are incapable of telling coherent stories about their relationships with parents and other people. This category corresponds with the disorganized attachment classification in infancy; these disorganized adults, like those in infancy, have difficulty forming relationships and have more problems with mental health and well-being than other attachment groups.

Differences in parenting

The earliest developmental psychologists were mainly interested in learning why parents' relationships with their children differed so widely. In the mid-20th century researchers began to realize that different forms of parenting behavior in a wide

Children like these who believe that other people are trustworthy and supportive are more likely to have happy and satisfying relationships with others. Those who remember their childhood experiences are also more likely to become secure and autonomous adults.

Research into attachment in adolescence and adulthood (see p. 124) has shown that parenting and childrearing will play a part in the way that teenagers interact with each other. Internal working models of relationships are based on relationships formed in childhood.

variety of cultures could be described by using two "dimensions" or attributes—parental warmth or acceptance and parental control or restriction of the child's behavior. In this research scientists found that while some parents tended to be warm, loving, and affectionate toward their children, others were neutral or hostile, negative, and rejecting. Some parents were highly restrictive and controlling of their children's behavior, some were moderately firm in their control, while others exercised very little control over their children.

Warmth and control—the two main aspects of parenting behavior—were shown to be independent of each other. One parent could be very warm and loving toward her children, but also highly restrictive, demanding that they behave according to her standards. In contrast, another parent might be warm and loving while exercising very little control. Thus it became clear from this research that to describe and understand parenting and its effects on children, psychologists would need to consider the extent to which each parent was warm and controlling.

Baumrind's parenting styles

In the 1960s and 1970s Diana Baumrind's theory and research were a major influence on this area of psychology. Baumrind proposed that these two dimensions of parenting behavior could be used to define several meaningful categories of parenting types or styles. She argued that these different parenting styles were extremely important because they could help explain why some children are better behaved and adjusted than others. Baumrind believed that certain parenting styles were more effective at promoting appropriate behavior and healthy social and emotional development.

Authoritative parents are those who are relatively high in warmth and moderate to high in control of their children. Authoritative parents tend to be firm with their children and are certain to correct them for misbehaving. However, these parents exert this control while also making it clear to their children that they are loved and accepted. These parents can be thought of as those who have a close and warm relationship with their children, but who also make clear their expectations for appropriate behavior, and who redirect or discipline their children when necessary. Baumrind and others found that the children of authoritative parents are well adjusted, socially and emotionally mature, and competent. These children are most likely to do well in school and to have good relationships with their peers.

Authoritarian parents are like authoritative parents in that they exercise moderate to high levels of control. In contrast, they are harsh, negative, and sometimes hostile toward their children. In instances when authoritarian parents discipline the child, the interaction is likely to be conflict-ridden, harsh, and punitive. Baumrind discovered that these parents were less effective at promoting healthy social and emotional development in their children. This and subsequent research suggests that children of authoritarian parents are more likely to be immature, socially incompetent, and negative in their emotions. They tend to underperform at school and have less successful relationships with others.

Permissive parents are essentially the opposite of authoritarian parents. They exercise very little control over their children, typically ignoring misbehavior.

At the same time, they are also warm and supportive. Baumrind believed children brought up in such an environment would be lacking in the basic social skills needed to be competent in peer relationships and to do well in school.

Parenting style and the child

It is very important to consider other aspects of the family when thinking about the effect of parenting styles on children's development. Contemporary developmental psychologists do not

> *"Parentage is a very important profession, but no test of fitness for it is ever imposed in the interest of the child."*
> —*George Bernard Shaw, 1944*

believe that children are passive receivers of parenting. Instead, parents are also affected by children's behaviors, and children very actively think about and reconstruct in their own minds the experiences that they are having with their parents. We all recognize that the parent can affect the child, but it should

Exchanges between authoritarian parents and their children tend to be conflict-ridden and induce negative emotions in the child. This is parents' visiting day at a school in Pennsylvania, and the boy listens while being scolded by his mother for a poor performance.

also be borne in mind that the child can affect the parent, and that children can interpret their personal experiences in very different ways—it is perfectly possible that one child's happy homelife might be another's tale of misery and even abuse.

Daycare and development

If attachment to caregivers is formed in infancy, what happens to infants who are placed in daycare during the first or second year of life? Are these infants unable to form attachment relationships with their parents? Even if they can, are their attachment relationships somehow compromised or impaired by frequent separation from their mothers and fathers? And finally, aside from attachment, does being away from parents early in life lead to problems in social, emotional, or cognitive development?

There has been much interest in these questions in the past few decades, because the number of infants who are placed in childcare settings has increased massively during this time. Today most children in most industrial nations are in some form of nonparental childcare by the time they are three years old, and a significant minority of infants and toddlers are also placed in daycare. This shift in childrearing patterns has arisen as a result of dramatic changes in women's career development and adult employment patterns. Many more families now include a single parent or two parents who need or wish to work outside the home.

National differences

In spite of this general trend, there are still large national differences in the number of infants (birth to one year) who are placed in childcare. The United States is at one end of this spectrum, where there are some options for working mothers with infants. If the mother wants or needs to work, and there are no family members or other trusted individuals available to care for the infant, then some form of infant daycare is usually available. At the opposite end of the spectrum is Sweden, where infant daycare is virtually

---

FATHERING

PSYCHOLOGY & SOCIETY

Most psychological theories and research have emphasized the role of mothers in their children's development. There has been relatively little research on the role of fathers in their children's lives. In the 1970s this imbalance began to be resolved as developmental psychologists became more interested in the question "In what ways do fathers influence child development?"

Researchers discovered that there were very large cultural variations in the extent to which fathers had contact with their children and were involved in their daily rearing and care. The bulk of this research has focused on fathers in modern industrial countries such as those in Europe and North America. In these cultures most children are involved with their fathers, although the extent of paternal participation in childrearing is considerably lower than that of mothers. Several studies have shown that even in those families where both parents work fulltime outside of the home (for example, in dual-career couples), mothers do most of the day-to-

day caregiving of their children, and fathers are less involved. Mothers usually hold the primary responsibility for getting the children off to school, tending them in the evenings, taking them to the doctor, and so forth.

These studies have also demonstrated differences in the ways in which mothers and fathers interact with their children. Compared to the mother, fathers are more likely to engage in rough-and-tumble play, even with young infants. These interactions are very emotional and exciting, and some research has suggested that they are very important in helping children develop understanding and self-regulation of emotion in the preschool years. A secure father–infant relationship can compensate for an insecure attachment relationship with the mother, if that arises. Fathers are also a critically important source of support for the mother and the family. Traditionally, the father has been the primary source of income and resources; but even if he is not, he can still provide social and emotional backup for the mother in childrearing.

nonexistent because mothers are given an allowance by the government to offset a loss in wages so that they can stay at home with their infants. The likelihood that infants will be placed in daycare at an early age is decided as much by the nation in which they were born as by any other circumstance such as financial necessity.

Impact on attachment

In the 1980s researchers began studying the effect of infant daycare on infant attachment and other developmental outcomes that can be observed in infants. A huge debate arose as a result of this work because the findings were not conclusive. Jay Belsky claimed these studies showed that infants who were placed in daycare in the first year of life for more than 20 hours a week were more likely to have an insecure attachment relationship with their mothers. Meanwhile, Alison Clarke-Stewart argued that the Strange Situation was not valid for infants who had become used to regular separations from and reunions with their mothers. However, the most recent longitudinal study, conducted by the National Institutes of Child Health

> "It would be a mistake to conclude that a lot of time in child care, especially started early in life, is creating psychopaths."
> —Jay Belsky, 2000

and Development in the United States, suggests that for most infants being placed in daycare does not present a risk to the attachment relationship with the parents—a sensitive and responsive mother is more important to the

Father and child. Most psychological studies focus on the relationship between the mother and child. It was not until the 1970s that researchers started to question the influence of the father on the development of the child. Most of this research has focused on families in industrial societies.

formation of a secure attachment relationship, regardless of whether the infant attends daycare. Recent studies have also shown links between daycare and other aspects of development. Some research goes so far as to suggest that daycare can even have a positive influence on children's cognitive development, particularly those in higher-risk home circumstances—for example, those who live in poverty or with delinquent parents.

Some studies show that extensive daycare early in life may cause some children to be aggressive and uncompliant with parents and teachers. However, these results have not been confirmed by other experiments. The results are mixed across different studies, and most of the experiments have relied on small, nonrepresentative samples.

Studies into the long-term consequences of early childcare are still being carried out, so any resolution to this controversial debate still seems a long way off.

CONNECTIONS

- Psychoanalysis: Volume 1, pp. 52–65
- Cognitive Psychology: Volume 1, pp. 104–117
- Emotion and Motivation: Volume 2, pp. 86–109
- Infant Cognition: pp. 24–39
- Stages of Development: pp. 58–77
- Social Development: pp. 130–149

Social Development

"Man is born an animal."

Harry Stack Sullivan

People are distinct from all other animals in the complexity of their social behavior. Yet we come into the world with no understanding of others, lacking the basic communication skills required to interact. Our idea of "self" is shaped by how others see us and how we see them. Our ability to see things through other people's eyes contributes to our shared moral values. Early friendships are the key to having healthy social relationships throughout our lives.

Before you can know others, you must know yourself. Theories about the development of the "self"—our identity and the concepts that we have about our interests and abilities—have been proposed by social scientists for more than a century. In 1902 the American sociologist Charles Horton Cooley (1864–1929) proposed that the "self" is a reflection of how others see us—the looking-glass self. If our parents, siblings, and peers tell us that we are clever, good looking, and athletic, then we are likely to perceive ourselves in these ways. If people treat us as though we are dull and unattractive, then that is also the way we are likely to see ourselves.

We use the looking-glass "test" all the time. For example, when you are getting dressed for a date and wonder how your date will react to your appearance, you are doing the looking-glass test. When you hesitate to speak up in class because you worry that what you say might sound foolish, you are imagining how you will appear through other people's eyes.

Members of a swimming team proudly exhibit their gold medals. According to Charles Cooley's theory of the looking-glass self, their concepts of themselves as successful sportswomen will be reinforced by the perceptions of other members of the group as well as their parents and siblings.

A sense of others

American social psychologist George Mead (1863–1931) elaborated on Cooley's ideas. A key part of Mead's theory is that children's understanding of self and others develops simultaneously through social interactions. As children develop the skills that enable them to communicate with others, they acquire knowledge about themselves and learn how to see the world from other people's points of view. You can see how young children use their knowledge of themselves and others in "pretend games" such as "mommies and daddies" when they act out being both themselves and the parents.

> *"It is impossible to fully interpret or control the process of instruction without recognizing the child as a self and viewing his conscious processes from the point of view of their relation in his consciousness to his self, among other selves."*
> *— George Mead, 1910*

Throughout life we use role-play to define our sense of self and others. You don't have to be a parent or even a grownup to understand how mothers and fathers behave, and most of us have some idea of how we would behave if we became a mother or father. We also act out roles that we will probably never play in real life. For example, not many of us grow up to become detectives or astronauts, but most of us have imagined solving a crime or traveling to another planet in a spaceship. In acting out these roles, we use our generalized knowledge of detectives or astronauts and apply what we know to our own selves.

SELF-AWARENESS

How can we establish when our sense of self develops? It is not possible to interview infants about who they are and how they've come to that understanding—you can try, but you won't get very far! Researchers

who study the emerging sense of self-awareness have had to rely on experimental procedures. In the rouge test a researcher secretly places one red spot on the nose of a child (*see* Vol. 1, pp. 104–117), who is then placed in front of a mirror. The researcher watches to see how the child reacts to the reflection. The young child is thought to have some sense of self-recognition if she or he reacts by touching her own nose when she sees the mirror reflection. If she touches the red spot on the mirror image, it suggests that she has not yet developed the ability to recognize herself visually. From about 15 to 24 months of age infants develop the ability to recognize themselves. Until that age infants show no indication that they recognize themselves in the mirror.

How animals compare

Questions have been raised about the rouge test and what it measures. Perhaps it tests only perception skills? Chimpanzees reared in isolation show no evidence of self-awareness in the rouge test, so self-concept does depend on social exposure. Such comparative research on nonhuman primates—and with nonprimates such as

CASE STUDY

FACE-TO-FACE: LET'S TAKE TURNS

Although newborn children and young infants may seem as if they do not understand the rules of communications, research on the give and take of face-to-face interaction between a caregiver and baby suggests otherwise.

In one study T. Berry Brazelton and his colleagues observed mothers and their young infants in natural, face-to-face interactions. These observations led to the discovery that long before they are able to speak, infants are capable of taking turns in their interactions with their mothers. Involving smiles, frowns, surprises, lip movements, and sounds like cooing, the face-to-face

interaction between mother and baby has a conversational quality. Very young infants were not skilled at taking turns, but over the following months they became much more skilled at give-and-take interactions. The researchers described this quality of interaction as coherence and proposed that patterned interactions are a central part of the infant's developing social skills. Interestingly, the research also demonstrated that infants who were born prematurely were less likely to experience these coherent interactions with their mothers, perhaps because their nervous systems were not as mature.

dolphins—suggests that people are not the only animals able to recognize themselves.

An important change in the interaction between babies and caregivers occurs in the first year of life—a shift from primary to secondary intersubjectivity. The intimate, face-to-face eye contact between a caregiver and an infant is termed primary intersubjectivity and occurs from early in life. During these exchanges the infant learns important new skills about turn-taking—an essential part of social communication (*see* box above).

Toward the end of the first year of life secondary intersubjectivity appears. Infant and caregiver interact with each other as they did before, but they are now able to include other things—objects, people, the family dog, or a loud noise—into their "conversation." For example, a mother and her infant may be looking at each other and smiling, when suddenly the infant notices a toy lying nearby. The mother reacts by picking up the toy and saying, "Oh, look at that. Isn't it funny? Listen to the noises it makes!" and shakes the toy as it makes its sounds. The infant looks at the toy, then at the mother, then back at the toy, and may reach out to grasp the object.

As infants gets older, they become better at pointing out objects and other people to their mothers, and this expands these interactions. Throughout the development of these skills infants are

learning about the social rules of communication and about their ability to act on the world and other individuals. This shift from primary to secondary intersubjectivity is critical to infants' emerging sense of self-identity and their learning that they have control over other people and objects.

The "still face" paradigm

One of the most important things that infants learn from social interactions with caregivers is that they can have expectations about the social world. That is, people are predictable beings. Understanding that someone will behave in a predictable ways helps us communicate our thoughts and feelings.

Infants develop expectations about other people's social behavior from a surprisingly young age. This discovery was made using an experimental procedure called the still face. The researcher places an infant in a baby seat and asks a familiar person (such as the mother) or a stranger to sit in front of the infant. The adult engages the infant in face-to-face interaction by making eye contact, talking, and cooing. The infant responds by making eye contact, smiling, and making sounds and facial expressions. After a few minutes the adult freezes her face into a neutral expression. Infants do not like this. Although they respond in different ways, many infants show signs of frustration or anger; they may start crying, fussing, and fidgeting. Other infants seem fearful or sad; they may withdraw and look away and become very still. The infant knows that a rule of normal social behavior has been broken. Once the adult unfreezes her face and begins interacting normally again, the infant is usually able to resume face-to-face interaction.

During the first six to eight weeks of life infants smile using just the lower portions of the face. These early smiles are reflexive and can be triggered by the infants' physical state, such as gas, or by stroking their cheeks. Although all parents enjoy these newborn smiles, most realize that the smiles are not voluntary or social in nature. From two to three months of age infants begin responding with true social smiling—a voluntary smile that involves the entire face. Parents and others are able to make infants smile by speaking to them, making close face contact, or by showing them something amusing.

Initially, any person is able to elicit these social smiles, but from three to six months infants start showing a preference for their caregivers. John Bowlby (1907–1990), the British attachment theorist, believed that social smiling is essential to the formation of a strong and secure attachment relationship; infants truly enjoy interacting with their parents, and parents feel special when their infants smile at them.

SOCIAL REFERENCING

Another important component of social skills is learning how to communicate our emotions with others. Social referencing occurs when an infant looks to the face of a caregiver to gain information about how she or he should be feeling. Social referencing is a critical skill for infants because it helps them learn about their own feelings in ambiguous situations. For example, imagine a nine-month-old boy playing with his father in the park. One of his father's friends who has never before met the baby suddenly appears and joins

them. He bends over and begins talking to the baby, asking his name and trying to touch him. The infant is uncertain and feels frightened. But the father is allowing the stranger to get close. The baby looks at his father's face. Because he is smiling and reassuring, the baby understands that he need not be afraid. With further encouragement the baby starts smiling and laughing with his father's friend.

> "[Social] referencing...stretches beyond infancy to meander through the life span. It lies at the razor's edge interface of the individual and society, as one of the critical ways in which the individual's construction of reality is socially influenced."
> — Saul Feinman, 1992

Self-concept

Psychologists use the term "self-concept" to describe the complete set of ideas that individuals hold about themselves. Children's self-concepts change over time as they gain new experiences and as their brains develop and provide them with better skills for thinking and problem

Infants do not develop the ability to smile socially until they are about two or three months old. The social smile has been identified as one of the essential elements in the relationship between parents and their children—the child enjoys smiling, and it makes the parent feel good.

solving. Many psychologists have studied changes in children's self-concepts from infancy to adolescence. Developmental psychologist H. Rudolph Schaffer summarized their findings and suggests that the changes can be described in five ways.

First, the self-concept changes from being very simple to being highly complex. While young children describe themselves using the most general terms

> "The social, productive nature of human existence, and the range and extent of the human capacity to communicate... have made human history not so much one of biological but social evolution...."
> — Stephen Rose, 1976

("I am a good boy"), older children and adolescents give longer and more precise descriptions that take many factors into account ("I am a trustworthy friend and terrible at school, but I'm getting better at school since we moved last year").

Second, young children are notoriously unreliable in their self-descriptions. Until recently, with the development of puppet-based assessments of self-concepts (see box, p. 135), it was almost impossible to gain a clear understanding of the self-concepts of children much younger than six or seven years of age. As children get older, they become more consistent in their descriptions, in part as a result of their growing knowledge about the continuity of personality over time and situations.

Third, self-concepts change from being focused on concrete terms to emphasizing abstract ideas. For example, young children are more likely to talk and think about themselves in terms of what they look like and what they are good at ("I am a girl," "I am tall," "I am a fast runner"). As they get older, their self-understanding and descriptions turn toward internal states or feelings and the functioning of the mind ("I care about

people," "I am trustworthy," or "I am a complicated person").

Fourth, self-concepts increasingly emphasize comparisons with others. Younger children are likely to think of themselves in absolute terms, without reference to others ("I am not strong"). As they develop, children compare themselves to other children ("I am not as strong as other children"). This shift toward social comparison can be a problem for children because of its potentially negative effect on developing self-esteem—the concept that the self is worthy of other people's love and positive regard.

Fifth and finally, there is an important change in the public versus private nature of the self. Although preschool children can sometimes distinguish between their public acts and private thoughts, children do not begin thinking about the privacy of the self-concept until late in middle childhood. Adolescents spend much time pondering their private sense of identity, a change that is accompanied by greater self-consciousness and concern about how others see them. By young adulthood most of us have formed an understanding that acknowledges the conscious and

In dressing up for Halloween, these children are playing with their emerging sense of self-identity and how others see them. As children grow up, they begin to define themselves in relation to their friends. It is not until adolescence and young adulthood that people become aware of the relationship between how we see ourselves and how other people see us.

CASE STUDY

YOUNG CHILDREN'S SELF-CONCEPTS

One way to get young children to provide information about their self-concepts is to engage them in puppet play, using two puppets that describe different types of children. One puppet represents a child who likes to watch lightning during a storm, while the other puppet represents a child who does not like watching lightning and hides during a storm. After watching the puppets act out their roles, the children choose the puppet they are most like. In this way it is possible to gain some insight into four- and five-year-old children's self-concepts. More reliable reports can be gathered if the children are not forced to make a choice between the two puppets. Instead of asking the children to choose which puppet they are most like, the researcher asks, "What are you like?"

Research like this helps developmental psychologists measure the self-concepts of preschool children. The challenge for psychologists is to develop methods that will allow them to assess these concepts even earlier in life, with the difficulty being that younger children are unable to describe themselves using spoken language.

These teachers are using puppets to communicate with children in an early childhood development program. This is one method used to find out about children's self-concepts.

unconscious links between how we see ourselves and how others see us.

Understanding the self goes hand in hand with learning about other people. Researchers have identified five stages of development in children's understanding of others. During the first stage (from about three to five years of age) children's understanding of others is poorly developed and highly egocentric—they do not understand that other people's views may be different from their own.

During the second stage (about five to eight years of age) children come to recognize that people can, and often do, have different perspectives, but they are not yet able to integrate these different perspectives into their understanding of self versus other. During the third stage (about eight years of age to the end of childhood) children begin to think about their own and others' viewpoints; they are now able to be introspective about possible differences between themselves and others. However, they cannot hold these multiple perspectives in mind at the same time. That skill is acquired in the

fourth stage, early adolescence. During the fifth and final stage (from midadolescence to adulthood) teenagers develop the skills to compare many perspectives (including their own) to many others. They can understand the viewpoints of abstract groups, such as society at large or a certain cultural or ethnic group. This ability to consider the beliefs and thinking of an abstract group of people is essential to moral development—the development of a system of personal values about what is right and what is wrong.

THEORY OF MIND

As individuals, we are unable to experience another person's thoughts or feelings directly. Since each of our minds is distinct, how are we able to interpret other people's thoughts and intentions? Our ability to "read" other people's minds is one of the key aspects of the developing sense of self and understanding of others that underlie much of our social behavior and moral development.

We use phrases such as "putting myself in someone else's shoes" to describe how we understand other people's thoughts and feelings, and how they influence behavior. Psychologists use the term "theory of mind" to describe the same thing. Theory of mind is the understanding that other people possess mental states that involve ideas and views of the world that are different from our own. Although it is not yet clear at what age children develop a rudimentary theory of mind, the preschool years (three to five years of age) are a watershed period. The cognitive scientist Steven Pinker gives the example

> "The fallacy of conceiving consciousness to be something different from the feeling...has arisen in a great measure, from the use of the personal pronoun 'I.'"
> — Thomas Brown, 1824

of a toddler playing with his mother who hands him a banana and tells him the phone is ringing. Even though the child knows that the banana is a banana, he understands what his mother wants him to do and pretends that the banana is a telephone instead of eating it.

Children learn to interpret other people's minds in early childhood, but it is not easy to test their theory-of-mind abilities. Methods of testing theory of mind can be flawed. While some children who do not perform well on theory-of-mind tests genuinely do not understand other people's minds, others who do have a

theory of mind, and therefore understand other people's minds, still do badly on the tests because they are impulsive by nature and may not understand what the tests are trying to discover.

Autism

In the most extreme cases individuals who are diagnosed with autism may lack any understanding of other people's minds. Autism (*see* Vol. 6, pp. 68–91) is a developmental disorder, or learning disability, usually first detected during infancy. The distinctive feature of autistic children is their inability to interact socially; they are totally self-absorbed and show little or no interest in other people. Their failure to develop social relationships with others is usually accompanied by severe delays in the development of language and other communication skills.

While it is possible that autism is biological in origin, the onset and severity of symptoms are probably influenced by a range of environmental factors. Research has shown that although some autistic individuals have remarkable abilities in certain areas, such as memory tests, drawing, or music, even relatively high-functioning autistic people perform poorly on theory-of-mind tests.

SELF-ESTEEM

An important part of our self-concept is our self-esteem—how good or bad we feel about ourselves. Self-esteem emerges as we develop an understanding of our own strengths

The child sitting on the wall is having difficulties forming social relationships with the other children in the playground. To get on well with others, children need to have a well-developed theory of mind: They need to understand how others think and feel or at least be aware that others' views and feelings are different from their own.

THE FALSE BELIEF TASK

In a classic 1983 study Heinz Wimmer and Josef Perner proposed that a child has a theory of mind if he or she appreciates that people can hold false beliefs. To test their ideas, they developed a series of games involving dolls and objects, the best-known being the Sally-Anne task.

In this game the child is shown two dolls (Sally and Anne), a small box, a small basket, and a marble. Sally plays with the marble and then puts it in the basket (covered with a cloth) and leaves the room to play outside. Anne takes the marble from the basket and plays with it, then puts the marble inside the box (also covered from sight). Now Sally returns to the room, and the child is asked, "Where will Sally look for her marble?" Older children appreciate immediately that Sally holds a false belief about the location of the marble; she believes it is in the basket because that is where she put it, but it is a false belief because we know that Anne moved the marble to the box. If the child says that Sally will look in the basket, it indicates she understands that Sally holds this false belief and that the child has some form of a theory of mind. Most children younger than four years of age say Sally will look in the box, but over the next one or two years their ability to consider the perspectives and thoughts of other individuals develops rapidly.

and weaknesses compared to those of others. The process of comparing ourselves to others becomes particularly important in middle childhood and adolescence. Unlike other components of the self-concept, self-esteem varies widely between individuals and is very dynamic—our feelings about our own worthiness and competence can change dramatically over time, across situations, and depending on the circumstances even from moment to moment.

Five dimensions

In the 1980s Susan Harter devised tests that measure five dimensions of children's self-esteem: athletic/physical, social, physical attractiveness, behavior, and academic. In these tests children describe whether they are more or less athletic than others, better or worse at school, more or less attractive, and so on. Also, they describe the extent to which these abilities or attributes are or are not important to them. Children can think they are terrible at schoolwork, but that will not have a negative effect on their self-esteem if schoolwork does not matter to them. The same is true for the other dimensions of self-esteem. Low self-esteem arises when children have low self-worth regarding abilities that truly matter to them. Harter's research demonstrated the complexity of

self-esteem in childhood and adolescence. A child may have high self-esteem when it comes to some aspects of self-perception (for example, feeling attractive and being an excellent student), but may have low self-esteem in other domains like athletics and social relationships.

While the self-esteem of some individuals goes up and down for no obvious reasons, some children,

> *"The importance of self-esteem for creative expression appears to be almost beyond disproof."*
> —S. Coopersmith, 1967

adolescents, and adults have high self-esteem most of the time. The variation in self-esteem affects people's social and emotional development. Individuals with high self-esteem tend to be more ambitious and more successful in achieving their goals—provided that over-confidence does not blind them to their weaknesses. Individuals with low self-esteem are more likely to suffer from depression and anxiety and to withdraw from social interactions with other people.

The final outcome of the developing sense of self in early and middle childhood is the formation of a stable personal identity. Erik Erikson (*see* Vol. 1, pp. 52–65) proposed that adolescence is the crucial period in the development of identity formation. It is during adolescence that we understand who we are and where we are going.

Identity exploration and commitment

In the 1960s James Marcia, professor of psychology at the University of California, San Francisco, tested some of the ideas in Erikson's theory. From interviews with young adults about their beliefs about various aspects of their lives, including their employment choices and political attitudes, Marcia identified two aspects of identity formation: identity exploration and identity commitment.

Identity exploration occurs when adolescents investigate their own beliefs, plans for the future, and understanding of the past. Typically, it involves thinking about parents, other family members, peers, and close friends, and who they are as individuals. Some adolescents consider these matters carefully and are able to describe their exploration, while others do not seem to consider them at all.

During adolescence we develop a sense of identity—who we are and what we are going to do in life. This can be a difficult and challenging time as individuals analyze their own past and future, and also challenge the beliefs and behavior of family members and their peer group.

Identity commitment is the degree to which the adolescent or young adult holds a firm belief in her own attitudes and aspirations. While some adolescents have a strong desire to realize their goals, others take few steps toward fulfilling their plans.

Marcia also identified four patterns, called statuses, in adolescents' search for an identity. They are broadly age related, but they do not occur in any order, and few individuals go through all of them.

Four identity statuses

Identity diffusion is the term given by Marcia to the status of adolescents and young adults who do not actively explore their personal identities, and who lack clear goals and commitments. Identity diffusion is most common among young adolescents and becomes less common in late adolescence and early adulthood.

Identity moratorium occurs among individuals who are in the midst of deep exploration but have not yet committed to a particular identity. They may be thinking about what they believe and who they are; after a period of exploration they arrive at an answer and commit themselves to their new beliefs and goals.

Identity foreclosure occurs when an individual commits to an identity before he or she has examined carefully his or her own beliefs, experiences, and goals. Foreclosure is a fairly common pattern in which the adolescent or young adult commits to safe and conventional goals without exploring other options. These individuals are most likely to adopt the values and aspirations of their parents or friends without having given much thought to whether they really share them.

Finally, identity achievement occurs among those individuals who have thoroughly examined their beliefs and aspirations and have formed a strong commitment to their emerging identity. Identity achievement is rare among young adolescents, but becomes the most common pattern by late adolescence and young adulthood as the individual achieves a greater degree of maturity.

Another important component of the self-concept is the understanding of one's own gender. An individual's sex—male or female—is biologically determined, but that is only the beginning of the story. Apart from the natural variations in masculinity and femininity that occur among boys and girls, social and environmental influences also affect the development of our sexual identity. Many psychologists make a distinction between "sex" and "gender." When they talk about an individual's sex, they are referring to biological makeup and anatomy. Gender is used to refer to the behavior, attitudes, and goals society considers appropriate for males and females. Research on the formation of gender differences in behavior and the development of self-concepts has produced a considerable amount of information.

Early boy/girl differences

From an early age (before two or three years of age) boys and girls begin to show differences in their toy preferences. Boys are more likely to be attracted by vehicles and similar objects, while girls are more likely to play with dolls. Because parents, family members, and other children reinforce this gender-stereotyped play, it is

virtually impossible to know whether early toy preferences are due to biological differences or the result of socialization. Around this time a difference in overt physical aggression emerges. From about two years old throughout childhood and into adulthood males show more aggression than females. Girls can be aggressive, too, but boys are more likely to show physical or verbal aggression, while girls are more likely to be aggressive using subtler means, such as excluding children from play or by spreading rumors.

From about three years of age until midadolescence children have a strong preference for playing with same-sex peers. Casual observation of any schoolyard shows that children spend nearly all of their play time with children of the same sex. There is also an emerging gender difference in children's networks of peers and friends. From preschool years onward girls' groups of friends are smaller and more exclusive than boys' groups. Boys play with a larger number of other boys in groups that are less exclusive than girls' groups. The same patterns have been observed in several other cultures and species. The fact that it is very difficult to get the children to behave otherwise suggests to some researchers that this behavior is biologically determined.

From an early age boys prefer playing with masculine toys such as guns, while girls prefer feminine toys such as dolls. The extent to which this is innate (inborn) or is a result of being socialized by parents and others has long been debated.

KEY POINTS

- Gender differences in behavior emerge in early childhood as a complex transaction between biology and socialization.
- Moral development, which occurs gradually from childhood through adulthood, has important links to development of the self, reasoning ability, and behavior that is beneficial to others.
- Once children begin school, peer relationships and close friendships become central to their social development and mental health. This remains true throughout adolescence and adulthood.

In the schoolyard girls nearly always play with other girls, and boys play with other boys. Children learn from an early age whether they are a girl or a boy, and gender stereotypes tend to be reinforced by the reactions of parents, teachers, and peers to the children's behavior.

GENDER CONCEPTS

Researchers exploring children's concepts of gender have found a clear developmental progression during early and middle childhood. In the first several years of life children acquire the labels for "boy" and "girl" and learn to apply these labels to themselves and to others. This is the result of socialization.

Children of this age also learn to distinguish between "men" and "women." They rely heavily on obvious physical features, however. For instance, it is easy to deceive a four-year-old child by asking whether men can wear dresses or women can have short hair. From around the age of six or seven children acquire an adult-like understanding of gender. Although they still tend to rely principally on physical appearances to make judgments about gender, they nevertheless can now understand that gender and physical appearance can be distinct; for example, a man can have long hair, or a woman can wear trousers.

For decades developmental psychologists have debated how children's concepts of gender influence their behavior. While some psychologists argue that children's behavior is shaped by their beliefs about how boys and girls should behave, others assert that boys and girls behave differently before they have any understanding of gender differences. On one hand, gender differences are seen as genetic (inherited), and according to the other theory they are socialized (learned).

These two approaches have been integrated in a theory that recognizes there are both biological influences on children's behavior and environmental influences on children's understanding about sex differences. The theory is called the gender schema theory—a schema being a kind of mental framework of ideas and memories that help tell an individual appropriate behavior or how to behave in different circumstances.

Biological and social definitions

The gender schema theory suggests that children's understanding of gender is filtered through their existing ideas of how girls and boys look and behave. These ideas include both biological and social definitions of gender. Children are more likely to notice and remember events or objects that are consistent with their

FALSE APPEARANCES

CASE STUDY

In studies carried out in the 1970s and 1980s B. Lloyd and C. Smith asked women who were themselves mothers to look after six-month-old babies whom they had not met before. Some of the infants were cross-dressed and cross-named; boys were presented as girls, girls as boys. Regardless of the children's biological sex, the women treated them in a way that was consistent with their apparent gender. When a woman played with a baby named and dressed as a boy, she usually offered it a masculine toy, such as a rubber hammer. If she thought it was a girl, she gave it soft, furry toys. The women also responded differently to how the babies played. If a child named and dressed as a boy played in a physically robust way, the women joined in and encouraged the child. If a "girl" behaved in the same way, the women saw this as a sign of distress and talked soothingly to the child.

current understanding of gender-typical behavior. For example, if a young boy says, "Look how strong I am," and his mother or father replies, "Oh yes, I bet you'll be a linebacker on the high school football team," the response confirms the boy's existing belief that physical strength is a desirable attribute in males. When a young girl dresses up, and her father or mother tells her how pretty she looks, it confirms her idea that physical attractiveness is a desirable feminine quality. In countless ways like these children's emerging ideas of what it means to be a boy or girl are reinforced.

Concepts about gender vary from culture to culture, and there have been dramatic shifts in history regarding what is appropriate behavior for women and men. For example, it is now commonplace for women to have occupations that were once viewed as male professions and for girls to take part in sports that were previously considered the sole domain of boys. These shifts in behavior can be easily accommodated by children's gender schemas. Even so, regardless of the precise behaviors that define "male" and "female," identification with one's own gender is

A female architect at work. Traditionally architecture has been viewed as a male profession, but women are now enjoying careers in this field. Notions about acceptable careers or hobbies for men and for women have changed throughout the centuries and also vary between cultures.

critically important to the healthy social and emotional development of every individual.

From the first few days of life a newborn's parents talk about the baby in terms that are consistent with gender stereotypes (the characteristics that a particular culture holds to be typical of boys and girls). "It's a boy!" or "It's a girl!" are often the parents' first proud announcement to friends and relatives. Newborn babies enter the world color-coded according to gender—blue for boys, pink for girls. These colors are regarded as such infallible guides to gender that they can fool adults into misidentifying boys and girls (*see* box above).

Long before actual sex differences in behavior appear (for example, the emergence of higher levels of aggression in boys during the third year of life), parents and others behave differently toward girls and boys. Mothers spend more time talking and vocally interacting with infant daughters than they do with infant sons. Men are more likely than women to play with their children in a physically engaging, rough-and-tumble way, particularly if it is play with a son. Mothers and fathers also prefer their children to play with gender-appropriate toys (so do children's peer groups). In conversations with their daughters mothers use more terms that describe emotions than

Two girls fight in a high school corridor. Aggressive behavior is widely held to be unacceptable, but female aggression is often viewed as more deviant than male aggression.

they do with their sons. Parents will often tolerate—or even encourage—aggression in a son; but if a daughter behaves aggressively, she is likely to be told: "Little girls don't do things like that."

ETHNIC IDENTITY

For most children, especially those belonging to minority groups, ethnic identity is another important component of the developing sense of self. From preschool years children show an awareness of their own and others' ethnicity (for example, Asian, African, white). At this age they rely on physical features such as skin tone and facial features to define ethnic groups, much as they do when labeling children as girls or boys. By middle childhood all children are aware of their own ethnicities, and they tend to use more subtle but important aspects of cultural practices and attitudes—such as religion, diet, or dress—to define ethnic groups.

The development of ethnic identity is a complex process that evolves over time and is influenced by experiences and social influences. In the 1990s Jean Phinney, professor of psychology at the University of California, Los Angeles, proposed that the labels we apply to ourselves and others are only part of this identity. How children evaluate their own group membership is also important. For example, do they feel happy or unhappy about being members of a particular ethnic group? Do they feel that they belong in that group or not? To what extent do they adopt the behaviors and practices of their ethnic group?

Phinney believes that adolescence is a critical period in the development of ethnic identity. Before adolescence children do not closely examine their ethnic identity. They are aware of the labels that apply to their ethnic group (for example, "I am African American"), but they haven't had many opportunities to test their understanding of what it means to be a member of that ethnic group. Exploration of ethnic identity occurs when young teenagers become more aware of differences in cultural practices and behaviors, and when they learn about the social, political, and economic injustices that often exist for ethnic minorities. During this stage of development the adolescent no longer takes for granted the attitudes and behaviors of the majority ethnic group, but begins to question and challenge them. In the final stage, at the end of adolescence, young adults achieve a coherent ethnic identity. If they resolve many of the issues and concerns during the exploration phase, they become committed to their ethnicity.

UNDERSTANDING MORALITY

In 1932 the Swiss psychologist Jean Piaget (*see* pp. 64–76) proposed that morality develops in stages during childhood, and that moral development goes hand in hand with children's ability to reason. Although it may seem hard to believe now, at the time Piaget's beliefs were revolutionary. Until then psychologists had not considered seriously the notion that morality was a product of our developing minds.

Based on his own observations of children, Piaget described three stages of moral reasoning that all children move through at about the same age. During stage one (birth to four years of age) children lack even the most basic abilities to ponder questions of morality. Although young children are capable of learning basic social rules, they exercise them as a result of social learning, not because they have considered the logic behind the moral treatment of others ("Do as you would be done by").

During stage two (four to nine years) children acquire an understanding of why we have rules and codes of conduct. However, their understanding about why the rules exist and are enforced is naive. They believe that the rules cannot be changed. Adults enforce the rules, and children comply in deference to their unquestioned authority.

It is during the third and final stage (nine years of age and later) that children develop the ability to evaluate their own and others' behaviors. They become aware that the rules of moral conduct are a part of our culture, and that they can and do change. Perhaps most importantly, children begin to understand that we comply with the rules of morality because we choose to adhere to a high principle or standard, and not out of simpleminded obedience to authority.

As influential as Piaget's theory has been, it has limitations. The three stages that he described do not capture all the changes in moral reasoning. Also,

developmental psychologists believe that moral development does not end in middle childhood; there are important changes in adolescence and adulthood.

Lawrence Kohlberg (1927–1987), an American psychologist who studied under Piaget, addressed these limitations, using methods of assessing moral development that were more systematic and scientific than those used by Piaget.

Like Piaget, Kohlberg believed that moral reasoning developed through a series of stages, but he identified a total of six stages that span three levels of

> *"Although moral education has a forbidding sound to teachers, they constantly practice it."*
> — *Lawrence Kohlberg, 1981*

moral reasoning. Although individuals can progress from one stage to the next, very few individuals proceed to the final stage in moral development.

Levels of morality

The first level of moral reasoning, which Kohlberg called preconventional morality, has two stages. During stage one (before seven or eight years of age) children determine what is right and wrong based on rules and punishment, and they make decisions about how to behave based on their attempts to avoid punishment. At

The early teenage period is a critical time for people to begin questioning the values of the society in which they live. Such explorations may involve taking part in social projects. Here young Californians plant trees on behalf of the Los Angeles Conservation Corps.

Young children learn basic acceptable social behavior from their parents. This initial stage was labeled "preconventional morality" by Kohlberg. Children learn what is right and wrong from an adult's authority and by avoiding punishment. It is not until they are older that they develop the ability to contemplate questions of morality.

this stage children are unable to understand others' perspectives; they see morality as being based largely on their own obedience to authority. In stage two (eight to ten years of age) children come to see morality as a simple formula for justice based on equal treatment of self and other. They understand that other people's needs and wants are important; at the same time, they expect their own needs and wants to be met. For example, if a boy playing with friends sticks to the rules of a game, he expects his friends to follow the rules, too. This is an important step because it allows children to negotiate rules of conduct with other children without the intervention of an adult. Without this new flexibility children would not be able to get along without constant supervision by adults.

Level two, conventional morality, includes the next two stages. During stage three (10 or 11 years of age and later) the emphasis in moral reasoning shifts from acting in one's own interests toward doing what pleases and helps others. There is a comparable transition toward considering our own and others' intentions and motives, and this internal motivation (rather than the desire to comply with external authority figures) becomes the driving force behind moral behavior.

During stage four—adolescence and young adulthood—individuals emphasize the importance of the group's (society, culture) standards of behavior. Being good means obeying authority and respecting the social order in order to avoid chaos.

Level three, postconventional morality, includes two more stages and is acquired in adulthood by a small minority of individuals. During stage five individuals gain an understanding that laws and social rules are framed by fallible people, are not necessarily fair in all circumstances, and can be changed or challenged. Laws should be respected because they protect society; but if a particular law harms individual rights and cannot be changed by legal means, the individual is justified in breaking that law.

> *"People often fail to use their highest stage of moral judgement when reasoning about the moral dilemmas encountered in everyday life."*
> *— Jeremy Carpendale, 2000*

During stage six the individual is no longer guided by socially defined rules, but instead follows universal moral principles—codes of conduct that override the majority view about what is and is not appropriate behavior. A universal moral principle for some people is that it is wrong to take life in any circumstances. Faced with the choice of ignoring a universal moral principle or breaking a law, the individual who reaches this final stage of moral development is prepared to break the law and suffer the consequences as a result.

THE ROLE OF FRIENDSHIP

Psychologists now know that children's friendships play a crucial role in social development. In a theory published in the 1950s the American psychiatrist Harry Stack Sullivan theorized that much socialization occurs within relationships

KOHLBERG'S MORAL DILEMMAS: THE HEINZ STORY

CASE STUDY

In order to assess moral development, Kohlberg used short stories that presented the individual with a moral dilemma that he or she was then asked to solve. The classic dilemma involves a man named Heinz who had a dear wife who was very ill. Without a particular medication Heinz' wife would die. A pharmacist had the necessary drug, but he charged a very high price for it and refused to sell it to Heinz at a price he could afford. In desperation Heinz stole the drug so that his wife could live, even though he realized that by doing so he was breaking the law and would probably go to prison.

Should Heinz have stolen the drug? Why or why not? What else could he have done? What would you do if you were in this situation, and why? According to Kohlberg, only people who reach the final stage of moral development break the law for universal moral principles.

between close childhood and adolescent friends. Sullivan believed that these "chumships" were critical to the formation of individual identity and, eventually, to healthy romantic relationships. Although it may seem surprising to us now, few psychologists up till then had even considered that friends and peers were an important part of children's social worlds.

Since Sullivan's theory was published, researchers have addressed numerous questions about the formation of and changes in friendships, how children form and change their social standing in the larger peer group, and how these relationships affect children's mental health and development.

Forming friendships

Friendships are typically defined as close and lasting relationships between two people. They differ from social relationships with peers, parents, and siblings in the types of activities that friends carry out and the levels of intimacy and loyalty that are shown. One theory is that as children's abilities to reason develop, so does their understanding of how and why friendships are formed and maintained. When stable friendships first emerge in children's lives

Friendships play a crucial role in social development. The nature of friendship changes as the person matures. Young children play together and share toys, whereas teenagers rely on friends for emotional support.

(typically when they start preschool or school), the emphasis is on proximity and being friendly. Typical five- or six-year-olds will say that another child is their friend because they are in the same class, and because they are friendly and share toys. At this stage most children show frequent changes in who they label as their friend.

In middle childhood children's concepts of friendship become more mature. They are more likely to define their friendships in terms of loyalty and trust as well as shared attributes or desires (for example, "I know he's my friend, and we both love to play football"). In the transition to adolescence there is another important shift when children come to understand friendships as being opportunities for intimacy and emotional support. At this stage and beyond, adolescents and adults describe their friendships in terms of closeness, affection, and trust.

Psychotherapist John Gottman devised an experiment to study the formation of friendships in childhood. He took children of the same age who did not know each other and randomly paired them. The children met for several play sessions for a month, and their interactions were videotaped. Some pairs of children became and remained friends, while others didn't. Gottman identified several factors that accounted for which children became friends.

Future friends were children who were likely to discuss and agree on a shared activity that they both enjoyed, while the children who did not become friends were less likely to explore and discover shared interests. The children who became friends were also more likely to disclose information about themselves and exchange other information. Their personal disclosures served to show that they trusted each other—an important building block in friendship formation. Friends-to-be were also clearer in their communication with each other, which reduced the risk of conflict between them. Even when conflict did occur, they were better at resolving their differences.

Conflict resolution

Gottman's research showed that friendships are a training ground for conflict resolution. Friendships are not always placid and easy-going. Children get into arguments and fights with their closest friends, just as adults do. However, what distinguishes healthy friendships is the way in which children can resolve conflicts. Stable and supportive friendships develop between partners who are able to sort out their disagreements and learn how to avoid future conflicts. By contrast, friendships that are more likely to end are those where this learning about conflict resolution does not occur. Highly aggressive children are the ones who find it most difficult to form lasting friendships. Reacting to conflict by hitting or shouting at your friend does not build trust and companionship.

An aggressive child having a temper tantrum. Aggressive children find it most difficult to form lasting friendships. That is because hitting, shouting, and screaming do not resolve conflicts.

Status in the group

When you watch a group of children playing together, it is obvious that there is a social hierarchy within the group, with some children more popular than others. From about the age of four children gain a status within their peer groups (for instance, at preschool or school and in the neighborhood) as being popular, well-liked, and the center of attention or unpopular and a person to be avoided.

That some children are rejected while others are accepted raises many questions about the social worlds of children. Why are some children popular and others ignored or even targeted for ridicule and bullying? How does this status form initially? Is it stable over time, or can it change over a period of time? Perhaps the most important question is what are the implications for those children who are rejected and ignored or mocked by their peers—does this experience affect their social and emotional development?

Researchers learned some answers to these questions by using a technique called *peer sociometric ratings*, which allows scientists to study and evaluate children's status in their peer groups. Although there are a variety of ways to conduct sociometric ratings, the basic method involves interviewing each child in a group separately (for example, all of the children in a classroom or a school). During the interview the child is given a

> *"Although most children have opportunities to participate in the rewarding world that comes with good peer relationships, there are others whose relationships with peers are much less satisfying."*
> — *Steven Asher, 1990*

list of names of all the children in that group and is asked a series of questions such as: (1) Who are your closest friends? (2) Name the children that you like the most. (3) Name the children that you like the least. (4) Name the children who start fights a lot, and so forth. From the answers, the investigator gets an idea of who is liked or disliked, and who children think is well-behaved or badly behaved.

Psychologists use these ratings to classify children into groups. Popular children are those named by many other children as being well-liked. Rejected children are those who are named by many other children as being disliked. Neglected children are those who are not named at all by any other children—it's as though their peers don't even notice them. Average or typical children, who form by far the largest group, are those who, like most adults, are mentioned by some of their peers as being well-liked, but mentioned by others as being disliked. Each child's status in the peer group can

remain the same or change over a period of time, although many of the children who are rejected by their peers do tend to remain in the rejected group.

Rejection by peers

In most groups of school-age children and adolescents there is a minority of individuals who are rejected by the majority. Their status is evident from observations of the children at play and in the classroom, where the rejected children tend to have fewer and more hostile peer interactions than other children. Why do their peers reject these children, and what are the effects of rejection? Several decades of research have produced some preliminary answers and suggestions for future investigators to consider. A number of studies have demonstrated that peer rejection is more likely if the child is aggressive. If a child enters a new group

FORMATION OF PEER STATUS

CASE STUDY

Are children rejected because they are aggressive? Or do children become aggressive because of rejection? Psychologists have attempted to answer these questions by conducting a number of experiments. In the 1980s Ken Dodge and other researchers took individual children from different schools and placed them together, at random, in new play groups so that they were playing with children they had never met before. Before the experiment began, the researchers collected peer sociometric ratings so they knew who was accepted and who was rejected in the individual children's own schools.

When the children were placed in the new groups, the researchers observed their behavior and measured their status many times throughout the experiment. Those children who had been rejected in the previous school quickly reestablished their rejected status in the new groups. Even though it was not possible for a child's reputation to affect his or her status in the new group, the rejected child tended to be rejected again. The rejected children were more likely to be hostile and aggressive and have few communication skills, for example, to enter a game or conversation. It is not clear whether the children learned these behaviors after being rejected or vice versa. Well-liked children are less aggressive and have more skills for entering a conversation or game with a group of children.

(for example, on starting school) and reacts to conflicts with other children by hitting and screaming at them, the other children quickly identify the aggressive child and avoid him or her. Although this process has unfortunate consequences for the rejected child, it is understandable. Why would anyone want to play with another child who is unpredictable and temperamental, unable to share, and tries to hurt others?

Give a dog a bad name

Once this reputation is established, it is difficult (but not impossible) to lose. Peer rejection is part of an ongoing cycle that reinforces the child's problems with social skills. Children who then move to a new group and who are aggressive do not know how to enter a game or solve a group problem; they are far more likely to be rejected again by their peers. The more they are isolated from peer interactions, the further they fall behind in social skills, so they become even less successful in the peer group. These effects have been observed in natural settings (for example,

on school playgrounds) as well as in child development experiments, such as those conducted by Ken Dodge and his colleagues (*see* box, p. 147).

Many psychologists argue that children's peers are even more important socializing influences than their parents. As children move through the early school years and into adolescence, they spend less and less time with their parents and siblings and more and more time with their friends. As they get older, they begin to take on the values, attitudes, and styles of behavior of their friends. These values and ways of behaving and dressing tend to be different from those of their parents, leading to what is described as the "generation gap" between parents and their offspring.

Although children tend to be like their friends in terms of personality, academic achievement, and attitudes, it is not clear how friendship similarity arises. Is it because children choose friends who are most like themselves—which is referred to as selection—or is it because children who spend a lot of time together teach

Close friends share the same interests and beliefs, dress like each other, and enjoy spending time together. It is a complex issue whether or not close friends imitate each other because they spend so much time together or because they have chosen friends with the same values and tastes.

each other how to behave and what to believe (referred to as socialization)? The answer to this question is not simple: part of the reason we share interests and beliefs with our closest friends is because we have chosen them as friends, and part of the reason we chose them as friends is because we have discovered that we share interests and beliefs. Friends also influence each other's interests and beliefs.

Recent research has shown how selection and socialization influence friendships among antisocial and delinquent youths. In middle childhood aggressive children (many of whom are also unruly and disruptive in the classroom) are likely to be rejected by their peers. If they do not change their behavior, it becomes increasingly difficult for them to find children who are willing to be friends. Not surprisingly, by the time they are young adolescents, they are likely to have only a few friendships, which tend to be with similarly antisocial youths. These relationships are less stable and poorer in quality than the friendships that develop between well-liked children.

> *"Friendship... is one of those things that gives value to survival...."*
> — *C. S. Lewis, 1960*

Research by Thomas Dishion at the University of Oregon and others has shown that antisocial adolescents teach each other how to become even more antisocial—they socialize one another. Psychologists describe this as deviancy training. Deviant behavior can include drug abuse and the use of violence. Researchers have also measured the effect of peer group pressure on underage smoking and drinking alcohol. When delinquent teenagers are together, they frequently talk and laugh about committing antisocial and often illegal acts, even when they know they are being watched and videotaped. During these conversations they reinforce each other's

A young couple in a car being stopped by the police. During adolescence teenagers spend less time with their parents and more time with their friends. This often means that they adopt similar values and attitudes. Research has shown that antisocial teenagers teach each other deviancy.

antisocial attitudes by showing approval for delinquent acts. By discussing their activities and attitudes, they also teach each other new antisocial behaviors. Friendships in adolescence can, therefore, undermine healthy development and result in deviant behavior being learned.

These socializing effects can be so subtle yet powerful that they occur even in group treatment settings with skilled therapists. Antisocial acts and attitudes become the social "glue" for delinquent teenagers' relationships, which can involve group drug use and promiscuous unprotected sexual activity. When antisocial adolescents and young adults form romantic attachments, partners tend to be alike in prior and current antisocial behaviors, suggesting that the cycle of selection and socialization continues into adulthood.

CONNECTIONS

- Psychoanalysis: Volume 1, pp. 52–65
- Cognitive Psychology: Volume 1, pp. 104–117
- Problem Solving: Volume 3, pp. 136–163
- Stages of Development: pp. 58–77
- Relating to Others: Volume 5, pp 28–49
- Abnormality in Development: Volume 6, pp. 68–91

Applications and Future Challenges

—Relating developmental psychology to the real world and considering the future.—

Psychological study of human development from fetus to adulthood is a rapidly changing field. Psychologists have utilized technological advances such as genetic profiling, which are expected to bring about improved treatments of mental illnesses. Other research is focused on improving the nurturing of children as they develop in a world full of new problems and challenges.

During the last 100 years there have been many major advances in our understanding of human biology. These, coupled with other studies looking at environmental influences on psychological traits, have led psychologists to radically alter the way they view subjects such as childhood development, the nature and importance of families, and mental disorder. Multidisciplinary research into genetics, the development of the brain, and the broader significance of national

A NEW LOOK AT JUNG'S PERSONALITY THEORY

FOCUS ON

Like any branch of science, psychology is constantly evolving, and cornerstone theories and ideas are frequently reviewed or reinterpreted. For example, in his seminal *Psychological Types* (1921) Swiss psychoanalyst Carl Gustav Jung (1875–1961) (*see* Vol 1, pp. 52–65) suggested that people's personalities could be divided into one of two discrete groups—introvert or extrovert. According to Jung's criteria, introversion involves a concern with subjective experience, with one's mental processes, and with the world of one's thoughts and fantasies. By contrast, extroversion involves a predominant interest in objective experience, in the external world of appearances, and in outside reality. Introverts are not solely preoccupied with themselves, however, but are concerned with the hidden meaning of all things and with the nature of reality, rather than with its visible and possibly superficial appearance.

Widely accepted for many years, Jung's personality theory has come under close scrutiny recently. The theory is limited because it is insufficiently rooted in scientific method. It simplifies the widely observable tendency of people to switch from introversion to extroversion according to the situation. They may be outgoing when they feel at ease, but reticent when they are uncomfortable. Psychologists now suggest that most people are ambiverts—a blend of introvert and extrovert.

Carl Jung in the study of his house in Bollingen, Germany. Early in his career Jung worked closely with Sigmund Freud (1856–1939), but disagreements over Freud's approach to libido and incest led to personal and professional schism. Nonetheless, Jung and Freud were key pioneers in the field of personality research.

and cultural influences have embedded within psychology a range of scientific principles. This is in contrast to many early researchers (*see* box p. 150) who used methods such as introspection (*see* Vol. 1, pp. 30–39), which have been criticized for their lack of externally verifiable objectivity.

Studying brain development

For many years, scientific opinion was divided over whether human personality and development were dependent on biological causes (nature) or on the external influence of circumstance and the environment (nurture). Psychologists now recognize that people develop through constant interaction between the two. Research in several disciplines has helped them reach this conclusion, notably genetics (the study of heredity and its influences) and cognitive neuroscience (the study of brain and its processes).

The last quarter of the 20th century saw a dramatic increase in the quantity and quality of research into brain development in infancy and early childhood. Advances in this field gave scientists important new insights into how early experiences, such as rejection by a parent or malnutrition, may influence subsequent cognitive and social-emotional development through their effects on the brain. Technological advances have led to many discoveries in the field of brain development. These new techniques include functional magnetic resonance imaging (fMRI, *see* Vol. 2, pp. 20–39) and diagnostic tools that use habituation procedures.

Meanwhile, there remains some debate among neuroscientists and psychologists about whether the early years really are the most important in brain development. Some researchers think that the brain is an organ that can adapt to change throughout life, regardless of experiences in infancy and childhood. Nor is it clear how much the development of the brain depends on external environmental cues, or how lasting the effects of influences such as malnutrition and poverty are on the brains of young children (*see* box p. 152).

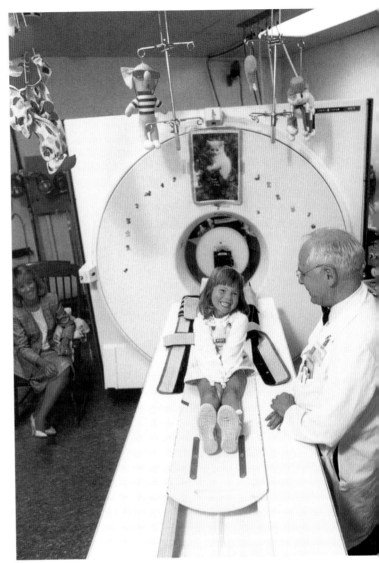

This girl is preparing to undergo an MRI scan. The MRI scanner contains a powerful magnet that causes different chemicals within the brain to emit distinctive radio signals. Using these signals, a series of 2-D slices through the brain can be shown.

Despite these uncertainties, modern psychologists know a great deal about the way the brain grows and functions in early childhood, and how the functions of the nervous system influence thought, the emotions, and behavior. This knowledge helps them advise on child development with increasing conviction.

Research into brain development has allowed psychologists to draw conclusions about possible treatments of psychological problems that occur from birth to old age. First, it is now known that when we are

POVERTY AND THE DEVELOPING BRAIN

According to research by the World Bank, more than one billion people worldwide live on the local equivalent of less than one U.S. dollar a day. Psychologists have learned that poverty adversely affects brain development and many other aspects of mental and physical health.

Extreme lack of material resources leads to malnutrition, increased susceptibility to disease, inadequate healthcare and education, and dangerous housing. Conditions of poverty can also have severe effects on the neurological and psychological development of children. In Brazil, for example, as many as eight million children and adolescents live on the streets of major cities or in favelas (shantytowns). Drug use, violence, and sexually transmitted diseases are

Poverty, malnutrition, and ill health are endemic in places such as this favela or shantytown in Rio de Janeiro, Brazil.

rampant, and many of the children living in favelas are slowly poisoned by environmental contaminants, such as lead.

Children living in deprived conditions like these are likely to have problems with their cognitive, emotional, physical, and social development. They display a high incidence of learning disabilities, suffer more from abuse, and have high rates of injury and illness. Despite numerous initiatives to improve the living circumstances of these children, it is unclear whether these programs have been or will be effective. But the causes of their plight have been identified—they suffer from psychological problems because they live in the favelas, but they do not live there because they are somehow unfit for society.

These children live in Ronciha Favela in Rio de Janeiro. Children from deprived areas stand a high risk of suffering from psychological disorders.

born, the brain is not intact; it continues to develop rapidly—often in spurts—throughout childhood and adolescence. Evidence from studies of animals suggests the brain reorganizes as a result of changes in the levels of hormones (messenger chemicals) during puberty. As a result, problems in brain development may be more easily rectified than once thought.

Second, scientists have shown that brain growth partly depends on exposure to particular stimuli. For some parts of the brain these stimuli must be received at a precise stage of development, while for other parts the stimuli may be effective regardless of the developmental stage at which they occur. By studying the timing and nature of the stimuli, it is possible that developmental psychologists will soon be able to determine the treatments needed to reverse the effects of some neurological disorders.

Third, it has been discovered that even though the brain develops most rapidly early in life, it is capable of change throughout its existence. For example older adults who consistently use their brains to solve problems, play computer games, or work creatively are more likely to retain the use of neural systems that may otherwise deteriorate if the brain is not actively engaged. As with muscular strength, brain power may need regular exercise to stay in shape. So to retain a sharp mind and good memory as old age approaches, the advice is clear—use it or lose it. By further investigating these changes in brain development throughout the human life span, psychologists hope to find treatments that will reduce the deterioration in mental function that is normally associated with senility.

The genetics of psychology

In addition to the rapid progress of research into brain development, scientists are making discoveries about the influence of genetics on a range of psychological attributes. These include intelligence, personality, emotions, and mental illnesses and disorders. Over the next few decades there is likely to be a proliferation of research and applications using these novel genetic techniques, which may lead to new treatments and possibly to cures.

Psychologists have long considered the contribution of genetic factors to human social and emotional development. Years of behavioral studies using identical and nonidentical twins, full and half siblings, and unrelated adoptive and step-siblings have shown that genetic heritage can have a major influence on many psychological attributes, including personality traits (*see* Vol. 5, pp. 142–163).

Although the importance of genetic influences is now universally recognized, how they actually operate to produce psychological characteristics such as personality and emotions is poorly understood. However, there have been recent advances in scientific techniques for acquiring and analyzing human deoxyribonucleic acid (DNA). DNA is the molecule that forms the basis of the genetic code that people inherit from their parents, and scientists can now investigate human DNA for the genetic

HABITUATION AND BRAIN FUNCTIONING

EXPERIMENT

Testing for brain habituation is a useful diagnostic tool for children with pervasive developmental disorders or mental retardation. It can provide a good measure of brain functioning that does not require an assessment of verbal or other communication skills and therefore can be conducted when infants are very young.

Researchers have discovered that if they present something like a sound or a visual signal repeatedly to a healthy infant, the baby's attention to the stimulus gradually decreases; the infant habituates, or gets used to, the stimulus. When a new stimulus, such as a new sound or image, is presented, the infant typically exhibits a dramatic increase in attention—the child notices the change in the stimulus. This is called dishabituation.

People vary widely in the rate at which they show habituation to a repeated stimulus and dishabituation to a new stimulus. This variation is highly predictive of basic neurological development and functional ability. These tests can therefore be used as a simple test of brain health, particularly with infants.

As simple as this test is, it has been shown to be robust over time, and its results do correlate with later intelligence test performances. The discovery of the habituation technique led to the extensive study of cognitive development in infancy and early childhood, and triggered research in this field on other species.

The habituation method also shows promise as a way of testing for brain abnormalities in unborn fetuses. Scientists can use loud sounds outside the womb to measure habituation in healthy fetuses and those with known disorders such as Down syndrome (a genetic disorder that affects mental functioning). Fetuses react to these sounds if they notice them—they may move, and their heart rate changes. The researchers can measure these variables to determine how soon a fetus habituates to these sounds. Healthy fetuses are likely to show normal habituation, while fetuses with Down syndrome show slower habituation or no habituation at all. With further research habituation may soon be used as a diagnostic tool for measuring fetal brain development.

signatures of a variety of traits, including intelligence, schizophrenia, depression, aggression, and dementia.

Most of the psychological research programs emerging from this genetic revolution are concerned with making improvements in diagnosis and new types of treatments. Examples include prenatal tests for Down's syndrome, fragile-X syndrome, and phenylketonuria (see Vol. 5, pp. 142–163). These disorders account for many cases of mental retardation. Several genetic markers for Alzheimer's disease—an incurable disease that causes loss of memory and other cognitive skills in later life—have also been identified. In addition, genetic signatures have been identified as possible causes of attention deficit hyperactivity disorder (ADD).

Geneticists and psychologists hope that many more discoveries are imminent— breakthroughs that may make it possible to identify DNA patterns that show a person's predisposition to psychological maladies such as depression, anxiety disorders, and schizophrenia. Although identifying the cause does not necessarily lead to a cure, research in this field is still an important step in the right direction.

Much remains to be discovered before the benefits of these research projects are fully realized. Most of the research currently conducted is experimental and highly exploratory, and new

These little girls are identical twins. Researchers have used both identical and nonidentical twins extensively to try to shed more light on the "nature versus nurture" question of personality, cognitive development, and psychological disorder. Recent research has also involved the use of genetic sequencing in a bid to resolve these problems.

discoveries are occurring at a rapid rate. Psychologists are only just beginning to appreciate the enormous complexities of genetic influences. In addition, these recent scientific breakthroughs are leading many psychologists to reflect on the ethics of genetic treatments and research. For how long, and in what ways should we store and protect the genetic material of research volunteers? Is it right or wrong to alter people's DNA in order to change their lives according to a psychological preconception of normality? These and many other ethical questions remain the subjects of intense scrutiny and debate.

ADAPTING TO CHANGING TIMES

Psychologists increasingly recognize the importance of studying the rearing environments or "contexts" of child development. The study of changes in contexts has provided them with a mass of information about the ways we adapt to our surroundings. Understanding these adaptations may lead to new treatments that improve the general psychological health of the population.

One of the most astounding contextual changes over the last century has been the improvements in medical technology that have enabled many more "high-risk" infants to survive than ever before. This includes infants that are born prematurely and well below a healthy birthweight. Questions of critical importance about these children and their families must be answered before the impact of these contextual changes on psychological development can be assessed. What, if any, are the long-term

DNA in Psychological Research

The key to heredity is the genetic code, or genome: a sequence of chemicals that determine how cells develop. At the heart of the code is deoxyribonucleic acid, or DNA. Researchers are beginning to study DNA to help them analyze the influence of inherited factors in a range of psychological fields. This allows them to study molecular genetics within the framework of traditional environmentally based studies of development.

One widely used and inexpensive method of DNA harvesting involves the collection of human cells from the mouth. Research participants have the insides of their cheeks scraped gently with cotton swabs that are then placed in a preserving solution in a plastic container. As long as storage conditions are kept optimal, cells obtained in this way can be kept indefinitely and used much later for DNA analysis and research.

DNA is used in psychological research in a variety of ways. If it is collected from a very large group of people, scientists can scan entire sets of human genes and look for associations between particular psychological attributes and particular locations within the genome. Genome scans have already led to many important discoveries, such as the identification of the single gene that causes phenylketonuria (PKU). Infants that are found to have the PKU gene can be treated simply and effectively by a change in diet that greatly reduces the chances that the children will suffer from mental retardation later in life.

Psychologists also can identify "candidate genes" and test their effects on a wide variety of psychological traits. For example, scientists can select specific genes that are already known to code for brain chemicals known as

neurotransmitters, which are linked to some psychological traits. Researchers routinely test for the effects of dopamine and serotonin genes on the symptoms of depression, anxiety, and attention deficit disorders.

Although it will take time, and much more work needs to be done, psychologists are hopeful that genetic research will lead to important discoveries that will greatly improve the tests and treatments for a variety of psychological maladies.

A DNA molecule. The chemicals that form the genetic code in DNA bond together to form a long ladderlike structure. They bond at a slight angle, twisting the structure to form a "double-helix" shape. Scientists have only recently started to implement genetic techniques into traditional psychological research.

results of premature birth or low birthweight? Are there psychological treatments that can ensure better lives for these individuals? When, if ever, is a fetus "too young"; and what size of embryo is "too small"? Should we, as a society, decide where these cutoff points should be and legislate appropriately? If not, who should make these decisions?

In many nations it is now common for babies who are born before 27 weeks gestation or that weigh less than two pounds (0.9 kg) to survive and grow to adulthood. This is due largely to the widespread establishment of neonatal intensive care units (NICUs). These institutions have equipment and trained staff who are able to keep premature babies alive long enough for their bodies and brains to "catch up" in developmental terms. Also, doctors now understand that these high-risk infants should not be isolated, but instead must have frequent physical contact with parents and other caregivers for them to develop normally.

Longer-term studies of high-risk infants, such as the project focusing on the children of Kauai (*see* box below), have demonstrated that some parenting factors are critical for the subsequent health and development of a child. Once an infant is well enough to leave hospital, the mother's health and behavior toward

With increasing numbers of premature babies surviving each year, psychologists are studying the longer-term effects of premature birth on psychological health.

THE ROOTS OF RESILIENCE

CASE STUDY

Many of the world's children and adolescents live without adequate shelter, food, water, or healthcare. But even in situations of extreme deprivation, some children still develop normally. Researchers have long been interested in the roots of resilience—the ability that some of these high-risk children have not only to survive but to thrive. Psychologists hope that the identification of these resiliency factors will lead to new treatments that will dramatically improve the mental health of many high-risk children and their families around the world.

In a famous research program, psychologists Emmy Werner and Ruth Smith studied an entire group of infants born on the Hawaiian island of Kauai in 1955. They followed the children and their families through infancy, adolescence, and into adulthood, and conducted many assessments of a wide range of outcomes.

Of nearly 700 children who were first included in the study, about one-third were known to be at risk of developmental problems. The risks were caused by factors including birth complications, such as premature

birth and low birthweight, poverty, and mentally ill parents. Despite these factors, however, the researchers found that many of these high-risk children developed into healthy, happy adults.

Werner and Smith discovered a specific set of factors that explained why these high-risk infants were thriving. They included having a close sibling relationship, good attention from caregivers in early childhood, strong family ties in the immediate and extended family, and few stressful life events, such as the death of a parent, divorce, or other upheavals.

This study showed that the response of children to deprivation is highly variable—each case is different, and each child must be treated as an individual. By implementing findings such as these, psychologists hope one day to develop prevention programs for high-risk young people from deprived areas. These programs will hopefully produce positive outcomes for other young children who might otherwise suffer from a range of developmental problems.

that infant become extremely important. Mothers who are not depressed, who have low levels of parenting-related stress, and who have ample social and emotional support from their partners, other family members, and friends are likely to be sensitive and responsive to the needs of their children. This maximizes the chances of the infants showing normal emotional, social, and cognitive development.

However, even the most sensitive and nurturing caregiving will not create a child who is psychologically healthy if profound damage has occurred to the central nervous system or other key organs within the infant's body. Babies of low birthweight may face many years of health and developmental problems, causing intense strain for parents and family members alike. As more of these infants survive, higher numbers of families will need increased support from medical and psychological professionals.

The human-computer interface

Another dramatic social change of the last two decades of the 20th century has been the increase in the use of computers and computer games by children and adolescents. Psychologists have studied the effects of this transformation on children's lives. They have also looked at some of the ways these technologies may be used to improve the lives and mental

This girl is chatting with a friend on the Internet. The long-term social and developmental effects of spending hours each day online are the focus of a great deal of research.

health of children and their families. Several questions remain unanswered. What are the long-term psychological consequences of computer and computer game use? Are there benefits for the social, emotional, and cognitive development of children? If so, are there also costs? What specific aspects of these new technologies promote optimal development, and how can we provide more children with these advantages, given that many families cannot afford their own computers?

Computers have become common in many family homes, and are also widely available in schools, community centers, and libraries. They are often connected to the Internet, providing young people with an array of information on a diverse range of topics. Surveys of parents have found that they typically purchase a computer and Internet access for educational purposes. Nonetheless, these studies have shown that computers are primarily a source of entertainment for children and adults alike—computer games and surfing the net are the most common recreational activities of today.

Computer games, although widely available to children of both sexes, tend to be more widely used by boys than by girls. Many of these games require fast thinking, strategy-building, attention, and visual-spatial skills. There is some evidence that playing games that require the use of perceptual and cognitive faculties may help strengthen these skills. Some studies, for example, have suggested that players of computer games have faster reaction times and are better at maintaining their attention than people who do not. Research examining the links between playing computer games and performance at school are less clear, with mixed and inconclusive results. There is also growing interest in the effects of computer use on children's social lives. Computers and computer games have the potential to create problems for children who are already in danger of becoming socially isolated, while the same technologies may provide benefits to children who are not at risk. Although children and adolescents have opportunities to meet others online (some young people describe two clearly differentiated strata of friends—"offline" and "online"), those who spend long periods using computers interact less with friends and family members than they would in the absence of such distractions. Some early research findings suggested that young people who spend many hours each week surfing the net are likely to suffer from depressive symptoms such as feelings of sadness and isolation, although it is unclear whether there is a real causal link between the two.

There is mounting concern about the use of computer video games that depict violence. Studies of the games used most frequently by children and adolescents suggest that nearly all the popular games contain at least some degree of violence. This research also has shown that some of the more violent games can promote aggression in children. However, it is important to remember that young people who are already aggressive are more likely to seek out and enjoy playing these games, so it is difficult to distinguish between cause and effect. Just how the use of these and other video games influences the development of social behavior remains an important question, which future research on computer use and child development will need to address.

CULTURAL DIFFERENCES

While studying adaptations to a changing world, psychologists have also begun to study differences in human development between different cultures (*see* Vol. 1, pp. 152–161). Why do they need to know about and understand these variations?

First, the study of cultural influences may lead to discoveries about specific environmental factors that contribute to psychological development. Psychologists can compare and contrast two different cultural groups in which a particular child-rearing practice is common in one but rare or absent in the other. That enables them to determine the possible effects of particular child-rearing practices on the social, emotional, and cognitive development of children.

Computer games and video consoles almost always include a degree of violence. Some, such as Grand Theft Auto 3, *have been banned in many countries due to their violent content. Psychologists are looking at the long-term effects of games like these on psychological traits such as aggression.*

LESBIAN AND GAY PARENTS

Over the last decade psychologists researching cultural variations in child-rearing practice have broadened their studies to include the development and psychological health of children raised in households with two mothers or two fathers. Are children with lesbian or gay parents psychologically different when compared to the children of heterosexual parents?

Social attitudes to homosexuality have changed radically over the last 30 years, and during the early 1990s psychologists realized that more and more same-sex parent households were forming. There have been relatively few studies to date, and none at all have examined the long-term effects of such family structures. However, the data so far suggest that most of these children do not stand a significantly higher risk of developing social and emotional problems as long as they are part of a stable household.

As with other family structures, healthy psychological development of children living in single-sex households appears to depend on the provision of love, attention, and the opportunities for learning that the children need.

These children have been raised by a same-sex couple. Studies suggest that parent sexuality has little effect on children's psychological development.

Second, diagnostic tests and treatments that are developed in a single cultural context may not work as well or even at all in other societies—the identification of "culture-specific" mechanisms will greatly improve the accuracy of diagnosis and the effectiveness of treatments.

Some now-defunct theories of child development assumed that people grow and learn in the same way because they are all members of the same species, but research in psychology and the related fields of cultural anthropology and sociology has shown that this is not the case. In fact, studies of child-rearing practices in different cultural groups have revealed remarkable variations in the experiences of children and adolescents.

Psychologists have known for years that children show better psychological health and development when they have several adult caregivers to nurture them. Research into parenting in nations such as the United Kingdom and the United States has focused on two-parent families, and especially on the relative contributions of each parent to the care of the child. These studies have shown that in most western cultures there is a consistent pattern of gender differences in parenting. Compared to most mothers, most fathers are less involved in the day-to-day care of their children. They spend less time with them, even when both parents work full time outside the home, and the mother tends to be the preferred parent when a child needs to be comforted. Some of the variations can be ascribed to biological differences between men and women. Mothers are better suited biologically to the child-rearing role, and fathers are biologically predisposed to play a less direct auxiliary role.

However, the conclusion that these differences are due solely to biology has been challenged by cross-cultural research. Recently, psychologists have studied naturally occurring variations in the ways that men and women divide child-rearing tasks in different contexts, ranging from gay- and lesbian-parent households in North America (*see* box p. 159) to polygamous (one person with several partners) communities in Africa. These studies have revealed some surprising information about family structure, gender, and parenting behaviors. Though much remains to be learned, these studies suggest that although family structures adapt to economic, social, and political forces, a child's need for nurturing and attentive caregiving exists in all cultural settings. Both men and

These are the children of Chinese silk-farm laborers. While their parents work, tending the silkworms or making precious silk from the cocoons, a nurse cares for their children. Research suggests that as long as the quality of care is good, young children suffer few ill effects on their psychological well-being as a result of being cared for in a group like this. Quality of care is more important than the relationship of child to caregiver.

women—whether biological parents or not—are capable of meeting this need.

For example, anthropologists have conducted much research on the family structure of the Aka people of Central Africa. In this hunter-gatherer culture fathers spend much more time holding their infants and toddlers than they do in other cultures. Another important difference is the way Aka fathers behave when holding and interacting with their children. Studies of western fathers have demonstrated that a significant amount of the contact with their children involves "rough-and-tumble" play—rollicking games that stimulate the children and strengthen their relationship with the father. Aka fathers engage in very few of these physical behaviors. Instead, Aka mothers and fathers alike spend most of their playtime with their infants in face-to-face social interaction. Aka fathers are more likely to soothe and calm, clean, and show love and affection for their

children than are the mothers. By contrast, the bulk of the mothers' physical contact with their children involves feeding and carrying them. The caregiving behaviors of Aka women and men challenge our western stereotypes of the separate nature of "fathering" and "mothering." Studies such as this undermine the theory that biology alone accounts for differences between genders in parenting.

Investigating group childcare

According to the attachment theory of John Bowlby (1907–1990), infants begin to form strong and enduring emotional bonds with their caregivers (typically their mothers) during the first year of life. The formation of this bond is of critical importance to the child's subsequent psychological development and mental health. For decades, the prevailing view has been that an infant's psychological development may be compromised by frequent, prolonged separations from the mother. At the same time, we have witnessed dramatic changes in social attitudes about the use of group care for infants and preschool children. It is now common for young children to be placed in family day care (small facilities that operate from the proprietor's own home) or day-care centers (large, specialized childcare facilities). Some psychologists have suggested that this shift in childcare practice has placed the mental health of whole generations of children in jeopardy, while others have maintained that this risk has been exaggerated. An intensive research effort is now under way, and comparisons between different cultural groups have been particularly useful in informing this debate.

Researchers have begun to realize that group child rearing is not a new phenomenon, and that there are many differences between the types of care used

Babies form strong ties with their mothers over the first year of life. Without this important bonding, the psychological development of the infant can be affected.

CHILDCARE AND NATION: PSYCHOLOGY AND SOCIAL POLICY

Psychologists who study cultural variations in childcare have discovered that it is impossible to ignore the role of government social policy; this is a good example of how psychology and politics are often linked. Many psychologists now argue that these national social policy differences have a direct effect on the daily lives and psychological development of children.

In many European nations group childcare for infants under one year of age is rare because governments provide subsidies to families. These subsidies allow parents to take time off work to care for their infants. By contrast, in the United States government and society place strong emphasis on childcare being the responsibility of employers and parents. There is no

government-mandated paid maternity leave, although employees have a limited period of family leave during which their jobs are protected. Therefore it is not uncommon for infants in the United States to be placed in group childcare settings so that their mothers can return to work—sometimes when the children are as young as two months old.

This has led to sometimes-bitter public debate among psychologists, public health officials, and child advocates. In the future researchers will be able to inform this debate by studying cultural differences in childcare practices. This will allow all children to receive the high-quality care they need, regardless of the society in which they happen to have been born.

A caregiver plays with preschool children at a daycare center. Many European governments subsidize a period of maternity leave before and after birth, but this does not happen in the United States. Thus psychologists are studying the influence on psychological attributes in later life of this early maternal separation.

by various cultural groups and nations. One example of group childcare emerged after 1948 in the kibbutzim of Israel. (A kibbutz—plural kibbutzim—is a farm or factory in which all wealth is held in common, and all the children living there are reared collectively.) On a kibbutz the whole community shares the provision of services, food, and shelter, and there is a strong emphasis on an equal distribution of wealth. There may be rules prohibiting

or minimizing private ownership of material goods. From early in their lives children living on a kibbutz spend lots of time during the day in groups with a care-giver. Shared care-giving for children is a way of life that is consistent with the kibbutzim philosophy, with its emphasis on equality and egalitarianism.

The long-standing presence of group childcare in Israeli kibbutzim, along with the rapid increases in group childcare in

other nations such as the United States, has led psychologists to study how these contexts influence the psychological development of children. Researchers have found that children living on a kibbutz do not stand a higher risk of relationship problems with their parents than other Israeli children. Nor does the kibbutz lifestyle put them at a higher risk of behavioral or emotional problems. Similarly, studies of the effects of group childcare on child development in North America and Europe suggest that group care of sufficiently good quality does not negatively affect development.

Research suggests that the quality of care matters more than the social setting, or the relationship of the child to the caregiver. A bad parent may put a child at greater risk of developmental problems than a good nanny, and long days spent in a communal nursery may be less

A kibbutz beside the sea of Galilee in Israel. People who live on a kibbutz share work, food, and material possessions, and their children are cared for by the community from an early age.

harmful than the constant attention of cruel or inadequate parents.

However, other research projects have shown that millions of children around the world are exposed to inadequate childcare in group settings. Solving this conundrum is one of the biggest challenges faced by developmental psychologists in the 21st century.

CONNECTIONS

- Brain-imaging Techniques: Volume 1, pp. 96–103
- Cross-cultural Psychology: Volume 1, pp. 152–161
- Biology of the Brain: Volume 2, pp. 20–39
- People as Social Animals: Volume 5, pp. 6–27
- Relating to Others: Volume 5, pp. 28–49
- Nature and Nurture: Volume 5, pp. 142–163
- Personality: Volume 5, pp. 94–117
- Abnormality in Development: Volume 6, pp. 68–91

Set Glossary

abnormality Within abnormal psychology abnormality is the deviation from normal or expected behavior, generally involving maladaptive responses and personal distress both to the individuals with abnormal behavior and to those around them.

abnormal psychology The study and treatment of mental disorders.

acquisition The process by which something, such as a skill, habit, or language, is learned.

adaptation A change in behavior or structure that increases the survival chances of a species. Adjective: adaptive

addiction A state of dependence on a drug or a particular pattern of behavior.

adjustment disorder A mental disorder in which a patient is unable to adjust properly to a stressful life change.

affect A mood, emotion, or feeling. An affect is generally a shorter-lived and less-pronounced emotion than mood.

affective disorder A group of mental disorders, such as depression and bipolar 1 disorder, that are characterized by pronounced and often prolonged changes of mood.

agnosia A group of brain disorders involving impaired ability to recognize or interpret sensory information.

Alzheimer's disease A progressive and irreversible dementia in which the gradual destruction of brain tissue results in memory loss, impaired cognitive function, and personality change.

amnesia A partial or complete loss of memory.

amygdala An almond-shaped structure located in the front of the brain's temporal lobe that is part of the limbic system. Sometimes called the amygdaloid complex or the amygdaloid nucleus, the amygdala plays an important role in emotional behavior and motivation.

anorexia nervosa An eating disorder in which patients (usually young females) become obsessed with the idea that they are overweight and experience dramatic weight loss by not eating enough.

antidepressants A type of medication used to treat depression.

antianxiety drugs A type of medication used to treat anxiety disorders.

antipsychotic drugs A type of medication used to treat psychotic disorders such as schizophrenia. Sometimes known as neuroleptics.

anxiety disorder A group of mental disorders involving worry or distress.

anxiolytics *See* antianxiety drugs

aphasia A group of brain disorders that involve a partial or complete loss of language ability.

arousal A heightened state of awareness, behavior, or physiological function.

artificial intelligence (AI) A field of study that combines elements of cognitive psychology and computer science in an attempt to develop intelligent machines.

attachment theory A theory that describes how infants form emotional bonds with the adults they are close to.

attention The process by which someone can focus on particular sensory information by excluding other, less immediately relevant information.

attention deficit disorder (ADD) A mental disorder in which the patient (usually a child) is hyperactive, impulsive, and unable to concentrate properly.

autism A mental disorder, first apparent in childhood, in which patients are self-absorbed, socially withdrawn, and engage in repetitive patterns of behavior.

automatization The process by which complex behavior eventually becomes automatic. Such a process may be described as having automaticity or being automatized.

autonomic nervous system A part of the nervous system that controls many of the body's self-regulating (involuntary or automatic) functions.

aversion therapy A method of treating patients, especially those suffering from drink or drug addiction, by subjecting them to painful or unpleasant experiences.

axon Extension of the cell body of a neuron that transmits impulses away from the body of the neuron.

behavioral therapy A method of treating mental disorders that concentrates on modifying abnormal behavior rather than on the underlying causes of that behavior.

behaviorism A school of psychology in which easily observable and measurable behavior is considered to be the only proper subject of scientific study. Noun: behaviorist

bipolar I disorder A mental (affective) disorder involving periods of depression (depressed mood) and periods of mania (elevated mood).

body image The way in which a person perceives their own body or imagines it is perceived by other people.

body language The signals people send out to other people (usually unconsciously) through their gestures, posture, and other types of nonverbal communication.

Broca's area A region of the brain (usually located in the left hemisphere) that is involved with processing language.

bulimia nervosa An eating disorder in which patients consume large amounts of food in binges, then use laxatives or self-induced vomiting to prevent themselves putting on weight.

CAT scan *See* CT

causality The study of the causes of events or the connection between causes and effects.

central nervous system The part of the body's nervous system comprising the brain and spinal cord.

cerebellum A cauliflower-shaped structure at the back of the brain underneath the cerebral hemispheres that coordinates body movements.

cerebral cortex The highly convoluted outer surface of the brain's cerebrum.

cerebrum The largest part of the brain, consisting of the two cerebral hemispheres and their associated structures.

classical conditioning A method of associating a stimulus and a response that do not normally accompany one another. In Pavlov's well-known classical conditioning experiment dogs were trained so that they salivated (the conditioned response or CR) when Pavlov rang a bell (the conditioned stimulus or CS). Normally, dogs salivate

(an unconditioned response or UR) only when food is presented to them (an unconditioned stimulus or US).

clinical psychology An area of psychology concerned with the study and treatment of abnormal behavior.

cognition A mental process that involves thinking, reasoning, or some other type of mental information processing. Adjective: cognitive

cognitive behavioral therapy (CBT) An extension of behavioral therapy that involves treating patients by modifying their abnormal thought patterns as well as their behavior.

cognitive psychology An area of psychology that seeks to understand how the brain processes information.

competency In psycholinguistics the representation of the abstract rules of a language, such as its grammar.

conditioned stimulus/response (CS/CR) *See* classical conditioning

conditioning *See* classical conditioning; instrumental conditioning

connectionism A computer model of cognitive processes such as learning and memory. Connectionist models are based on a large network of "nodes" and the connections between them. Adjective: connectionist

consciousness A high-level mental process responsible for the state of self-awareness that people feel. Consciousness is thought by some researchers to direct human behavior and by others simply to be a byproduct of that behavior.

cortex *See* cerebral cortex

cross-cultural psychology The comparison of behavior, such as language

acquisition or nonverbal communication, between different peoples or cultures.

cross-sectional study An experimental method in which a large number of subjects are studied at a particular moment or period in time. Compare longitudinal study

CT (computed tomography) A method of producing an image of the brain's tissue using X-ray scanning, which is commonly used to detect brain damage. Also called CAT (computerized axial tomography).

culture-specific A behavior found only in certain cultures and not observed universally in all humankind.

declarative knowledge A collection of facts about the world and other things that people have learned. Compare procedural knowledge

declarative memory *See* explicit memory

defense mechanism A type of thinking or behavior that a person employs unconsciously to protect themselves from anxiety or unwelcome feelings.

deficit A missing cognitive function whose loss is caused by a brain disorder.

delusion A false belief that a person holds about themselves or the world around them. Delusions are characteristic features of psychotic mental illnesses such as schizophrenia.

dementia A general loss of cognitive functions usually caused by brain damage. Dementia is often, but not always, progressive (it becomes worse with time).

Dementia of the Alzheimer's type (DAT) See Alzheimer's disease

dendrite A treelike projection of a neuron's cell body that conducts nerve impulses toward the cell body.

dependency An excessive reliance on an addictive substance, such as a drug, or on the support of another person.

depression An affective mental disorder characterized by sadness, low self-esteem, inadequacy, and related symptoms.

desensitization A gradual reduction in the response to a stimulus when it is presented repeatedly over a period of time.

developmental psychology An area of psychology concerned with how people develop throughout their lives, but usually concentrating on how behavior and cognition develop during childhood.

discrimination In perception the ability to distinguish between two or more stimuli. In social psychology and sociology unequal treatment of people based on prejudice.

dysgraphia A brain disorder involving an ability to write properly.

dyslexia Brain disorders that disrupt a person's ability to read.

eating disorders A group of mental disorders that involve disturbed eating patterns or appetite.

echoic memory See sensory memory

ego The central part of a person's self. In Freudian psychology the ego manages the balance between a person's primitive, instinctive needs and the often conflicting demands of the world around them.

egocentric A person who is excessively preoccupied with themselves at the expense of the people and the world around them.

eidetic An accurate and persistent form of visual memory that is generally uncommon in adults (often misnamed "photographic memory").

electroconvulsive therapy (ECT) A treatment for severe depression that involves passing a brief and usually relatively weak electric shock through the front of a patient's skull.

electroencephalogram (EEG) A graph that records the changing electrical activity in a person's brain from electrodes attached to the scalp.

emotion A strong mood or feeling. Also a reaction to a stimulus that prepares the body for action.

episodic memory A type of memory that records well-defined events or episodes in a person's life. Compare semantic memory

ethnocentricity The use of a particular ethnic group to draw conclusions about wider society or humankind as a whole.

event-related potential (ERP) A pattern of electrical activity (the potential) produced by a particular stimulus (the event). EVPs are often recorded from the skull using electrodes.

evoked potential See event-related potential (ERP)

evolution A theory suggesting that existing organisms have developed from earlier ones by processes that include natural selection (dubbed "survival of the fittest") and genetic mutation.

evolutionary psychology An approach to psychology that uses the theory of evolution to explain the mind and human behavior.

explicit memory A type of memory containing information that is available to conscious recognition and recall.

flashbulb memory A very clear and evocative memory of a particular moment or event.

fMRI (functional magnetic resonance imaging) An MRI-based scanning technique that can produce images of the brain while it is engaged in cognitive activities.

functionalism An approach to psychology that concentrates on the functions played by parts of the mind and human behavior.

generalized anxiety disorder (GAD) A type of nonspecific anxiety disorder with symptoms that include worry, irritability, and tension.

genes A functional unit of the chromosome that determines how traits are passed on and expressed from generation to generation. Adjective: genetic

Gestalt psychology A psychology school that emphasizes the importance of appreciating phenomena as structured wholes in areas such as perception and learning, as opposed to breaking them down into their components. Most influential in the mid-1900s.

gray matter The parts of the nervous system that contain mainly nerve cell bodies.

habituation See desensitization

hallucination A vivid but imaginary perceptual experience that occurs purely in the mind, not in reality.

heritability The proportion of observed variation for a trait in a specific population that can be attributed to genetic factors rather than environmental ones. Generally expressed as a ratio of genetically caused variation to total variation.

hippocamus A part of the limbic system in the temporal lobe that is thought to play an important role in the formation of memories.

Humanism A philosophy that stresses the importance of human interests and values.

hypothalamus A small structure at the base of the brain that controls the autonomic nervous system.

hysteria A type of mental disturbance that may include symptoms such as hallucinations and emotional outbursts.

implicit memory A type of memory not normally available to conscious awareness. Sometimes also known as procedural or nondeclarative memory. Compare explicit memory

imprinting A type of learning that occurs in a critical period shortly after birth, such as when chicks learn to accept a human in place of their real mother.

individual psychology An approach to psychology that focuses on the differences between individuals. Also a theory advanced by Alfred Adler based on the idea of overcoming inferiority.

information processing In cognitive psychology the theory that the mind operates something like a computer, with sensory information processed either in a series of discrete stages or in parallel by something like a connectionist network.

ingroup A group whose members feel a strong sense of collective identity and act to exclude other people (the outgroup).

innate A genetically determined trait that is present at birth, as opposed to something that is acquired by learning.

instinct An innate and automatic response to a particular stimulus that usually involves no rational thought.

instrumental conditioning A type of conditioning in which reinforcement occurs only when an organism makes a certain, desired response. Instrumental

conditioning occurs, for example, when a pigeon is trained to peck a lever to receive a pellet of food.

internalize To make internal, personal, or subjective; to take in and make an integral part of one's attitudes or beliefs:

introspection A behaviorist technique of studying the mind by observing one's own thought processes.

language acquisition device (LAD) According to linguist Noam Chomsky, a part of the brain that is preprogrammed with a universal set of grammatical rules that can construct the rules of a specific language according to the environment it is exposed to.

libido The sexual drive.

limbic system A set of structures in the brain stem, including the hippocampus and the amygdala, that lie below the corpus callosum. It is involved in emotion, motivation, behavior, and various functions of the autonomic nervous system.

long-term memory A type of memory in which information is retained for long periods after being deeply processed. Generally used to store events and information from the past. Compare short-term memory

longitudinal study An experimental method that follows a small group of subjects over a long period of time. Compare cross-sectional study

maladaptive Behavior is considered maladapative or dysfunctional if it has a negative effect on society or on a person's ability to function in society.

medical model A theory that mental disorders, like diseases, have specific underlying medical causes, which must be addressed if treatment is to be effective.

mental disorder A psychiatric illness such as schizophrenia, anxiety, or depression.

metacognition The study by an individual of their own thought processes. *See also* introspection

mnemonic A technique that can be used to remember information or improve memory.

modeling The technique by which a person observes some ideal form of behavior (a role model) and then attempts to copy it. In artificial intelligence (AI) people attempt to build computers that model human cognition.

modularity A theory that the brain is composed of a number of modules that occupy relatively specific areas and that carry out relatively specific tasks.

morpheme The smallest unit of a language that carries meaning.

motor neuron *See* neuron.

MRI (magnetic resonance imaging) A noninvasive scanning technique that uses magnetic fields to produce detailed images of body tissue.

nature–nurture A long-running debate over whether genetic factors (nature) or environmental factors (nurture) are most important in different aspects of behavior.

neuron A nerve cell, consisting of a cell body (soma), an axon, and one or more dendrites. Motor (efferent) neurons produce movement when they fire by carrying information *from* the central nervous system *to* the muscles and glands; sensory (afferent) neurons carry information *from* the senses *to* the central nervous system.

neuropsychology An area of psychology that studies the connections between parts of the brain and neural processes, on one hand, and different cognitive processes and types of behavior, on the other.

neurotransmitter A substance that carries chemical "messages" across the synaptic gaps between the neurons of the brain.

nonverbal communication The way in which animals communicate without language (verbal communication), using such things as posture, tone of voice, and facial expressions.

operant conditioning *See* instrumental conditioning

outgroup The people who do not belong to an ingroup.

parallel processing A type of cognition in which information is processed in several different ways at once. In serial processing information passes through one stage of processing at a time.

peripheral nervous system All the nerves and nerve processes that connect the central nervous system with receptors, muscles, and glands.

personality The collection of character traits that makes one person different from another.

personality disorder A group of mental disorders in which aspects of someone's personality make it difficult for them to function properly in society.

PET (positron emission tomography) A noninvasive scanning technique that makes images of the brain according to levels of metabolic activity inside it.

phenomenology A philosophy based on the study of immediate experiences.

phobia A strong fear of a particular object (such as snakes) or social situation.

phoneme A basic unit of spoken language.

phrenology An early approach to psychology that studied the relationship between areas of the brain (based on skull shape) and mental functions. Phrenology has since been discredited.

physiology A type of biology concerned with the workings of cells, organs, and tissues.

positive punishment A type of conditioning in which incorrect responses are punished.

positive reinforcement A type of conditioning in which correct responses are rewarded.

primary memory *See* short-term memory

probability The likelihood of something happening.

procedural knowledge The practical knowledge of how to do things ("know-how"). Compare declarative knowledge

prosody A type of nonverbal communication in which language is altered by such things as the pitch of someone's voice and their intonation.

psyche The soul or mind of a person or a driving force behind their personality.

psychiatry The study, classification, and treatment of mental disorders.

psychoanalysis A theory of behavior and an approach to treating mental disorders pioneered by Austrian neurologist Sigmund Freud. Adjective: psychoanalytic

psychogenic A mental disorder that is psychological (as opposed to physical) in origin.

psycholinguistics The study of language-related behavior, including how the brain acquires and processes language.

psychosurgery A type of brain surgery designed to treat mental disorders.

psychotherapy A broad range of treatments for mental disorders based on different kinds of interaction between a patient and a therapist.

psychosis A mental state characterized by disordered personality and loss of contact with reality that affects normal social functioning. Psychosis is a feature of psychotic disorders, such as schizophrenia. Adjective: psychotic

reaction time The time taken for the subject in an experiment to respond to a stimulus.

recall The process by which items are recovered from memory. Compare recognition

recognition The process by which a person realizes they have previously encountered a particular object or event. Compare recall

reductionism A philosophy based on breaking complex things into their individual components. Also, an attempt to explain high-level sciences (such as psychology) in terms of lower-level sciences (such as chemistry or physics).

reflex An automatic response to a stimulus (a "knee-jerk" reaction).

reflex arc The neural circuit thought to be responsible for the control of a reflex.

rehearsing The process by which a person repeats information to improve its chances of being stored in memory.

representation A mental model based on perceptions of the world.

repression In psychoanalysis an unconscious mental process that keeps thoughts out of conscious awareness.

response The reaction to a stimulus.

reuptake The reabsorption of a neurotransmitter from the place where it was produced.

risk aversion A tendency not to take risks even when they may have beneficial results.

schema An abstract mental plan that serves as a guide to action or a more general mental representation.

schizophrenia A mental disorder characterized by hallucinations and disordered thought patterns in which a patient becomes divorced from reality. It is a type of psychotic disorder.

secondary memory *See* long-term memory

selective attention *See* attention

self-concept The ideas and feelings that people hold about themselves.

semantic memory A type of long-term memory that stores information based on its content or meaning. Compare episodic memory

senses The means by which people perceive things. The five senses are vision, hearing, smell, touch, and taste.

sensory memory An information store that records sensory impressions for a short period of time before they are processed more thoroughly.

sensory neuron *See* neuron

serotonin A neurotransmitter in the central nervous system that plays a key role in affective (mood) disorders, sleep, and the perception of pain. Serotonin is also known as 5-hydroxytryptamine (5-HT).

shaping A type of conditioning in which behavior is gradually refined toward some ideal form by successive approximations.

short-term memory A memory of very limited capacity in which sensory inputs are held before being processed more deeply and passing into long-term memory. Compare long-term memory

social cognition An area of psychology that combines elements of social and cognitive psychology in an attempt to understand how people think about themselves in relation to the other people around them.

social Darwinism A theory that society behaves according to Darwinian principles, with the most successful members thriving at the expense of the least successful ones.

social psychology An area of psychology that explores how individuals behave in relation to other people and to society as a whole.

sociobiology A theory that seeks to explain social behavior through biological approaches, notably the theory of evolution. *See also* evolutionary psychology

somatic Something that relates to the body as opposed to the mind; something physical as opposed to something mental.

stereopsis The process by which the brain assembles one 3-D image by combining a pair of 2-D images from the eyes.

stimulus A type of sensory input that provokes a response.

subject The person studied in a psychological experiment.

synapse The region across which nerve impulses are transmitted from one neuron to another. It includes the synaptic cleft (a gap) and the sections of the cell membranes on either side of the cleft. They are called the presynaptic and postsynaptic membranes.

synesthesia A process by which the stimulation of one sense (such as hearing a sound) produces a different kind of sensory impression (such as seeing a color).

thalamus A structure in the forebrain that passes sensory information on to the cerebral cortex.

theory of mind The realization by an individual (such as a growing child, for example) that other people have thoughts and mental processes of their own. It is universally accepted that humans have a theory of mind, and research has shown that some other animals, such as chimpanzees and dolphins, might also have a theory of mind, but this is still debated. Theory of mind is of interest to developmental psychologists since it is not something people are born with, but something that develops in infancy.

tranquilizers A type of medication with sedative, muscle-relaxant, or similar properties. Minor tranquilizers are also known as antianxiety or anxiolytic drugs; major tranquilizers are also known as antipsychotic drugs.

unconditioned stimulus/response (US/UR) *See* classical conditioning

unconscious In psychoanalytic and related theories the area of the mind that is outside conscious awareness and recall but that informs the contents of such things as dreams. In general usage *unconscious* simply refers to automatic cognitive processes that we are not aware of or the lack of consciousness (that is, "awareness") at times such as during sleep.

working memory *See* short-term memory

Resources

Further Reading

Altmann, G. T. M. *The Ascent of Babel: An Exploration of Language, Mind, and Understanding.* Cambridge, MA: Oxford University Press, 1999.

American Psychiatric Association. *Diagnostic and Statistical Manual of Mental Disorders, 4th edition, Text Revision.* Washington, DC: American Psychiatric Press, 2000.

Argyle, M. *The Psychology of Interpersonal Behaviour (5th edition).* London, UK: Penguin, 1994.

Asher, S. R. and Coie, J. D. (eds.). *Peer Rejection in Childhood.* Cambridge, UK: Cambridge University Press, 1990.

Atkinson, R. L. *et al. Hilgard's Introduction to Psychology (13th edition).* London, UK: International Thomson Publishing, 1999.

Barnouw, V. *Culture and Personality.* Chicago, IL: Dorsey Press, 1985.

Baron, J. *Thinking and Deciding.* Cambridge, UK: Cambridge University Press, 1994.

Barry, M. A. S. *Visual Intelligence: Perception, Image, and Manipulation in Visual Communication.* Albany, NY: State University of New York Press, 1997.

Beck, J. *Cognitive Therapy: Basics and Beyond.* London, UK: The Guildford Press, 1995.

Bickerton, D. *Language and Species.* Chicago, IL: The University of Chicago Press, 1990.

Blackburn, I. M. and Davison, K. *Cognitive Therapy for Depression and Anxiety: A Practitioner's Guide.* Oxford, UK: Blackwell, 1995.

Boden, M. A. *Piaget (2nd edition).* London, UK: Fontana Press, 1994.

Brehm, S. S., Kassin, S. M., and Fein, S. *Social Psychology (4th edition).* Boston, MA: Houghton Mifflin, 1999.

Brody, N. *Intelligence (2nd edition).* San Diego, CA: Academic Press, 1997.

Brown, D. S. *Learning a Living: A Guide to Planning Your Career and Finding a Job for People with Learning Disabilities, Attention Deficit Disorder, and Dyslexia.* Bethesda, MD: Woodbine House, 2000.

Bruhn, A. R. *Earliest Childhood Memories.* New York: Praeger, 1990.

Buunk, B. P. "Affiliation, Attraction and Close Relationships." *In* M. Hewstone and W. Stroebe (eds.), *Introduction to Social Psychology: A European Perspective.* Oxford, UK: Blackwell, 2001.

Cacioppo, J. T., Tassinary, L. G., and Berntson, G. G. (eds.). *Handbook of Psychophysiology (2nd edition).* New York: Cambridge University Press, 2000.

Cardwell, M. *Dictionary of Psychology.* Chicago, IL: Fitzroy Dearborn Publishers, 1999

Carson, R. C. and Butcher, J. N. *Abnormal Psychology and Modern Life (9th edition).* New York: HarperCollins Publishers, 1992.

Carter, R. *Mapping the Mind.* Berkeley, CA: University of California Press, 1998.

Cavan, S. *Recovery from Drug Addiction.* New York: Rosen Publishing Group, 2000.

Clarke-Stewart, A. *Daycare.* Cambridge, MA: Harvard University Press, 1993.

Cohen, G. *The Psychology of Cognition (2nd edition).* San Diego, CA: Academic Press, 1983.

Cramer, D. *Close Relationships: The Study of Love and Friendship.* New York: Arnold, 1998.

Daly, M. and Wilson, M. *Homicide.* New York: Aldine de Gruyter, 1988.

Davis, R. D., Braun, E. M., and Smith, J. M. *The Gift of Dyslexia: Why Some of the Smartest People Can't Read and How They Can Learn.* New York: Perigee, 1997.

Davison, G. C. and Neal, J. M. *Abnormal Psychology.* New York: John Wiley and Sons, Inc., 1994.

Dawkins, R. *The Selfish Gene.* New York: Oxford Universty Press, 1976.

Dennett, D. C. *Darwin's Dangerous Idea: Evolution and the Meanings of Life.* Carmichael, CA: Touchstone Books, 1996.

Dobson, C. *et al. Understanding Psychology.* London, UK: Weidenfeld and Nicolson, 1982.

Duck, S. *Meaningful Relationships: Talking, Sense, and Relating.* Thousand Oaks, CA: Sage Publications, 1994.

Durie, M. H. "Maori Psychiatric Admissions: Patterns, Explanations and Policy Implications." *In* J. Spicer, A. Trlin, and J. A. Walton (eds.), *Social Dimensions of Health and Disease: New Zealand Perspectives.* Palmerston North, NZ: Dunmore Press, 1994.

Eliot, L. *What's Going on in There? How the Brain and Mind Develop in the First Five Years of Life.* New York: Bantam Books, 1999.

Eysenck, M. (ed.). *The Blackwell Dictionary of Cognitive Psychology.* Cambridge, MA: Blackwell, 1991.

Faherty, C. and Mesibov, G. B. *Asperger's: What Does It Mean to Me?* Arlington, TX: Future Horizons, 2000.

Fernando, S. *Mental Health in a Multi-Ethnic Society: A Multi-Disciplinary Handbook.* New York: Routledge, 1995.

Fiske, S. T. and Taylor, S. E. *Social Cognition (2nd Edition).* New York: Mcgraw-Hill, 1991.

Franken, R. E. *Human Motivation (5th edition).* Belmont, CA: Wadsworth Thomson Learning, 2002.

Freud, S. and Brill, A. A. *The Basic Writings of Sigmund Freud.* New York: Modern Library, 1995.

Gardner, H. *The Mind's New Science: A History of the Cognitive Revolution.* New York: Basic Books, 1985.

Garnham, A. and Oakhill, J. *Thinking and Reasoning.* Cambridge, MA: Blackwell, 1994.

Gaw, A. C. *Culture, Ethnicity, and Mental Illness.* Washington, DC: American Psychiatric Press, 1992.

Giacobello, J. *Everything You Need to Know about Anxiety and Panic Attacks.* New York: Rosen Publishing Group, 2000.

Gazzaniga, M. S. *The Mind's Past.* Berkeley, CA: University of California Press, 1998.

Gazzaniga, M. S. (ed.). *The New Cognitive Neurosciences (2nd edition).* Cambridge, MA: MIT Press, 2000.

Gazzaniga, M. S., Ivry, R. B., and Mangun, G. R. *Cognitive Neuroscience: The Biology of the Mind (2nd edition).* New York: Norton, 2002.

Gernsbacher, M. A. (ed.). *Handbook of Psycholinguistics.* San Diego, CA: Academic Press, 1994.

Gigerenzer, G. *Adaptive Thinking: Rationality in the Real World.* New York: Oxford University Press, 2000.

Goodglass, H. *Understanding Aphasia.* San Diego, CA: Academic Press, 1993.

Gordon, M. *Jumpin' Johnny Get Back to Work! A Child's Guide to ADHD/Hyperactivity.* DeWitt, NY: GSI Publications Inc., 1991.

Gordon, M. A *I Would if I Could: A Teenager's Guide to ADHD/Hyperactivity.* DeWitt, NY: GSI Publications Inc., 1992.

Goswami, U. *Cognition in Children.* London, UK: Psychology Press, 1998.

Graham, H. *The Human Face of Psychology: Humanistic Psychology in Its Historical, Social, and Cultural Context.* Milton Keynes, UK: Open University Press, 1986.

Grandin, T. *Thinking in Pictures: And Other Reports from my Life with Autism.* New York: Vintage Books, 1996.

Greenberger, D. and Padesky, C. *Mind over Mood.* New York: Guilford Publications, 1995.

Groeger, J. A. *Memory and Remembering: Everyday Memory in Context.* New York: Longman, 1997.

Gross, R. and Humphreys, P. *Psychology: The Science of Mind and Behaviour.* London, UK: Hodder Arnold, 1993.

Halford, G. S. *Children's Understanding: The Development of Mental Models.* Hillsdale, NJ: Lawrence Erlbaum Associates, 1993.

Harley, T. A. *The Psychology of Language: From Data to Theory (2nd edition).* Hove, UK: Psychology Press, 2001.

Harris, G. G. *Casting out Anger: Religion among the Taita of Kenya.* New York: Cambridge University Press, 1978.

Hayes, N. *Psychology in Perspective (2nd edition).* New York: Palgrave, 2002.

Hearst, E. *The First Century of Experimental Psychology.* Hillsdale, NJ: Lawrence Erlbaum Associates, 1979.

Hecht, T. *At Home in the Street: Street Children of Northeast Brazil.* New York: Cambridge University Press, 1998.

Hetherington, E. M. *Coping with Divorce, Single Parenting, and Remarriage: A Risk and Resiliency Perspective.* Mawah, NJ: Lawrence Erlbaum Associates, 1999.

Higbee, K. L. *Your Memory: How It Works and How to Improve It (2nd edition).* New York: Paragon 1993.

Hinde, R. A. *Individuals, Relationships and Culture: Links between Ethology and the Social Sciences.* Cambridge, UK: Cambridge University Press, 1987.

Hogdon, L. A. *Solving Behavior Problems in Autism.* Troy, MI: Quirkroberts Publishing, 1999.

Hogg, M. A. (ed.). *Social Psychology.* Thousand Oaks, CA: Sage Publications, 2002.

Holden, G. W. *Parents and the Dynamics of Child Rearing.* Boulder, CO: Westview Press, 1997.

Holmes, J. *John Bowlby and Attachment Theory.* New York: Routledge, 1993.

Hughes, H. C. *Sensory Exotica: A World Beyond Human Experience.* Cambridge, MA: MIT Press, 1999.

Hyde, M. O. and Setano, J. F. *When the Brain Dies First.* New York: Franlin Watts Inc., 2000.

Ingersoll, B. D. *Distant Drums, Different Drummers: A Guide for Young People with ADHD.* Plantation, FL: A.D.D. WareHouse, 1995.

Jencks, C. and Phillips, M. *The Black-White Test Score Gap.* Washington, DC: Brookings Institution Press, 1998.

Johnson, M. J. *Developmental Cognitive Neuroscience.* Cambridge, MA: Blackwell, 1997.

Johnson, M. H. and Morton, J. *Biology and Cognitive Development. The Case of Face Recognition.* Cambridge, MA: Blackwell, 1991.

Johnson-Laird, P. N. *The Computer and the Mind: An Introduction to Cognitive Science.* Cambridge, MA: Harvard University Press, 1988.

Jusczyk, P. W. *The Discovery of Spoken Language.* Cambridge, MA: MIT Press, 1997.

Kalat, J. W. *Biological Psychology (7th edition).* Belmont, CA: Wadsworth Thomson Learning, 2001.

Kaplan, H. I. and Sadock, B. J. *Synopsis of Psychiatry: Behavioral Sciences, Clinical Psychiatry.* Philadelphia, PA: Lippincott, Williams and Wilkins, 1994.

Karen, R. *Becoming Attached: First Relationships and How They Shape Our Capacity to Love.* New York: Oxford University Press, 1998.

Kirk, S. A. and Kutchins, H. *The Selling of DSM: The Rhetoric of Science in Psychiatry.* New York: Aldine de Gruyter, 1992.

Kinney, J. *Clinical Manual of Substance Abuse.* St. Louis, MO: Mosby, 1995.

Kleinman, A. *Rethinking Psychiatry: From Cultural Category to Personal Experience.* New York: Free Press, 1988.

Kosslyn, S. M. and Koenig, O. *Wet Mind: The New Cognitive Neuroscience.* New York: Free Press, 1992.

Kutchins, H. and Kirk, S. A. *Making Us Crazy: DSM: The Psychiatric Bible and the Creation of Mental Disorders.* New York: Free Press, 1997.

LaBruzza, A. L. *Using DSM-IV; A Clinician's Guide to Psychiatric Diagnosis.* St. Northvale, NJ: Jason Aronson Inc., 1994.

Leahey, T. A. *A History of Psychology: Main Currents in Psychological Thought (5th edition).* Upper Saddle River, NJ: Prentice Hall, 2000.

LeDoux, J. *The Emotional Brain.* New York: Simon and Schuster, 1996.

Levelt, W. J. M. *Speaking: From Intention to Articulation.* Cambridge, MA: MIT Press, 1989.

Lewis, M. and Haviland-Jones, J. M. (eds.). *Handbook of Emotions (2nd edition).* New York: Guilford Press, 2000.

Lowisohn, J. H. *et al. Substance Abuse: A Comprehensive Textbook (3rd edition).* Baltimore, MD: Williams & Wilkins, 1997.

McCabe, D. *To Teach a Dyslexic.* Clio, MI: AVKO Educational Research, 1997.

McCorduck, P. *Machines Who Think: A Personal Inquiry into the History and Prospects of Artificial Intelligence.* San Francisco: W. H. Freeman, 1979.

McIlveen, R. and Gross, R. *Biopsychology (5th edition).* Boston, MA: Allyn and Bacon, 2002.

McLachlan, J. *Medical Embryology.* Reading, MA: Addison-Wesley Publishing Co., 1994.

Manstead, A. S. R. and Hewstone M. (eds.). *The Blackwell Encyclopaedia of Social Psychology.* Oxford, UK: Blackwell, 1996.

Marsella, A. J., DeVos, G., and Hsu, F. L. K. (eds.). *Culture and Self: Asian and Western Perspectives.* New York: Routledge, 1988.

Matlin, M. W. *The Psychology of Women.* New York: Harcourt College Publishers, 2000.

Matsumoto, D. R. *People: Psychology from a Cultural Perspective.* Pacific Grove, CA: Brooks/Cole Publishing, 1994.

Matsumoto, D. R. *Culture and Modern Life.* Pacific

Grove, CA: Brooks/Cole Publishing, 1997.

Mazziotta, J .C., Toga, A. W., and Frackowiak, R. S. J. (eds.). *Brain Mapping: The Disorders.* San Diego, CA: Academic Press, 2000.

Nadeau, K. G., Littman, E., and Quinn, P. O. *Understanding Girls with ADHD.* Niagara Falls, NY: Advantage Books, 2000.

Nadel, J. and Camioni, L. (eds.). *New Perspectives in Early Communicative Development.* New York: Routledge, 1993.

Nobus, D. *Jacques Lacan and the Freudian Practice of Psychoanalysis.* Philadelphia, PA: Routledge, 2000.

Oakley, D. A. "The Plurality of Consciousness." *In* D. A. Oakley (ed.), *Brain and Mind*, New York: Methuen, 1985.

Obler, L. K. and Gjerlow, K. *Language and the Brain.* New York: Cambridge University Press, 1999.

Ogden, J. A. *Fractured Minds: A Case-study Approach to Clinical Neuropsychology.* New York: Oxford University Press, 1996.

Owusu-Bempah, K. and Howitt, D. *Psychology beyond Western Perspectives.* Leicester, UK: British Psychological Society Books, 2000.

Paranjpe, A. C. and Bhatt, G. S. "Emotion: A Perspective from the Indian Tradition." *In* H. S. R. Kao and D. Sinha (eds.), *Asian Perspectives on Psychology.* New Delhi, India: Sage Publications, 1997.

Peacock, J. *Depression.* New York: Lifematters Press, 2000.

Pfeiffer, W. M. "Culture-Bound Syndromes." *In* I. Al-Issa (ed.), *Culture and Psychopathology.* Baltimore, MD: University Park Press, 1982.

Pillemer, D. B. *Momentous Events, Vivid Memories.* Cambridge, MA: Harvard University Press, 1998.

Pinel, J. P. J. *Biopsychology (5th edition).* Boston, MA: Allyn and Bacon, 2002.

Pinker, S. *The Language Instinct.* New York: HarperPerennial, 1995.

Pinker, S. *How the Mind Works.* New York: Norton, 1997.

Porter, R. *Medicine: A History of Healing: Ancient Traditions to Modern Practices.* New York: Barnes and Noble, 1997.

Ramachandran, V. S. and Blakeslee, S. *Phantoms in the Brain: Probing the Mysteries of the Human Mind.* New York: William Morrow, 1998.

Ridley, M. *Genome: The Autobiography of a Species in 23 Chapters.* New York: HarperCollins, 1999.

Robins, L. N. and Regier, D. A. *Psychiatric Disorders in America.* New York: Free Press, 1991.

Robinson, D. N. *Toward a Science of Human Nature: Essays on the Psychologies of Mill, Hegel, Wundt, and James.* New York: Columbia University Press, 1982.

Rugg, M. D. and Coles, M. G. H. (eds.). *Electrophysiology of the Mind: Event-Related Brain Potentials and Cognition.* Oxford, UK: Oxford University Press, 1995.

Rutter, M. "The Interplay of Nature and Nurture: Redirecting the Inquiry." *In* R. Plomin and G. E. McClearn (eds.), *Nature, Nurture, and Psychology.* Washington, DC: American Psychological Association, 1993.

Sarason, I. G. and Sarason B. R. *Abnormal Psychology: The Problem of Maladaptive Behavior (9th edition).* Upper Saddle River, NJ: Prentice Hall, 1998.

Savage-Rumbaugh, S., Shanker, S. G., and Taylor, T. J. *Apes, Language, and the Human Mind.* New York: Oxford University Press, 1998.

Schab, F. R., & Crowder, R. G. (eds.). *Memory for Odors.* Mahwah, NJ: Lawrence Erlbaum Associates, 1995.

Segal, N. L. *Entwined Lives: Twins and What They Tell Us about Human Behavior.* New York: Plume, 2000.

Seeman, M. V. *Gender and Psychopathology.* Washington, DC: American Psychiatric Press, 1995.

Seligman, M. E. P. *Helplessness: On Depression, Development, and Death.* San Francisco, CA: W. H. Freeman and Co., 1992.

Shorter, E. *A History of Psychiatry: From the Era of Asylum to the Age of Prozac.* New York: John Wiley and Sons, Inc., 1997.

Siegler, R. S. *Children's Thinking (3rd edition).* Englewood Cliffs, NJ: Prentice Hall, 1998.

Simpson, E. M. *Reversals: A Personal Account of Victory over Dyslexia.* New York: Noonday Press, 1992.

Singer, D. G. and Singer, J. L. (eds.). *Handbook of Children and the Media.* Thousand Oaks, CA: Sage Publications, 2001.

Skinner, B. F. *Science and Human Behavior.* New York: Free Press, 1965.

Slavney, P. R. *Psychiatric Dimensions of Medical Practice: What Primary-Care Physicians Should Know about Delirium, Demoralization, Suicidal Thinking, and Competence to Refuse Medical Advice.* Baltimore, MD: The Johns Hopkins University Press, 1998.

Smith McLaughlin, M., Peyser Hazouri, S., and Peyser Hazouri, S. *Addiction: The "High" That Brings You Down.* Springfield, NJ: Enslow publishers, 1997.

Sommers, M. A. *Everything You Need to Know about Bipolar Disorder and Depressive Illness.* New York: Rosen Publishing Group, 2000.

Stanovich, K. E. *Who Is Rational? Studies of Individual Differences in Reasoning.* Mahwah, NJ: Lawrence Erlbaum Associates, 1999.

Symons, D. *The Evolution of Human Sexuality.* New York: Oxford University Press, 1979.

Symons, D. "Beauty is in the Adaptations of the Beholder: The Evolutionary Psychology of Human Female Sexual Attractiveness." *In* P. R. Abramson and S. D. Pinkerton (eds.), *Sexual Nature, Sexual Culture.* Chicago, IL: University of Chicago Press, 1995.

Tavris, C. *The Mismeasure of Women.* New York: Simon and Schuster, 1992.

Triandis, H. C. *Culture and Social Behavior.* New York: McGraw-Hill, 1994.

Tulving, E and Craik, F. I. M. *The Oxford Handbook of Memory.* Oxford, UK: Oxford University Press, 2000.

Vygotsky, L. S. *Mind in Society: The Development of Higher Psychological Processes.* Cambridge, MA: Harvard University Press, 1978.

Weiten, W. *Psychology: Themes and Variations.* Monterey, CA: Brooks/Cole Publishing, 1998.

Werner, E. E. and Smith, R. S. *Overcoming the Odds: High-Risk Children from Birth to Adulthood.* Ithaca, NY: Cornell University Press, 1992.

White, R. W. and Watt, N. F. *The Abnormal Personality (5th edition).* Chichester, UK: John Wiley and Sons, Inc., 1981.

Wickens, A. *Foundations of Biopsychology.* Harlow, UK: Prentice Hall, 2000.

Wilson, E. O. *Sociobiology: A New Synthesis.* Cambridge, MA: Harvard University Press, 1975.

Winkler, K. *Teens, Depression, and the Blues: A Hot Issue.* Springfield, NJ: Enslow publishers, 2000.

Wolman, B. (ed.). *Historical Roots of Contemporary Psychology.* New York: Harper and Row, 1968.

Wrightsman, L. S. and Sanford, F. H. *Psychology: A Scientific Study of Human Behavior.* Monterey, CA: Brooks/Cole Publishing, 1975.

Yap, P. M. *Comparative Psychiatry: A Theoretical Framework.* Toronto, Canada: University of Toronto Press, 1974.

Zarit, S. H. and Knight, B. G. *A Guide to Psychotherapy and Aging.* Washington, DC: American Psychological Association, 1997.

Useful Websites

Amazing Optical Illusions
http://www.optillusions.com
See your favorite optical illusions at this fun site.

Bedlam
http://www.museum-london.org.uk/MOLsite/exhibits/bedlam/f_bed.htm
The Museum of London's online exhibition about Bedlam, the notorious mental institution.

Bipolar Disorders Information Center
http://www.mhsource.com/bipolar
Articles and information about bipolar 1 disorder.

Brain and Mind
http://www.epub.org.br/cm/home_i.htm
An online magazine with articles devoted to neuroscience, linguisitics, imprinting, and a variety of related topics.

Exploratorium
http://www.exploratorium.edu/exhibits/nf_exhibits.html
Click on "seeing" or "hearing" to check out visual and auditory illusions and other secrets of the mind.

Freud and Culture
http://www.loc.gov/exhibits/freud
An online Library of Congress exhibition that examines Sigmund Freud's life and key ideas and his effect on 20th-century thinking.

Great Ideas in Personality
http://www.personalityresearch.org
This website looks at scientific research programs in personality psychology. Pages on attachment theory, basic emotions, behavior genetics, behaviorism, cognitive social theories, and more give concise definitions of terms as well as links to further research on the web.

Jigsaw Classroom
http://www.jigsaw.org
The official web site of the Jigsaw Classroom, a

cooperative learning technique that reduces racial conflict between schoolchildren. Learn about its history and how to implement the techniques.

Kidspsych

http://www.kidspsych.org/index1.html
American Psychological Association's childrens' site, with games and exercises for kids. Also useful for students of developmental psychology. Follow the "about this activity" links to find out the theories behind the fun and games.

Kismet

http://www.ai.mit.edu/projects/humanoid-robotics-group/kismet/kismet.html
Kismet is the MIT's expressive robot, which has perceptual and motor functions tailored to natural human communication channels.

Neuroscience for Kids

http://faculty.washington.edu/chudler/neurok.html
A useful website for students and teachers who want to learn about the nervous system. Enjoy activities and experiments on your way to learning all about the brain and spinal cord.

Neuroscience Tutorial

http://thalamus.wustl.edu/course
The Washington University School of Medicine's online tutorial offers an illustrated guide to the basics of clinical neuroscience, with useful artworks and user-friendly text.

Psychology Central

http://emerson.thomsonlearning.com/psych
Links to many useful articles grouped by subject as well as cool, animated figures that improve your understanding of psychological principles.

Schizophrenia.com

http://www.schizophrenia.com
Information and resources on this mental disorder provided by a charitable organization.

Seeing, Hearing, and Smelling the World

http://www.hhmi.org/senses
A downloadable illustrated book dealing with perception from the Howard Hughes Medical Institute.

Sigmund Freud Museum

http://freud.t0.or.at/freud
The online Sigmund Freud Museum has videos and audio recordings of the famous psychoanalyst—there are even images of Freud's famous couch.

Social Psychology Network

http://www.socialpsychology.org
The largest social psychology database on the Internet. Within these pages you will find more

than 5,000 links to psychology-related resources and research groups, and there is also a useful section on general psychology.

Stanford Prison Experiment

http://www.prisonexp.org
A fascinating look at the Stanford Prison Experiment, which saw subjects placed in a prison to see what happens to "good people in a bad environment." Learn why the experiment had to be abandoned after six days due to the unforeseen severity of the effects on participants.

Stroop effect

http://www.dcity.org/braingames/stroop/index.htm
Take part in an online psychological experiment to see the Stroop effect in action.

Quote Attributions

opening quote

quote

Each chapter in *Psychology* contains quotes that relate to the topics covered. These quotes appear both within the main text and at the start of the chapters, and their attributions are detailed here. Quotes are listed in the order that they appear in the chapter, and the page numbers at the end of each attribution refer to the pages in this volume where the quote appears.

Fetal Development

Eliot, L. *What's Going on in There? How the Brain and Mind Develop in the First Five Years of Life.* New York: Bantam Books, 1999, p. 6, p.11, p.15, p.22.

Campbell, D.M. *et al.* "Diet in Pregnancy and the Offspring's Blood Pressure 40 Years Later." *British Journal of Obstetics and Gynaecology,* **103**, p. 13.

Infant Cognition

Gesell, A. and Ilg, F. L. *Infant and Child in the Culture of Today: The Guidance of Development in Home and Nursery School.* New York: Harper, 1943, p. 25.

Leach, P. *Your Baby and Child : From Birth to Age Five.* New York: Random House, 1977, p. 26.

Cleverley, J. F. *Visions of Childhood: Influential Models from Locke to Spock.* New York: Teachers College Press, 1986, p. 29.

Pinker, S. *The Language Instinct.* New York: HarperPerennial, 1995, p. 30.

Markham, E. "Constraints Children Place on Word Meanings." *In* P. Bloom (ed.), *Language Acquisition: Core Readings.* Cambridge, MA: MIT Press, 1993, p. 32.

Skinner, B. F. "Education in 1984." *New Scientist,* **22**, 1964, p. 33.

Chomsky, N. *Aspects of the Theory of Syntax.* Cambridge, MA: MIT Press, 1965, p. 37.

B. F. Skinner (1904–1990).

Karmiloff-Smith, A. *Beyond Modularity: A Developmental Perspective on Cognitive Science.* Cambridge, MA: MIT Press, 1992, p. 38.

Perceptual Development

Kellman, P. J. and Arterberry, M. E. *The Cradle of Knowledge: Development of Perception in Infancy.* Cambridge, MA: MIT Press, 1998, p. 40.

Braun, J. (ed.). *Visual Attention and Cortical Circuits.* Cambridge, MA: MIT Press, 2001, p. 41.

Barrera, M. E. and Maurer, D. "Discrimination of Strangers by the Three-month-old." *Child Development,* **52**, 1981, p. 46.

Guttman, J. and Sekular, R. Lecture at the 1995 Meeting of the Canadian Society for Brain, Behavior, and Cognitive Science, in Halifax, Canada. 1995, p. 52.

Karow, J. "Pesticides and Parkinson's." *At* http://www.sciam.com, 2000, p. 55.

Velmans, M. "When Perception Becomes Conscious." *British Journal of Psychology,* **90**, 1999, p. 57.

Stages of Development

Vygotsky, L. *Mind in Society: The Development of Higher Psychological Processes.* Cambridge, MA: Harvard University Press, 1978, p. 59, p. 62, p. 63.

Vygotsky, L. *Thought and Language.* Cambridge, MA: MIT Press, 1962, p. 60.

Piaget, J. *The Construction of Reality in the Child.* New York: Basic Books, 1954, p. 65, p.75.

Boden, M. A. *Piaget.* London, UK: Fontana, 1979, p. 69.

Inhelder, B. and Piaget, J. *The Growth of Logical Thinking: From Childhood to Adolescence.* New York: Basic Books, 1958, p. 71.

Piaget, J. *The Origins of Intelligence in Children.* New York: International Universities Press, 1952, p. 76.

Memory Development

Wilde, O. F. O. (1854–1900). Unpublished quote, *c.* 1880. p. 78.

Darling, D. J. *Zen Physics: The Science of Death, The Logic of Reincarnation.* New York: HarperCollins, 1996, p. 83.

American Psychological Society. *Current Directions in Psychological Science, Volume 9.* New York: Cambridge University Press, 2001, p. 84.

Weaver, B. "Why Early Memories Elude Us: 'Childhood Amnesia' and Brain Development." *At* http://www.psychologicalscience.org/media/pr000401.html, 2000, p. 87.

Rovee-Collier, C. "The Development of Infant Memory." *Current Directions in Psychological Science,* **8**, 1999, p. 88.

Twain, M. "Chapters from Mark Twain's Autobiography, by Mark Twain." *North American Review*, 1907, p. 91.

Leonardo da Vinci. Notebook, *c*.1500, p. 93.

Problem Solving

Charles Kettering (1876–1958). Unpublished quote, p. 94.

Siegler, R. S. *Children's Thinking (3rd edition)*. Englewood Cliffs, NJ: Prentice Hall, 1998, p. 95.

Engel, S. *The Emergence of Story Telling during the First Three Years*. Washington, DC: Zero to Three, 1997, p. 97.

Willatts, P. "Development of Means-end Behavior in Young Infants: Pulling a Support to Retrieve a Distant Object." *Developmental Psychology*, **35**, 1999, p. 101.

Glick, J. "A Cultural-Historical Approach to the Cultural-Historical Approach: From Principles to Practices." *In* L. Resnick, R. Saljo, and C. Pontecorvo (eds.), *Discourse Tools and Reasoning*. New York: Springer Verlag, 1998, p. 102.

Cheng, P. W. and Holyoak, K. J. "Pragmatic Reasoning Schemas." *Cognitive Psychology*, **17**, 1985, p. 105.

Ball, L. J. "Working Memory, Metacognitive Uncertainty, and Belief Bias in Syllogistic Reasoning." *Quarterly Journal of Experimental Psychology*, **53A**, 2000, p. 107.

Galotti, K. M., Komatsu, L. K., and Voelz, S. "Children's Differential Performance on Deductive and Inductive Syllogisms." *Developmental Psychology*, **33**, 1997, p. 109.

Emotional Development

James, W. *The Principles of Psychology*. 1890, p. 115.

Erikson, E. Cited in R. I. Evans, *Dialogue with Erik Erikson*. New York: Harper and Row, 1967, p. 117.

Lorenz, K. *The Natural Science of the Human Species*. Cambridge, MA: MIT Press, 1995, p. 119.

Bowlby, J. *Attachment and Loss*. New York: Basic Books, 1969, p. 120.

Ainsworth, M. D. Cited in "On the Shaping of Attachment Theory and Research: An Interview with Mary D. Ainsworth, Fall 1994." *In* E. Waters *et al.* (eds.), "Caregiving, Cultural, and Cognitive Perspectives on Secure-base Behavior and Working Models: New Growing Points of Attachment Theory and Research." *Monographs of the Society for Research in Child Development*, **60**, 1995, p. 124.

Shaw, G. B. *Everybody's Political What's What?* London, UK: Constable, 1944, p. 127.

Belsky, J. Cited in an article by D. Brindle, *The Guardian*, April 7 2000, p. 129.

Social Development

Sullivan, H. S. *The Interpersonal Theory of Psychiatry*. New York: Norton, 1953, p. 130.

Mead, G. H. "The Psychology of Social Consciousness Implied in Instruction." *Science*, **31**, 1910, p. 131.

Feinman, S. *Social Referencing and the Social Construction of Reality in Infancy*. New York: Plenum Press, 1992, p. 133.

Brown, T. *Lectures on the Philosophy of the Human Mind*. Andover, U.K: Newman, 1822, p. 136.

Coopersmith, S. *The Antecedents of Self-esteem*. San Francisco: W. H. Freeman, 1967, p. 137.

Kohlberg, L. *Essays on Moral Development*. San Francisco: Harper and Row, 1981, p. 143.

Carpendale, J. I. M. "Kohlberg and Piaget on Stages and Moral Reasoning." *Developmental Review*, **20**, 2000, p. 144.

Asher, S. R. Cited in S. R. Asher and J. D. Coie (eds.), *Peer Rejection in Childhood*. Cambridge, UK: Cambridge University Press, 1990, p. 147.

Lewis, C. S. *The Four Loves*. New York: Harvest Books, 1960, p149.

Every effort has been made to attribute the quotes throughout *Psychology* correctly. Any errors or omissions brought to the attention of the publisher are regretted and will be credited in subsequent editions..

Noam Chomsky (born 1928).

Set Index